D1595895

Thomas Merton and the Inclusive Imagination

Thomas Merton

and the

Inclusive Imagination

Ross Labrie

UNIVERSITY OF MISSOURI PRESS

COLUMBIA AND LONDON

Library of Congress Cataloging-in-Publication Data

Labrie, Ross.
    Thomas Merton and the inclusive imagination / Ross Labrie.
        p.   cm.
    Includes bibliographical references and index.
    ISBN 0-8262-1382-0 (alk. paper)
    1. Merton, Thomas, 1915–1968—Criticism and interpretation.   2. Romanticism—
United States—History—20th century.   3. Christian poetry, American—History and
criticism.   4. Imagination in literature.   I. Title.
    PS3525.E7174 Z766   2001
    818'.5409—dc21

                                                                    2001041582

Designer: Stephanie Foley
Typesetter: The Composing Room of Michigan, Inc.
Printer and Binder: Thomson-Shore, Inc.
Typeface: Adobe Caslon

Acknowledgment is hereby made to New Directions Publishing Corporation for permission to quote from *The Collected Poems of Thomas Merton* and to HarperCollins Publishers
for permission to quote from *Entering the Silence: The Journals of Thomas Merton, Volume
Two, 1941–1952.*

Parts of the chapters "Nature and Time" and "Myth and Culture" appeared previously
in the following journals: "Merton and Time," *Merton Annual* 11 (1998): 121–37;
"Merton and America," *Cithara* 38 (May 1999): 21–31.

Contents

Preface

Anne E. Carr has justly described Thomas Merton as the "most influential and widely read American religious thinker of our time."[1] Some years ago I became interested in the romantic sources of Thomas Merton's thought, and, following the earlier work of Dennis McInerny, published an article about Merton's relationship to the American romantics. I had been aware of the scholarship of critics such as Michael Higgins and John Holmes in addressing the subject of Merton's relationship to Blake and wondered what more there might be to consider. In the late 1930s, when Merton was a young man on the threshold of deciding what path his life would take, he became almost simultaneously interested in romanticism and mysticism. He thought of romanticism and mysticism as having much in common, just as he later determined that his vocations as a monastic contemplative and poet did as well. One of the notable characteristics of Merton's writings, both in poetry and in prose, is his seamless intermingling of religious and romantic elements, an intermingling that, because of his enormous influence, has had the effect of making widespread a distinctive form of religious thought and expression.

At some point I began to wonder what it was about romanticism that had captured Merton's attention and held his attention virtually all of his life. In time there arose the conviction that it was his understanding

1. Carr, *A Search for Wisdom and Spirit: Thomas Merton's Theology of the Self*, 146.

of the importance of unity and wholeness. These were also the qualities that Merton appeared to value in the writings of the great mystics. Regarding Merton's understanding of mysticism it became apparent that his ostensible allegiance to the apophatic tradition of Western mysticism required revision, that in particular those many loving references to nature in Merton's voluminous journals had at the very least to be integrated into any conception of him as an apophatic contemplative. Even though he was on the whole not a systematic thinker, Merton's writings form a coherent whole when considered from the point of view of his emphasis on unity and wholeness. Conscious of the ubiquitous theme of unity in Merton's writings, I have linked aspects of his thought in framing the chapters, as he himself did in a number of essays, such as those in *Raids on the Unspeakable,* one of his finest collections. I have incorporated the material from the recent, full publication of Merton's journals, relating passages from these sources, where this seemed to be of use, to the texts of the originally published, selected journals. However, one of these selected journals, *Conjectures of a Guilty Bystander* (1966), incorporated so much new material that it can rightly be considered a separate work in its own right rather than simply a revised and selective version of Merton's journals. In the references to the English romantic poets I have cited the editions of these poets that Merton was reading in the 1930s when his thinking about them took its first large strides.

I should here like to acknowledge my indebtedness to Merton scholars whose writings and suggestions have been helpful in connection with this work, seeking the forgiveness in advance of any whom I have forgotten to mention: Christine Bochen, Anne E. Carr, Lawrence Cunningham, Thomas Del Prete, Robert Faricy, Patrick Hart, Michael Higgins, Robert Inchausti, George Kilcourse, David Leigh, Dennis McInerny, Patrick O'Connell, William Shannon, Lynn Szabo, Bonnie Thurston, Robert Waldron, and Monica Weis. I am grateful to the University of Sydney, Australia, for granting me visiting-scholar privileges during the study leave while I wrote this book. I am grateful as well to Jonathan Montaldo for his help with the Merton Collection at Bellarmine University and to Paul Spaeth and Lorraine Welsh for their help with the Merton Collection at St. Bonaventure University. I also thank the interlibrary loan divisions of the University of Sydney Library and the

University of British Columbia for their efficient and generous assistance. Finally, I acknowledge with gratitude the Humanities and Social Sciences grants from the University of British Columbia, which allowed me to travel to collections of Merton's published and unpublished writings at Columbia University, Bellarmine University, and St. Bonaventure University.

Thomas Merton and the Inclusive Imagination

1

Romanticism and Mysticism

In an early poem titled "The Philosophers," Thomas Merton wrote a parody of the famous concluding lines of Keats's "Ode on a Grecian Urn" in order to satirize what he considered to be the prevailing materialism of twentieth-century culture: "Body is truth, truth body, Fat is all / We grow on earth, or all we breed to grow."[1] In the late 1960s in his long poem *Cables to the Ace,* Merton made a similarly irreverent allusion to the romantic poets:

> O God do I have to be Wordsworth
> Striding on the Blue Fells
> With a lake for sale and Lucy
> Locked in the hole of my camera?[2]

The passage illustrates both Merton's identification with the romantics and his attempt to create a space of his own for himself as a writer. In *The Seven Storey Mountain* (1948), he confided that through William Blake, who was the offshoot of Protestant dissenters, he had paradoxically found his way to the Roman Catholic Church. Both Blake and the romantics generally had a profound influence on the formation of Merton's fundamental ideas as a thinker and artist. On the whole, Merton was more engaged by the first generation of romantic poets (Blake,

1. Merton, "The Philosophers," in *The Collected Poems of Thomas Merton,* 3.
2. Merton, *Cables to the Ace,* in ibid., 444.

Coleridge, and Wordsworth) than by the second (which included Keats, Shelley, and Byron). The reason was that the first generation was more hospitable to religion than the second—with Blake exhibiting a radical, iconoclastic, and visionary Christianity, whereas Coleridge and Words-worth returned in time to the spirituality of the Church of England. While Merton was more partial to the first generation of romantic po-ets, he shared the general conviction of romantic artists that reason and empiricism contributed to only a partial understanding and knowledge about reality, particularly about ultimate reality.

While working toward his M.A. at Columbia University beginning in 1938, Merton took courses in the English romantic poets, the notes of which are housed at St. Bonaventure University in upstate New York, the campus (then called St. Bonaventure College) at which Merton taught in the early 1940s. His Columbia course notebooks contain both what he thought important enough to write down as well as entries that are clear-ly glosses of his own. In the summer of 1938, for example, he noted that romanticism was obviously a religious phenomenon even if, he cautioned, not necessarily Christian. In the case of Blake, however, he was impressed by the union of the artist and the mystic, and he recognized that Blake was a devout Christian, even if a heterodox one. In fact, in Merton's eyes Blake had lived a saintly life. Also attractive to Merton was Blake's alienation from eighteenth-century deism and his putative acquaintance with the re-ligions of the East, the connection to the East being something that he had in common with American romantics such as Thoreau and Emerson.[3] Blake believed that the philosophy of the East taught, as he conveyed through the character of Ezekiel in "The Marriage of Heaven and Hell," the "first principles of human perception," a view that Merton shared.[4]

---

3. Merton, "Nature and Art in William Blake," in *The Literary Essays of Thomas Mer-ton*, 451. See also Merton's letter to Robert Lax in 1938 in which he asserted that Blake was "full of Indian and Chinese theories of art" and that he believed Blake had read the Bhagavad Gita (*The Road to Joy: The Letters of Thomas Merton to Old and New Friends*, 142–43). Michael Cox states that Blake was "conversant with Hinduism" (*A Handbook of Christian Mysticism*, 226).

4. Blake, "The Marriage of Heaven and Hell," in *Poetry and Prose of William Blake*, 186. This is the edition of Blake's poems that Merton mentioned buying in *The Seven Storey Mountain*.

What Merton especially valued in the romantics was their addressing of what he called the "intimate, that is, ontological sources of life," the primary kind of understanding and knowledge sought by Blake, Wordsworth, and Coleridge.[5] For Merton, as for the romantics, the psychological and the ontological were coextensive since it was the self that could attain the most searchingly introspective yet also the most comprehensive, ontological reality. Since Merton had been reading the English romantic poets for his course at Columbia while at the same time reading about Christianity, he was particularly careful in his M.A. lecture notes to distinguish pantheism, which he detected in the early Wordsworth, from orthodox Christianity, which he noted in Coleridge. At the same time, in his Columbia lecture notes from a course called "The Art of Poetry" in 1938, he was evidently encouraged by the fact that Wordsworth had returned to formal Christianity later in life.[6]

Generally speaking, both the English and the American romantics had been influenced by Neoplatonism—especially Blake, and his was the strongest influence on Merton. In this connection, for Blake, as Kathleen Raine has demonstrated, matter was a shallow form of reality, whereas in contrast the mind was profoundly real both in itself and as the underlying source of reality in matter. While Blake was not a pantheist, and indeed detested the pantheism that he perceived in Wordsworth, he did believe in divine immanence, not in nature, but in the human mind. Indeed, for Blake, the human mind, at least potentially, participated in the life of God. While Blake's Neoplatonism was of a more radical kind than Merton would ever adopt, Merton did, along with medieval mystics such as Meister Eckhart, come to see the divine as present in the human soul, to see the mind, as the American romantic Ralph Waldo Emerson had phrased it, as a "particle of God."[7] While Merton was never as Platonic in his thinking as Coleridge, he did tend, like Coleridge, to regard the universe as imbued with the divine mind.

5. Merton, "The True Legendary Sound: The Poetry and Criticism of Edwin Muir," in *Literary Essays,* 30.

6. Merton, "Romanticism," 93; Merton, "Art of Poetry," n.p.

7. Raine, *Blake and Tradition,* 1:290–95; Emerson, "Nature," in *Essays and Lectures,* 10.

Among other things this meant that the universe was permeated with an ethical and providential hue, something that is quite apparent in both Wordsworth and Merton. Furthermore, Merton tended to perceive truth, goodness, and beauty as aspects of a single, ultimate reality, as can be seen in the observation in his early journal *Run to the Mountain* that love is the epitome of moral beauty.[8]

The ability of the romantics to see into the spiritual reality underlying matter, to see a world in a grain of sand, as Blake had put it, derived from imaginative and intuitive consciousness. Merton was attracted to the inclusiveness of Blake's conception of reality with its graduated scale of perception ending in the fullest or fourfold vision, a powerful, imaginative discernment of all of being that Merton characterized as a participation in the mind of God. Although there is an elitism implicit in such a graduated level of consciousness, Blake thought that all levels of consciousness were accessible to human beings in the present time. In his M.A. thesis on Blake, Merton described the kind of perception Blake exhibited as a direct, intuitive contact with "pure intelligibility," noting Blake's belief that the artist and the mystic had the same kinds of intuitions.[9] Like the romantics, Merton tended to see intuition as a perceiving use of the intelligence, an instrument for seeing into ultimate reality. For Coleridge, the great theorist of English romantic thought, the term *imagination* could mean this or it could mean the creative use of the mind, a secondary use of the imagination analogous to Blake's lower levels of the imagination. Merton was certainly aware of Coleridge's classification of the imagination since he acknowledged reading the *Biographia Literaria* in the late 1930s, and he made it clear in *The Seven Storey Mountain* that he elevated the imaginer as "seer" and "prophet" above that of "maker."[10] All the same, one should not exaggerate the separation in romantic thought between use of the imagination as a means of discernment and as a creative instrument. The reason is that the discernment of ultimate reality required the imagination to be creative

8. Merton, Nov. 21, 1939, in *Run to the Mountain: The Story of a Vocation*, 94.

9. Merton, "Nature and Art in Blake," in *Literary Essays*, 444.

10. See Merton to Robert Lax, Aug. 11, 1938, in *Road to Joy*, 144. See also Merton, Nov. 27, 1940, in *Run to the Mountain*, 264. Merton, *The Seven Storey Mountain*, 190.

enough to generate alternative visions of the phenomenal world to those presented by conventional thinking. Regarding the use of the imagination as an instrument of discernment, Merton saw the romantics as using it, with its connection to both the concrete and the immaterial, as an instrument for uniting the natural and the supernatural. In his M.A. course notes on Coleridge, Merton epitomized the romantic view of the imagination as the power by which one came into contact with the divine. Furthermore, writing in his journal in 1941, he suggested that for some artists, including Wordsworth, the particular symbols chosen to convey an imaginatively perceived reality could be part of a master vision dominated by a comprehensive symbol of the artist's vision, "one big central figure," as he put it.[11]

For romantics such as Wordsworth, Coleridge, and Keats, the imagination was most sensitive as an instrument of ontological discernment when enveloped in darkness or half-light. As A. S. Byatt has commented, romantic sublimity required darkness with "occasional violent contrasts of light or livid light." In darkness Wordsworth imagined the nightingale awakening the inner lives of travelers in "The Solitary Reaper," while Keats achieved an imaginative fusion with the song of the nightingale and thereby with the vast reality of the nonself in his famous "Ode to a Nightingale." Darkness, as Jerome McGann has pointed out, permitted the romantic writer to pass through the multiplicity of particulars to the single reality, the "One Life" underlying them all.[12] Although ultimate reality was regarded by the romantics as accessible through the use of the imagination and by means of the intuitive understanding that flowed from it, that reality was considered inexhaustible and thus of a kind that transcended human comprehension. In this the romantics and mystics whom Merton was reading in the late 1930s were in complete agreement.

Darkness and partial darkness allowed the physical eye and the inner eye to mingle in an attempt to discern the ontological and spiritual re-

11. See Merton, "Romanticism," 74, 94; Merton, Apr. 9, 1941, in *Run to the Mountain*, 340.

12. Byatt, *Wordsworth and Coleridge in Their Time*, 254; McGann, *The Romantic Ideology: A Critical Investigation*, 134.

ality underlying the physical world. Thus, Thoreau, for example, an American romantic with whom Merton as hermit and artist came to identify, wrote in *Walden* that nature was a desirable object of consciousness because, although it led the mind to understanding and knowledge, nonetheless, like the ultimate reality that it tangibly represented, it was ultimately "mysterious and unexplorable." For this reason openness of mind was a signal virtue in romanticism, as Merton recognized in connection with William Blake, who in turn defined the fallen human condition as a state of fragmentation and the recovery of paradise as the opportunity to achieve "total vision."[13]

Because Merton, like Blake, perceived the artist and the mystic as one, he used the terms *imagination, intuition, contemplation,* and *mysticism* at different points in his writing as if they were interchangeable. In "Poetry and Contemplation: A Reappraisal" (1958), for example, while distinguishing between discrete levels of contemplation, he asserted that the poet was always akin to the mystic because of the prophetic "intuition" by which he or she perceived the spiritual reality that inhered in the object contemplated. Without the use of such a power the universe was merely material and hence meaningless. In this connection Merton noted approvingly on one occasion that Wordsworth had described poetry as closest to its "divine origin" when it breathed the "spirit of religion."[14] The triumvirate of imagination, art, and religion was typical of the generalist writing of the romantics, who tended in their search for inclusive understanding to reunite the parts of the mind and to unite this restored mind in turn with the objects that the mind observed. This open-ended nature of romantic consciousness has been remarked upon by Northrop Frye, who commented that romantic writing was "philosophy produced by an essentially literary mind." Merton focused on this inclusive trait in romantic thinking as its salient characteristic from his earliest acquaintance with it, commenting in the autumn of 1941 that

13. Thoreau, *Walden,* 317–18; Merton, "Blake and the New Theology," in *Literary Essays,* 6.

14. Merton, "Poetry and Contemplation," in *Literary Essays,* 345; Wordsworth, "Essay, Supplementary to the Preface," in *Poetical Works of Wordsworth,* 945. This was the edition of Wordsworth that Merton left at St. Bonaventure College in 1941 when he entered the Abbey of Gethsemani.

Blake presented views of objects that illuminated the "*moral character* of the universe as a whole." This, as Merton realized, was one of the reasons that the romantics made such an extensive use of symbolism in their work, even in the case of Wordsworth, where the particulars of the physical world had been so carefully observed. For the romantics, the specific and the general were joined in meditation, as Coleridge observed, in such a way that the particular contained "something generally true."[15]

Although Coleridge used the term *meditation* in speaking of the poet's intuitive access to ultimate reality, it is clear that he meant by that term essentially what Merton meant by *contemplation* and furthermore that the contemplation Merton associated with the mystics was similar in kind to that which he perceived in the romantics. As Merton recognized, the bridge between romanticism and mysticism was Platonism.[16] He explicitly noted Blake's indebtedness to Neoplatonism in his thesis on Blake, and even though he distinguished between the goals of art and those of mysticism in *The Ascent to Truth* (1951) as well as in two well-known essays on poetry and contemplation, written in 1947 and 1958 respectively, nevertheless the distinction seemed to lose its importance for him after the mid-1950s. Increasingly, following the mid-1950s and especially when he began to write more spontaneously and with not a great deal of effort given to revision, Merton used the writing of poetry as an opportunity for contemplation. Spontaneity itself, he recognized, was a feature of romantic composition, favored because it allowed the true self to respond to the subject at hand before the intervention of the rational self with its discourse of impersonal argumentation.[17] Moreover, and this is especially evident in his journals, his writing tended to blur the distinction between different modes of writing, between journal and poem, prose and poetry, expressing the moment in whatever form that seemed appropriate. The dissolution of the boundaries between prose and poetry and between one genre and another was another

15. Frye, "The Drunken Boat: The Revolutionary Element in Romanticism," 2; Merton, Oct. 11, 1941, in *Run to the Mountain*, 437; Coleridge, ["Shakspere 'Out of Time'"], in *Select Poetry and Prose*, 347. This was the edition Merton left at St. Bonaventure College in 1941 when he entered the Abbey of Gethsemani.

16. See Merton, "This Is God's Work," in *Thomas Merton in Alaska*, 78–79.

17. See Lilian Furst, *Romanticism in Perspective*, 244.

feature of romantic art, an attempt to undercut the rather rigid classification of reality and of discourse that had been prominent in eighteenth-
century thought. In spite of Coleridge's objection to Wordsworth's idea
that there was no essential difference between poetry and prose, Coleridge insisting that metrical arrangement was that difference, a number
of romantic writers in both Britain and the United States abandoned the
division of prose and poetry into watertight compartments. Whitman is
a conspicuous example.

As will be seen, Merton affirmed the organic nature of the reality depicted by the romantic writers, especially the correspondences, as Lilian
Furst has put it, that existed between the physical and the immaterial
and at the bottom of which lay the assumption that the cosmos was ontologically united. John Clubbe and Ernest Lovell have suggested that
the romantic sensibility emphasized the organic unity of the cosmos by
celebrating "process" and "growth." Similarly, A. S. Byatt has observed
that Coleridge perceived society not as a collection of individuals but as
analogous to an organism with the parts "subserving" the whole—like a
"poem." Blake considered the Fall as the dissolution that had overtaken
a primal cosmic unity. In *The Four Zoas*, for example, he depicted the ru-
ination caused by the dissolution within the self, symbolically dramatiz-
ing the various parts of the self at war with each other. Furthermore, in
his poem "London," he led his readers to see the social evils that resulted from a fragmentation of the self. Similarly, Wordsworth linked the
new industrial culture of the late eighteenth century with a fragmentation of mind and sensibility from which rural dwellers would be more
likely to be exempt. With the notable exception of Whitman, the romantics generally lamented the effect of urbanization, the "din / Of
towns and cities," as Wordsworth put it, on ontological perception.[18]
With his pronounced antipathy to the technological culture that modern industrialization has produced, Merton was especially sensitive as
well to this aspect of romantic thought.

Accompanying the romantic reaction against urbanization and in-

18. Ibid., 33, 172; Clubbe and Lovell, *English Romanticism: The Grounds of Belief,*
152; Byatt, *Wordsworth and Coleridge,* 154; see Wordsworth, "Preface to the Second Edition," in *Poetical Works of Wordsworth,* 935–36; Wordsworth, "Lines Composed a Few
Miles above Tintern Abbey," in *Poetical Works of Wordsworth,* 206.

dustrialization in the early nineteenth century was the idealization of medieval culture, a culture that was seen as both unified and pastoral, a culture whose final traces had been effaced by laissez-faire economics and industrialization.[19] Merton's attraction to medieval culture in the late 1930s was reinforced by his belief that, although there were exceptions and inconsistencies, a strong religious and ontological consciousness leavened the lives of medieval Europeans, making it possible for them to transcend materialism and to form a communitarian society. As a young man Merton believed that this medieval culture had survived into the modern world within monasticism, although as he grew older he saw this as less the case and became somewhat more detached from medieval culture as such, even if not from the influence of some of the great medieval mystics. In time he recognized that his early passion for medievalism, stimulated by scholars such as Etienne Gilson, was mythic and in that sense of perennial value. In his thesis on Blake he had attempted, rather unsuccessfully on the whole, to link the vision of human perfectibility and solidarity that he found in Blake with that of medieval Christendom. While this was a flawed account of intellectual history, it did express the kind of idea of human unity that absorbed him throughout his life.

Merton saw the obstacles to spiritual consciousness presented by modern empiricism as analogous to those presented to the romantics by the dominance of reason in the late eighteenth and early nineteenth centuries. Rather like Thoreau, who described the intellect as a cleaver, Merton identified with the romantics' wariness about the claims of reason and its misuse in the eighteenth century as an instrument for validating the status quo. Reason could travel further than empiricism in probing ultimate reality, as in metaphysical argument, but, left out, for both the romantics and Merton, was the sort of phenomenological contact with ultimate reality that took one beyond the rim of the world of ideas. Merton identified with Blake's pronouncement that in seeing the infinite in all things one thereby saw God.[20] His reading of Blake tend-

19. See Alice Chandler, *A Dream of Order: The Medieval Ideal in Nineteenth-Century English Literature*, 3.
20. Blake, "There Is No Natural Religion," in *Poetry and Prose*, 2d ser., 148.

ed to emphasize Blake's sensitivity to the existential and his wariness about rational abstractions. Thus, whereas Blake claimed to be able to see angels and indeed included angels in his poetry, for Merton this indicated a mind primarily attuned to life and to experience rather than to thought, since the angels that Blake saw were creatures, not ideas.[21] While Blake wrote that everything possible to be believed was an image of truth, Merton generally affirmed the imagination when it worked in tandem with experience. In his thesis on Blake he distinguished between the Thomistic separation of truth and beauty and the view of "Blake and the Hindus," who did not "trouble" to make the distinction. Moreover, in harmony with Eastern philosophy, Blake, Merton insisted, had not been interested in truth in an analytical sense but rather as part of a comprehensive apprehension of being.[22]

Having awakened to the spiritual magnitude of ultimate reality in the late 1930s, Merton looked for signs of such consciousness in the literature he was reading, and he found this consciousness in the romantics. Even his incidental observations about romantic poetry were sensitive to this aspect of their work, as can be seen in the comment in his journal about the song of the dead men in "The Rime of the Ancient Mariner." He noticed that Coleridge used the song of the dead men to demonstrate the power of spiritual reality to affect physical reality, just as the song moved through the dead men in such a way as to reveal their passiveness and their instrumentality to a higher spiritual power.[23] Because of the romantic quest for a unifying vision, these writers resisted the fragmentation of consciousness that they attributed to the acquisition of socialized knowledge. In the romantic view, society's need to reconcile competing claims and factions inevitably led to such fragmentation, discouraging absolute perceptions of reality because of their simplicity and intractability. Hence, Blake's vision of a latent unity in the human condition would have appeared childlike to many. Indeed, romantics such as Blake, Wordsworth, and Whitman espoused the child's vision because of its unity and openness, qualities that a restored,

21. See Merton, "Romanticism," 47.
22. Merton, "Nature and Art in Blake," in *Literary Essays*, 446.
23. Merton, Nov. 13, 1940, in *Run to the Mountain*, 257–58.

paradisal human consciousness needed, they maintained, to incorporate. Thus, Blake let it be known to a correspondent in 1799 that he thought his visions could be more readily understood by children than by those who called themselves adults. Similarly, in the "Immortality Ode," Wordsworth looked back to a time before the intervention of socialized consciousness when the mind and psyche were relatively pristine and thus not overlaid with the layers of acquired thought that would obscure the "celestial light" innate within them. In this context Wordsworth proclaimed that the child was father of the man and an eye among the blind. The romantic emphasis on the child's mind has generally been associated with Rousseau, who declared that everything that came from the Creator was good but that human consciousness degenerated when put into the hands of society and particularly of formal, collective education with its inevitable residue of social indoctrination.[24] Because of the child's vulnerable receptivity and inner unity, neither yet broken by the mediation of reason, the child's mind also became for the romantics a symbol of integrated intelligence in which, for example, there was a mingling of the conscious and unconscious levels of the mind.

Although Merton sided with Blake and against Wordsworth in their rather different perceptions of the spiritual significance of nature, the distinction became less important for him later in life. Initially, he had been sympathetic to Blake's observation that for Wordsworth nature was a divinity, a perception that clashed with Blake's sense that the only divinity lay in a spiritual dimension in which the human mind, particularly the imagination, participated. While Merton came to realize that Wordsworth had evolved from the apparent pantheism of the early poems to a more conventional religiosity in the later work, it is equally evident that Merton underwent a sea change of his own. Although he never forsook his belief in the transcendence of the divine, he came increasingly, in the last decade of his life particularly, to view matter as penetrated by the mind of God through the initial act of creation and through the Incarnation. Furthermore, throughout his writings Merton

---

24. Blake to Dr. Trusler, Aug. 23, 1799, in *Poetry and Prose*, 835; Wordsworth, "Ode: Intimations of Immortality from Recollections of Early Childhood," in *Poetical Works of Wordsworth*, 587; Rousseau, *The Emile of Jean-Jacques Rousseau*, 11.

exhibited a sensitivity to what he perceived as the beauty, power, and goodness of nature that was quite similar to that exhibited by the romantics. While Thoreau, for example, wrote about the "indescribable innocence and beneficence of Nature," Merton also saw nature as representative of the goodness of its Creator and as the occasion for a contemplative union with the Creator. Apart from this, Merton, like Wordsworth, Emerson, and Thoreau, considered human beings and nature as "essentially adapted to each other," as Wordsworth put it. In this connection Emerson wrote that in the wilderness he found something more "connate" than in "streets or villages." In a similar vein Merton wrote to Etienne Gilson in 1951 to say that he had nothing to say to anyone except that which could be said by the "oaks of our forest." Like Saint Bernard of Clairvaux, he added, he could go to the trees and "learn everything." Even in his depiction of human beings Wordsworth chose rustic subjects in the belief that, like children, perhaps, their minds would have been less blunted due to socialization because of their daily proximity to nature.[25] In this light one can understand the importance of solitude for the romantics, and for Merton as a latter-day romantic, as a retreat not only from the ephemeral distractions of collective life but, even more important, from the reductiveness of collective consciousness.

Apart from its being an icon of creation, nature for the romantics and for Merton drew the mind to combine with that which was external to it, including the body, in a restless search for unity. As M. H. Abrams suggested in a reading of Coleridge's "Dejection: An Ode," when the romantic poet confronted a landscape, the "distinction between self and not-self tended to dissolve." Similarly, Jerome McGann has remarked upon Wordsworth's nostalgic quest for the recovery and restoration within human consciousness of the "idea of unity." The sort of union sought by the romantics, with the exception of the most radically pantheistic works, preserved the identity of the self and the separateness of

---

25. Thoreau, *Walden*, 138; Wordsworth, "Preface to the Second Edition," in *Poetical Works of Wordsworth*, 938; Emerson, "Nature," in *Essays and Lectures*, 10; Merton to Gilson, Nov. 12, 1951, in *The School of Charity: The Letters of Thomas Merton on Religious Renewal and Spiritual Direction*, 31; see Wordsworth, "Preface to the Second Edition," in *Poetical Works of Wordsworth*, 935.

the individual. This was one of the features of romanticism that clearly appealed to Merton during his graduate courses at Columbia in the late 1930s, the fact that the flower or tree or person remained what they were while participating in the full richness of being. Merton recognized that Wordsworth's ontological journey had begun with an intuitive perception of his own existence and of the unifying, intelligible reality that underlay all existence. Years later, toward the end of his life, Merton reiterated the same idea: that Wordsworth, for example, had written poems essentially celebrating his intuition of the ground of being.[26] This was the sort of unifying perception that Merton had noted in Blake, in whom existence, art, ideas, and mysticism were all of a piece. While it might be argued that romanticism in an extreme form later gave rise to a radical individualism—in Nietzsche, for example—Merton was attracted to the fine balance struck between individualism and unity by the first generation of English romantic poets.

As was suggested earlier, the impulse toward unity was so strong in romanticism that Blake, according to Merton, defined the Fall in Genesis as a fall from unity into division.[27] By the same token, as Merton recognized, Blake's restored vision of human unity can be seen in these lines spoken by Los in book 2 of *Jerusalem:*

> Mutual in one another's love and wrath all renewing
> We live as One Man; for contracting our infinite senses
> We behold multitude; or expanding: we behold as one,
> As One Man all the Universal Family; and that One Man
> We call Jesus the Christ; and he in us, and we in him,
> Live in perfect harmony in Eden, the land of life.[28]

Although committed to a restoration of unity, Blake also paradoxically thought about reality dialectically, arguing in "The Marriage of Heaven and Hell" that without contraries there was no "progression." In

---

26. Abrams, *The Correspondent Breeze: Essays in English Romanticism,* 102; McGann, *Romantic Ideology,* 40; Merton, "Romantic Poets," 125; Merton, "Romanticism," 66; Merton, *The Springs of Contemplation,* 16.

27. Merton, "Nature and Art in Blake," in *Literary Essays,* 429.

28. Blake, "Jerusalem," in *Poetry and Prose,* book 2, stanza 38, p. 479.

his essay "Blake and the New Theology," written in 1968, Merton contended that Blake's vision went beyond a Hegelian synthesis of history to an inclusive vision of a "higher unity." Coleridge too aspired to a higher state of consciousness in which opposites, including good and evil, became reconciled in a higher and more comprehensive reality. In this context Geoffrey Hartman has commented that the romantic poets sought a return to a unity of being, relying primarily on intuitive consciousness as the means of reconciling contraries. The reconciling of opposites in the romantics later in the nineteenth century extended itself to accommodate what would later still become known as the Darwinian aspects of nature. Thus, Thoreau presented the following complaisant portrait of natural predation: "The perch swallows the grub-worm, the pickerel swallows the perch, and the fisherman swallows the pickerel; and so all the chinks in the scale of being are filled."[29] For a romantic such as Thoreau, this passage appears, unexpectedly, to have a great deal in common with the deism of the eighteenth century that the romantics had ostensibly rejected. Rather than being a justification of an eighteenth-century, exploitatively oriented hierarchy of being, however, Thoreau's passage was intended to illustrate the unified and existential richness of being.

For the romantics, the need to restore a unity of being applied primarily to the act of perception itself and especially to the conjoining of the mind and nature. Nature's value lay in the fact that it presented the mind with an object that was separate from socialized thought. In the union of mind and nature, as Coleridge suggested in the "Dejection: An Ode," a new understanding of existence emerged in which in unifying itself with nature the mind gave to nature, as it were, a fuller, more ontological intelligibility than it would otherwise have possessed. In spite of the charge by Blake that Wordsworth had deified nature and so attributed to it a reality that it did not possess, even in the early "Tintern Abbey" poem Wordsworth had associated nature with an underlying

29. Blake, "Marriage of Heaven and Hell," in *Poetry and Prose,* 181; Merton, "Blake and the New Theology," in *Literary Essays,* 6; on Coleridge, see Clubbe and Lovell, *English Romanticism,* 154; Hartman, "Romanticism and Anti-Self-Consciousness," 303; Thoreau, *Walden,* 284.

spiritual reality that permeated all of being. The later Wordsworth went much further in the direction of a belief in a transcendental deity without sacrificing his earlier consciousness of the immanence of the divine in nature. Although Merton preferred Blake's reading of nature to Wordsworth's because it emphasized that reality was primarily immaterial, he conceded that nature, for Wordsworth, was "God's greatest and most important creation" and that Wordsworth "saw God in nature." While Merton sided with Blake regarding the secondary ontological status of nature alongside the mind, it could be argued that he was finally closer to Wordsworth in his existentialism since Blake had argued platonically in "A Vision of the Last Judgment" that heaven was reserved for those who had "Cultivated their Understandings."[30]

In other respects as well Merton resembled Wordsworth more closely than he did Blake.[31] As opposed to the startling, otherworldly visions of Blake, for example, Merton, like Wordsworth, tended first to describe his observations and then to reflect in tranquillity upon the psychological, ethical, and ontological significance of what he had described. Both Merton and Wordsworth emphasized the value of spontaneous experience followed by a reflective reconsideration as memory and imagination intermingled in a subsequent, deeper reading and re-presentation of original experience. A further bond may have been Merton's awareness that Wordsworth's *Prelude* was the autobiographical record of a man in his midtwenties—a portrait of the artist—a type of autobiography that Joyce and others in the modern period had emulated.[32] Moreover, the inclination toward solitude, such as one finds in Wordsworth's poetry, arose from the need to separate the self from society in order to place it in an environment in which its ontological reality and hence its hidden nature and value could be experienced.[33] The hermit life that

30. Coleridge, "Dejection: An Ode," in *Select Poetry and Prose,* 106; Merton, "Nature and Art in Blake," in *Literary Essays,* 451; Blake, "A Vision of the Last Judgment," in *Poetry and Prose,* 649.

31. On the similarities between Wordsworth and Merton, see Monica Weis, "Beyond the Shadow and the Disguise: 'Spots of Time' in Thomas Merton's Spiritual Development."

32. Merton, "Art of Poetry," n.p.

33. See Thomas McFarland, *Romanticism and the Heritage of Rousseau,* 51.

Merton had sought for many years, which he had partially achieved in the 1960s, had been to some extent prefigured by the picture of solitude that Wordsworth had presented in poems such as "Tintern Abbey":

> Once again I see
> These hedge-rows, hardly hedge-rows, little lines
> Of sportive wood run wild: these pastoral farms,
> Green to the very door; and wreaths of smoke
> Sent up, in silence, from among the trees!
> With some uncertain notice, as might seem
> Of vagrant dwellers in the houseless woods,
> Or of some Hermit's cave, where by his fire
> The Hermit sits alone.[34]

Merton appreciated the importance of stillness and of silence in Wordsworth's poetry, and certainly the nexus of nature, contemplation, and wisdom that one finds in Wordsworth is ubiquitous in Merton's writings. Blake too emphasized the value of solitude and contemplation. In the *Poetical Sketches,* for example, the speaker asks who it is who dares to enter where only nature had trod and is told that it is "Contemplation," who with her "pure quill on every flower writeth Wisdom's name." Thoreau as well wrote that he found it "wholesome" to be "alone the greater part of the time," adding that as a rule he felt less lonely by himself and with nature than when in society.[35]

The romantics related their interest in ontological perception to the sovereignty of the self and they valued this kind of perception above all others. This sovereignty that they perceived in the self paradoxically opened up feelings of affinity and a desire for unity with other human beings, a desire that became distorted within a society in which collective relationships were the norm. As Blake, through his character Los, indicated in *Jerusalem:* "Man is adjoin'd to Man by his Emanative portion / Who is Jerusalem in every individual Man."[36]

The privileging of the self in romanticism led inevitably to an em-

---

34. Wordsworth, "Tintern Abbey," in *Poetical Works of Wordsworth,* 206.
35. Blake, "Poetical Sketches," in *Poetry and Prose,* 43; Thoreau, *Walden,* 135.
36. Blake, "Jerusalem," in *Poetry and Prose,* book 2, stanza 44, p. 490.

phasis upon individualism and to declarations such as Coleridge's to the effect that the great contributions to human culture had invariably been made by individuals rather than by groups. Because of this emphasis upon individual consciousness, Merton became aware of romanticism as a countercultural force. In the view of the English novelist and critic A. S. Byatt, it was the belief by the romantics in the latent "rationality and goodness" of human nature that led to their support of "revolutionary and republican politics" based upon the assumption that affairs of state could safely be entrusted to ordinary human beings. While the English romantics abandoned their initial support for the revolutionary politics of Europe in the beginning of the nineteenth century, the American romantics maintained their populist ideals, with Thoreau proclaiming that the federal government of the United States had not the "vitality and force of a single living man." Apropos of Thoreau's criticism of centralized government and of the dwarfing of human beings brought about by technological culture, Merton noted in his essay "Rain and the Rhinoceros" that Thoreau had sat in his hermitage cabin criticizing the railways while "I sit in mine and wonder about a world that has, well, progressed." Regarding the tension between the individual and institutionalized society, Merton had been attracted to Blake initially because of Blake's simultaneous rejection both of the morally insensitive political and religious authorities of his time and of reformers such as Voltaire and Rousseau, who were too secular to be acceptable within Blake's spiritual terms of reference. For this reason, Merton characterized Blake's iconoclastic nonconformism as fundamentally a "rebellion of the saints."[37]

Blake's influence on Merton was pronounced because Blake was both romantic and mystic, and the two ways of seeing were as overlapping for Merton as they had been for Blake. Just as the romantics challenged the deistic and pragmatic culture of the eighteenth century, the great mystics of Christianity, Merton discovered, had challenged or simply gone around the ponderous administrative and doctrinal aspects of

37. Coleridge, "Table Talk," in *Select Poetry and Prose,* 501; Byatt, *Wordsworth and Coleridge,* 130; Thoreau, "Resistance to Civil Government," in *Reform Papers,* 63; Merton, "Rain and the Rhinoceros," in *Raids on the Unspeakable,* 12; Merton, *The Seven Storey Mountain,* 87.

Christianity. Merton revealed that his attraction to mysticism was especially stimulated by Aldous Huxley's *Ends and Means,* by Jacques Maritain's *Art and Scholasticism,* and, as has already been suggested, by Blake's poetry. In a letter to a journalist in 1963, Merton named the works related to mysticism that had most influenced him, and here he included the sermons of Meister Eckhart, the poetry of Blake, the *Confessions,* the *Sermons on the Psalms* of Saint Augustine, the *Rule* of Saint Benedict, the Bhagavad Gita, and Thomas à Kempis's *Imitation of Christ.*[38] It is difficult to see how so ascetic and reclusive a figure as Thomas à Kempis fitted into Merton's thinking in 1963 when Merton seemed much more preoccupied with social analysis and social reform. On the other hand, Thomas à Kempis represented a strong link with the ascetic dimensions of the monastic life to which Merton remained ideologically committed throughout his life. Thomas à Kempis's deep distrust of nature, however, does not easily square with Merton's sensibility. As far as Merton's indebtedness to Saint Augustine is concerned, he remained always a towering intellectual figure in Merton's imagination, especially with regard to the contemplative ascent to enlightenment. Again, though, Saint Augustine's conception of nature was far more negative than Merton's was, particularly in the later period of Merton's life.

Saint Augustine and the other mystics who interested Merton, including Blake, were in the Neoplatonic tradition, followers of Plotinus (c. 205–270), who attempted to unite Christian theology with Platonic philosophy. Mystical experience, according to Plotinus, brought one closer to the absolute envisaged by Plato, a more impersonal and ontological state of being than the relatively anthropomorphic Christian deity of the Judeo-Christian tradition. Pseudo-Dionysius and Saint Gregory of Nyssa were Neoplatonic mystics in the Church's early history whom Merton admired, but his favorite mystics were Saint John of the Cross and Meister Eckhart. In Saint Gregory of Nyssa, however, were many of the elements that Merton turned to in Saint John of the Cross, especially the perceptual reversal of darkness and light in which the contemplative detached himself or herself from the external world, thereby

38. Merton, Nov. 27, 1941, in *Run to the Mountain,* 455; Merton to M. R. Chandler, July 19, 1963, in *Witness to Freedom: The Letters of Thomas Merton in Times of Crisis,* 166.

creating a darkness in which without other distraction the presence of God could be experienced. In *The Ascent to Truth,* Merton's most analytical study of Western mysticism, he described such a process not only as intellectual but also as ascetic, indicating that the "voyage in darkness" was not to be accomplished without pain because our "spirits were made for light, not for darkness."[39]

In *The Ascent to Truth,* Merton distinguished between the traditions of light and darkness in the Western contemplative tradition—with Saint Gregory of Nyssa and Saint John of the Cross, for example, belonging to the tradition of darkness or the so-called apophatic approach to God. Others, such as Saint Bernard of Clairvaux and Saint Thomas Aquinas, were part of the positive or analogical approach to God that involved a focus on creation as symbolic of God's being. In fact, though, as Merton pointed out, many contemplatives followed both approaches, moving back and forth from one to the other:

> The tradition of apophantic ("non-apparent") theology goes back beyond Pseudo-Dionysius and the Cappadocian Fathers of the fourth century, who long ago taught that if we say "God is," indicating that in Him is the fullness of all that we can conceive of as Being, we must complete it by saying also "God is not" to indicate that the fullness of His Being is far beyond anything that we can conceive of as existing. . . . However, we must remember that this tradition of mystical negation always co-exists, in Christianity, with a tradition of symbolic theology in which positive symbols and analogies of theological teaching are accepted for what they are: true but imperfect approximations which lead us gradually toward that which cannot be properly expressed in human language.[40]

Merton approached the same subject in a somewhat different way in a letter to the distinguished Buddhist scholar Daisetz Suzuki in 1959 in which he attempted to show how the Western mind, as in the philosophy of Saint Thomas Aquinas, moved through analogies between created things to God:

39. Merton, *The Ascent to Truth,* 51.
40. Merton, "Godless Christianity?" in *Faith and Violence,* 269.

> I would suggest a use of the term "analogical." This means that
> we describe something that we do not and cannot know directly, by
> a reference to something that we do know. The terms "being,"
> "power," "love," "wisdom," etc. applied to God are all *analogies*. We
> know what being, power, etc., are in the world of experience, but
> the things that we thus know are so infinitely far from the "being,"
> etc., of God that it is just as true to say that God is "no-being" as to
> say that He is "being."[41]

In communicating with Suzuki, Merton was fastidious in trying to show
how Christianity might be compatible with Buddhism, as is indicated
here in his use of the term *no-being*. In fact, though, the term probably
meant something quite different to Suzuki since all that Merton meant
to say was that the reality of God so transcended our limited conception
of being as to be in another dimension of being altogether. Whether
approached through an apophatic or analogical contemplative process,
however, Merton conceived of God as the fullness of being.

Christian contemplatives who emphasized the analogical, creational
path to God included Saint Francis of Assisi, whose spirituality came
close to drawing Merton as a young man into the Franciscan order. Saint
Francis of Assisi's thought was elucidated and systematized by Saint
Bonaventure, whose spirituality enveloped Merton when he taught at
St. Bonaventure College in upstate New York in the early 1940s. Saint
Francis, like Merton himself, saw creation and nature as a mirror of the
power, mind, and goodness of God. Meister Eckhart, a medieval German mystic whom Merton much admired, wrote about nature in an even
more elevated manner than Saint Francis of Assisi: "Nature works so
uniformly and resembles the first emanation, which is so like that of the
angels that Moses did not dare to write of it lest weak-minded persons
should worship it, because they are so much alike."[42] While Merton distanced himself from the heterodox pantheism that had led to the disciplining of Eckhart by ecclesiastical authorities, he nonetheless identified

---

41. Merton to Suzuki, Oct. 24, 1959, in *The Hidden Ground of Love: The Letters of
Thomas Merton on Religious Experience and Social Concerns*, 568.
42. Eckhart, Latin Sermon no. 9 ["Adolescens"], in *Meister Eckhart: An Introduction
to the Study of His Works with an Anthology of His Sermons*, 167.

with the mystic's intense appreciation of nature and with Eckhart's accompanying perception that nature was in some sense part and parcel of God even if God transcended nature.

The contemplative order to which Merton belonged, the Cistercians, had been founded by Saint Bernard of Clairvaux, who directed that Cistercian monasteries be built in secluded, wooded valleys and who confided that he had learned all of his wisdom from the trees of the forests. As Merton put it in *The Waters of Siloe* (1949), it would be difficult for anyone, "at least temporarily," not to succumb to the "charm of the typical Cistercian valley," adding that one such monastery had inspired Wordsworth's famous poem "Tintern Abbey."[43] Augmenting this positive view of nature and its integral relationship to Western monasticism was Merton's rather startling observation that in the contemplative tradition to which he belonged not only nature in general but also human nature in particular might be regarded as not having been fundamentally corrupted by the Fall:

> Saint Bernard is always careful to insist that human nature was in no way harmed, in its essence, by the fall. We always remain what God has made us *in our essence,* but the tragedy is that God's good work is overlaid by the evil work of our own wills. Hence our simplicity was not taken from us but, and this was far worse, it was concealed under the disfigurement of a duplicity, a hypocrisy, a living lie that was not and could not be natural to us or part of our nature, and yet which would inevitably cling to us as a kind of hideous second-nature.[44]

Saint Bernard of Clairvaux's view of the essential goodness of human nature, with which in this passage Merton is in obvious agreement, underlay much of Merton's paradisal consciousness. For Merton, and for others such as Eckhart who were similarly influenced by Neoplatonic mysticism, the human psyche contained a germ of divine substance that had survived the Fall. In the above passage Merton argues that the Fall was more the result of blindness and a perverse recklessness than of an

43. Merton, *The Waters of Siloe,* 273.
44. Merton, *Thomas Merton on St. Bernard,* 109.

innately corrupted human nature. In any case, he postulated an inner conflict in human beings between an extant, innate, primordial innocence and a foolish and willful waywardness in behavior that issued from a socialized human nature.

According to Richard T. Wallis, a major difference between Neoplatonism and Christian mysticism arose from Plotinus's conviction that one's "true self" was "eternally saved" and that what was required was one's awakening to this fact. Because in Plotinus's philosophy the natural world was considered a sufficient world, morally speaking, there was no sense of sin and consequently no need for redemption through supernatural intervention. While Merton always upheld the need for supernatural intervention through the Incarnation of Christ, increasingly in the later writings, especially as he came under the influence of Buddhism, this aspect of his belief was given less emphasis than his intense awareness of the sufficiency of being. The same sort of ontological emphasis can be seen in Saint Augustine, who had a profound influence on Merton and who defined God platonically as absolute reality. While one does not want to overstate the influence of Neoplatonism on Merton through both the romantics and the Western mystics, he himself acknowledged his affinity to Platonic idealism in an entry in his journal in 1960 in which he admitted that he had to some extent "always been a Platonist."[45] The approach to God as absolute and ultimate reality by Western mystics in the Neoplatonic tradition emphasized the mind, which in contemplation the mystic attempted to permeate with the presence, including the intuited viewpoint so to speak, of God. As with the romantics this intuitive apprehension of reality involved the mind at all levels since for Plotinus consciousness at the surface was only one of several levels of awareness, including what is now called the subconscious and the unconscious. Another such link between romanticism and Neoplatonic mysticism was the ontological conception of the universe as a living unity, as an organic whole.

As was suggested earlier, Merton was inclined to use the terms *imagination, contemplation, mysticism,* and *intuition* interchangeably. In addi-

---

45. Wallis, *Neo-Platonism,* 89–90; Merton, Oct. 24, 1960, in *Turning toward the World: The Pivotal Years,* 59.

tion, the understanding that resulted from the fruitful contemplative use of these faculties Merton generally called *wisdom*. In support of this interchangeable use of terminology, Evelyn Underhill suggested in her landmark study of mysticism that the sort of intuition involved in mystical understanding at its most basic level, if not at higher levels, was similar to that described by the English romantic poets. As Geddes MacGregor observed in connection with the philosophical views of Jacques Maritain, mystical experience involves a connatural knowledge, an "immediate inclination" toward wisdom or ultimate reality based upon a disposition toward this knowledge rooted in our psyches.[46] Furthermore, as Daisetz Suzuki, for whose views Merton had great respect, noted in connection with Eastern philosophy, a searching of ultimate reality required a broad use of the contemplative or mystic's mind:

> Intellect, however, is not the whole thing. There must be a deep power of imagination, there must be a strong, inflexible will-power, there must be a keen insight into the nature of man, and finally there must be an actual seeing of the truth as synthesized in the whole being of the man himself.
>
> I wish to emphasize this idea of "seeing." It is not enough to "know" as the term is ordinarily understood. Knowledge unless it is accompanied by a personal experience is superficial and no kind of philosophy can be built upon such a shaky foundation.[47]

In the sorts of mystical traditions in which Merton was interested, this kind of preparatory understanding was taken as a necessary prelude to mystical understanding in general. In the Western, in contrast with the Eastern, mystical tradition, however, it is not only enlightenment but also the experience of contact with God that is sought.

Moreover, if, according to Evelyn Underhill, Eastern mysticism was more acutely conscious of the evolutionary process of being than Western mysticism, Western mysticism has had, according to Underhill, a social dimension that was absent in Eastern mysticism, a feature of which

---

46. See Merton, *The Ascent to Truth*, 59, 189; Underhill, *Mysticism*, 285; MacGregor, *Aesthetic Experience in Religion*, 142.

47. Suzuki, *Mysticism: Christian and Buddhist*, 33–34.

Merton was obviously aware in his attempts throughout the 1960s to show the effects of contemplation on social action. Furthermore, in the Western tradition to which in most fundamental respects Merton belonged, there was a greater openness toward reason than in the East, as long as reason was balanced with the other faculties and levels of the mind. Thus, Merton praised Saint John of the Cross, for example, for his reconciling of mysticism and the rational formulations of theological doctrine. Furthermore, in a letter to Father Raymond Flanagan in the 1940s, Merton described Saint John of the Cross as having been wary of those who desired "visions, ecstasies, locutions, and indeed any other kind of faith experience."[48] Although written early in his monastic career, there is no reason to think that Merton altered his views or the sort of balance that he here reflects. Within that orientation toward balance, moreover, was a tendency toward inclusiveness and a corresponding distrust of a potential dominance by any one kind of intelligence or energy. Thus, in *The Ascent to Truth* he praised Saint John of the Cross for exhibiting a prudence that was not, however, subservient to a wooden formalism.

By the same token, with his orientation toward breadth, Merton was uncomfortable with a contemplative theology that focused exclusively on love, and in this respect he valued the contribution to mystical thought made by Saint Thomas Aquinas for whom the intellect was always an integral part of the soul's turning toward God. Although Merton was sensitive to the narrow dominance that reason could sometimes achieve in culture, he saw no fundamental opposition between mysticism and reason or between mysticism and science. Thus, in a letter to Ernesto Cardenal in 1963, he praised the fifteenth-century mystic Nicholas of Cusa for anticipating through imaginative discernment the "kind of relativity," as Merton put it, that in a modern scientific form would later become widely associated with Einstein.[49] The possibility of friction between reason and mysticism arose only in the case where one attempted, as Merton put it, to reach God solely through conceptual understanding, blocking the fuller, experiential illumination of the soul.

48. Merton to Flanagan [1946–1947], in *Witness to Freedom*, 232.
49. Merton to Cardenal, undated entry from 1963, in *The Courage for Truth: The Letters of Thomas Merton to Writers*, 143.

While his own reflective type of contemplative experience was quite different from the visionary contemplation of Saint Teresa of Avila, Merton valued the monastic reforms that she had effected, reforms that emphasized the centrality of solitude, the sine qua non, in Merton's view, of the contemplative life. Solitude paradoxically fostered a hospitable, unifying consciousness by making possible the emergence of the self under its own starry sky, which it then discovered was the same sky that ontologically vaulted all of being. In the estimation of the Buddhist scholar Daisetz Suzuki, this was the point where Western mysticism, represented by those such as Meister Eckhart, and Eastern mysticism converged:

> "A little point" left by God corresponds to what Zen Buddhists would call *satori*. . . . To have a *satori* means to be standing at Eckhart's "point" where we can look in two directions: God-way and creature-way. Expressed in another form, the finite is infinite and the infinite is finite.
>
> Eckhart's "little point" is the eye, that is to say, "The eye by which I see God is the same as the eye by which God sees me."[50]

In Aldous Huxley's *Ends and Means,* a work that increased Merton's respect as a young man for contemplative understanding, he read that a "direct intuition of ultimate reality," as Huxley had put it, could help to establish a union between the "soul" and the "integrating principle of the universe." This ontological intimacy between the individual and the cosmos gave rise to a sense of the immanence of the divine, a consciousness that Merton derived both from Western mystics such as Eckhart and from Eastern mystical works such as the Hindu Bhagavad Gita, which he identified as one of the chief influences on him in the 1930s.[51] Without becoming thoroughly pantheistic, Merton gradually became accustomed to thinking of the divine immanence in the soul as a way of seeing with God's point of view, as it were. The transcending of a merely

---

50. Suzuki, *Mysticism,* 63.

51. Huxley, *Ends and Means,* 293, 286. Regarding the influence of the Bhagavad Gita on Merton, see his essay, "The Significance of the *Bhagavad-Gita,*" in *The Asian Journal of Thomas Merton,* 348–53.

natural viewpoint did in at least one respect ostensibly thwart unifying consciousness since it seemed to distance the mind from nature. Merton believed, however, that the contemplative or mystic did not reject creation but rather sought a detachment from possessive feelings about it. In this way the mind was free to enjoy the natural world without being a captive to it.

Speaking of Meister Eckhart's contemplative understanding of the intimacy between the soul and God in *Zen and the Birds of Appetite* (1968), Merton wrote of a "basic unity" within the self at the "summit of our being" where one could become united with God. Eckhart, who, as has been suggested, had a profound influence on Merton's ideas about the contemplative life, held that God was "in the soul, with His nature, with His being, and with His Divinity, and yet He is not the soul." Because of the involvement of God in matter through Christ, Eckhart believed, human nature as such had been transformed in such a way that what it was to Christ it could also become to other human beings. This transformation Eckhart associated with a "spark" in the soul or psyche that was immune from the corruptive consequences of the biblical fall from grace. Through contemplation one could experience this spark in the soul as a higher understanding of the soul's character and relationship to ultimate being. Inevitably, both in Eckhart and in Saint John of the Cross, the new understanding that was thereby brought about was one of unity and reintegration, first of the self, then of the self in relationship to God and to others. Thus, in speaking of Saint John of the Cross, Merton indicated that if there was one kind of knowledge or understanding with which the soul was inevitably discontent, it was one that was "fragmentary, illusory and incomplete." Similarly, in commenting on the tradition of English mysticism in *Mystics and Zen Masters* (1967), Merton emphasized the importance of the consciousness of "wholeness" and in turn of the relationship of this to the paradisal, "primitive state of innocence." He was respectfully aware that for mystics such as the medieval female English mystic Julian of Norwich, wholeness meant that God needed to be perceived as both male and female. Moreover, in his reading of Buddhism as a young man, Merton became impressed by the importance of unity in Buddhist thought, noting in a review of Aldous Huxley's *Ends and Means* in 1938 that in Buddhism "separateness" was synonymous with "pain" and that such "manifestations of 'separateness' as anger, greed, self assertion, or even boasting" were the "lowest degradation."[52] Here was contained the link between separateness and moral evil that would mark Merton's thought through all of his life.

The push toward unity and inclusiveness within Western mysticism came largely from Neoplatonism through which the hierarchy of being was also a hierarchy of unity wherein the higher one ascended in one's consciousness of the spiral of existence, the more unity with the rest of being one perceived and felt. As has been intimated, for Merton these desirable ideas of unity and inclusiveness were also, preeminently, to be found in Eastern religion—as in Buddhism—where, he argued, the apparent centering on nothingness gave one only a partial and therefore a somewhat misleading view of Buddhist thought. When Westerners spoke of "fullness," he observed, they inevitably and ironically tended to imagine a "'content'" with a limit that defined and circumscribed that fullness. Buddhists, on the other hand, preferred to speak of "'emptiness,'" not because they conceived of the ultimate as mere nothingness and void, but because they were aware of the "non-limitation and nondefinition of the infinite."[53] Here Merton equated Buddhism with the apophatic tradition of Western mysticism in which the physical world is transcended by being submerged in a psychic darkness that freed the mind and soul to paradoxically seek a fuller reality, a reality that contained nature without being limited to it.

Romanticism and mysticism, which overlap in many respects, as has been suggested, awakened Merton as a young man to an idealized reality that was centered on unity and wholeness. Although in the 1940s he tended to marginalize this aspect of his thinking in favor of the cognitive certainty that he sought in the Roman Catholic Church, increasingly after this period he returned to the idea of wholeness as the fount

52. Merton, *Zen and the Birds of Appetite*, 11–12; Eckhart, Latin Sermon no. 12 ["Nolite Timere"], in *Meister Eckhart*, 184; Merton, *The Ascent to Truth*, 56; Merton, *Mystics and Zen Masters*, 139; Merton, "Huxley and the Ethics of Peace," in *Literary Essays*, 460.

53. Merton, *Zen and the Birds of Appetite*, 85.

of his thinking about a great many diverse matters. Although mysticism, as opposed to romanticism, did not emphasize the role of the child, it did virtually the same thing in summoning the mind back to a consciousness of its created innocence and therefore of the prospect of a recovered, paradisal awareness. Stimulated by an imagined wholeness and unity, such paradisal consciousness allowed both romantics and mystics to offset the friction caused by collective living, both in the depersonalized landscapes of industrialized society and in the often numbing pronouncements of ecclesiastical bureaucracy.

Furthermore, both romanticism and mysticism emphasized the importance of solitude, even if only the solitude of iconoclastic independence—as in the case of Blake—solitude that formed a bulwark against the deadening effects of collective and especially of institutionalized consciousness. For both romantic and mystic, individual consciousness lay at the center of any attempt to transcend materialism. So it did as well for Thomas Merton in spite of his durable connection, even if an increasingly strained one, to the elaborate organization of the Roman Catholic Church. The emphasis on individual consciousness in both romanticism and mysticism inevitably placed romantics and mystics in a state of tension with the institutions of both church and state. Nevertheless, the norms of unity and wholeness at the heart of both romanticism and mysticism pulled romantics and mystics toward other human beings through an intuitive, ontological perception of unity that surpassed the often specious cohesiveness of both secular and ecclesiastical society.

Growing up against the background of two world wars, which were to be followed by other regional wars, Merton experienced society as synonymous with divisiveness and nationalism. For this reason in part, perhaps, in the 1930s he looked outside of twentieth-century culture for an alternative vision. In Blake, Wordsworth, Saint John of the Cross, and Meister Eckhart he encountered such an alternative discernment of human existence. Essentially, this involved the recovery of the self and its latent unifying, transsocial orientation toward being and the consciousness of being. The romantics and mystics suggested to Merton not the need to find other worlds than this one but rather the need to find other worlds *in* this one, worlds that one could not only think about but also live in. In this sense, rooted in the past, Merton's newfound awareness was anachronistic, perhaps, but in its durable insight and surprising accessibility, he felt, it was paradoxically pertinent to his own culture and time.

2

Consciousness and Being

In *The Seven Storey Mountain*, Merton lamented the "dead" rationalism that had frozen his mind, as he put it, during his university years, and was grateful to Blake for having relieved him of that experience. Similarly, in a letter to the distinguished Protestant theologian Paul Tillich in 1959, he indicated that since he had been "subjected" to a Thomist "formation," the experience had left him a little wary of "technical" metaphysics and that he on the whole preferred the Franciscan "instinct for immediacy." By the same token he found himself as a contemplative more attracted to the mysticism of Saint John of the Cross than to the theological bent of mind that seemed to him to mark the founder of his own order, Saint Bernard of Clairvaux. In like fashion in his preface to the French edition of *The Ascent to Truth*, written in 1957, Merton reflected that were he to have revised that book he would have concerned himself less with medieval Scholastic philosophy than he had, initially, since Scholasticism was not after all the "true intellectual climate for a monk."[1]

Merton's expository writing, which included books such as *The Ascent to Truth*, show that he was capable of clear and sustained analytical writing. Furthermore, with respect to the knowledge and scholarship that

1. Merton, *The Seven Storey Mountain*, 190; Merton to Tillich, Sept. 4, 1959, in *Hidden Ground of Love*, 577; Merton to Dom Jean-Baptiste Porion, Feb. 9, 1952, in *School of Charity*, 33; Merton, *Honorable Reader: Reflections on My Work*, 28.

underlay his expository writing, he argued on a number of occasions that the contemplative life required a solid cultural underpinning, and he criticized those in the monastic life who seemed to make a virtue of ignorance. Nonetheless, while he respected the soundness of Aquinas's deductive brilliance, he felt uneasy at becoming enmeshed in the mechanism of deductive reasoning and uncomfortable at becoming locked platonically within the world of thought. Thus, in his late work *Zen and the Birds of Appetite,* he found himself wanting to emulate the approach of the great German mystic Meister Eckhart, who in Merton's view both had ideas and was "free of them." Merton's uneasy perception about the limits of systematic reasoning was intensified by his allergy to the legacy of Cartesianism with its "reification of concepts" and "idolization of the reflexive consciousness."[2] Even more than deductive reasoning, Cartesianism separated the mind from the world around it, shifting the center of gravity of perception toward solipsism and away from external reality. In Merton's view Cartesianism had infiltrated modern thought, especially scientific and technological culture, with such thoroughness that human beings had become alienated from the external world, including other human beings and nature, losing a sense of their affinity to their fellow creatures. Even religion had structured the world in a Cartesian hierarchy that separated human beings from the world around them, as Merton wryly suggested in the prologue to *The Geography of Lograire:* "In holy walks there is never an order. . . . In holy seas there is never so much religion."[3]

Throughout his life Merton attempted to short-circuit his deliberative tendencies in order to create a space for contemplation. A passage from his journal in the spring of 1965 is characteristic of this attempt. There he announced that he had not sought to be a "'solitary'" or anything else, since "'being anything,'" as he put it, was a "distraction." It was enough to "be" in an "ordinary human mode, with only hunger and sleep, one's cold and warmth, rising and going to bed." In this way he believed that he lived as his "fathers" had lived, and in order to make this

2. Merton, *Zen and the Birds of Appetite,* 10; Merton, *Conjectures of a Guilty Bystander,* 260. See also Merton, Mar. 19, 1963, in *Turning toward the World,* 304.

3. Merton, *The Geography of Lograire: The Collected Poems of Thomas Merton,* 460.

kind of living possible he pledged to learn over time to forget "program and artifice."[4] The passage reveals Merton's romantic primitivism in general and his attempt in particular to elude the habit of ego-centered calculation that obscured the face of the world beyond the self. Similarly, although he sometimes fretted over his abbot's refusal to permit him to travel and to change monasteries, he was grateful, finally, for the vow of stability that he had taken, a vow to stay in one place, because by doing so he could observe with each day's passing how "inexhaustibly rich and different" was the "'sameness'" of his life.[5]

As his own successful involvement in the administration of his monastery made evident, Merton was not opposed to the planning and performance of life's practical responsibilities. While he sought a life that fundamentally—with its own time and space—reached beyond planning and execution toward attentiveness and contemplation, this did not mean a life that became permanently suspended in timelessness. While for Merton contemplation, in its ultimate sense, involved a timeless awareness of the presence of God, in its proximate sense it was involved with the quotidian and with history. An example of this proximate kind of contemplation can be seen in a 1965 entry in the journal *Dancing in the Water of Life:* "Grey dawn. A blood red sun, furious among the pines (it will soon be hidden in clouds). That darn black hound is baying in the hollow after some rabbit he will never catch. Deep grass in the field, dark green English woods (for we have had good rains). The bombing goes on in Vietnam."[6] Opening the journal entry with an observation about his natural surroundings as was his custom, Merton moves through the colors and shapes in his surroundings with a renewed sense of the eternal freshness of creation. The sober intrusion of his concern about the war in Vietnam comes as a minor shock to the reader following the unfolding of the description of the new day. It is difficult to determine the inner dynamics of the passage, since many possibilities

4. Merton, June 18, 1965, in *Dancing in the Water of Life: Seeking Peace in the Hermitage,* 257.
    5. Merton, May 28, 1965, in ibid., 251.
    6. Merton, May 22, 1965, in ibid., 249. I am indebted to Christine Bochen for drawing my attention to this passage.

present themselves. It might be argued, for example, that the sight of the "blood red sun" oriented Merton so that the subsequent allusion to the war followed along an associative track. Before the thought of Vietnam occurs, however, the image of the bloodred sun has been offset by the relatively consoling image of the moist and verdant grass and of Merton's redolent sense of his growing up in England. Another possibility is that the passage described the process of awakening itself. In this context one can see the sharply offsetting thought about the war as a rising into a more diurnal consciousness whereby the pressures of actuality suddenly reassert themselves. The boundaries of the passage are fluid and inclusive, allowing for the meaning to surface in the various ways that have been suggested without the sense that either the reader or Merton need experience the anxiety of ambiguity.

It was because of his awareness of the limits of systematic reasoning and of the alienating separation of the mind from the external world brought about by Cartesianism that Merton placed such a high value on spontaneity. As an example of his penchant for spontaneity, in 1960 he approved of the slow development of the plan for the construction of his hermitage, which thus evolved, as he emphasized, without "premeditation."[7] Once installed in the hermitage, and stimulated by his growing interest in Zen Buddhism, which he termed a "non-systematic" and "direct" vision into the "ground of being,"[8] he settled softly into his surroundings with a sharp appreciation for the *"immediacy"* of his relationship to the creatures around him, the "sun, the summer tanager," the "clear morning, the trees, the quiet, the barely born butterfly from the cocoon under the bench."[9] Merton's sense of immediacy here increased his attentiveness to the actuality of the life around him, something that was frustrated, he believed, by the inevitable abstractionism of both Thomist and Cartesian analysis. His sense of immediacy and actuality can be seen in a poem from the mid-1950s titled "Stranger":

> One bird sits still
> Watching the work of God:

7. Merton, June 1, 1960, in *Turning toward the World,* 6.
8. Merton, *Opening the Bible,* 51.
9. Merton, June 3, 1963, in *Turning toward the World,* 326.

One turning leaf,
Two falling blossoms,
Ten circles upon the pond.

One cloud upon the hillside,
Two shadows in the valley
And the light strikes home. . . .

Now act is waste
And suffering undone
Laws become prodigals
Limits are torn down
For envy has no property
And passion is none.

Look, the vast Light stands still
Our cleanest Light is One![10]

While the poem proceeds through a host of particulars to a final unity, it is important to see how exactly this is accomplished. At the beginning of the poem the particular creatures met are counted, reflecting Merton's valued perception of each of them: one bird, one turning leaf, two blossoms, one cloud, two shadows. In the midst of such contemplative riches, act is indeed waste, especially just as the flooding light of the sun united all of the creatures just encountered in a supernal, unifying reality. The speaker measures the contemplative distance traveled not only in the images of the many leading to the one but also in the rhyming sounds, which carry the reader from the negatively charged fields of "undone" and "none" to the affirmed "One." The negatively charged words—"suffering," "Laws," and "envy"—are part of a conversion of the difficult friction of some experience into the sublimated, blissful state of consciousness that concludes the poem.

Similarly, in a poem in *Emblems of a Season of Fury* (1963) titled "O Sweet Irrational Worship" in deference to a similarly titled poem by e. e. cummings, Merton demonstrated a heightened attentiveness to being as well as the sort of epistemological uniting of subject and object that one encounters in the romantics or in the writings of the great mystics:

10. Merton, "Stranger," in *Collected Poems*, 290.

Wind and a bobwhite
And the afternoon sun.

By ceasing to question the sun
I have become light,

Bird and wind.

My leaves sing.

I am earth, earth

All these lighted things
Grow from my heart.[11]

Shedding the dialectics of the "questioning" mind, the speaker moves out into the creatures around him with a Keatsian negative capability, temporarily becoming, on the level of consciousness at any rate, one with an environment that draws him into the wider circle of being. Within this wider circle all of being flows through him, now that the privileged view of the ego has been temporarily set aside so that the center of perception shifts imperceptibly toward a dispersed yet unified field.

Given Merton's commitment as a writer not only to consciousness but also to work, to culture, and to social morality, such protracted attentiveness, which united self and object, was inevitably momentary and frequently curtailed. In 1968 he reflected upon the power of such moments to sweep away the clutter of life in a memorable scene in which he gazed at the great reclining Buddhas in Polonnaruwa, Sri Lanka (then called Ceylon). In looking at the figures he suddenly found his consciousness clearing, having transcended its habitual, "half-tied vision of things," as he put it in 1968. In spite of such transcendence Merton was not dismissive of ordinary life. In this connection, in 1960 he appeared to strike what he considered a desirable balance between contemplation and action in a pithy comment included in the preface to the Argentinean edition of his selected writings: "Contemplation," he observed, "cannot construct a new world by itself," but without contemplation "we cannot understand the significance of the world in which we

11. Merton, "O Sweet Irrational Worship," in ibid., 344.

must act." By understanding, Merton here meant a knowing without the attachment of either desire or fear so that the world of one's own experience is seen with ontological transparency, as it were, with a full sense of its participatory value in the fullness of being. Such a perception he thought of as an "intuitive and 'direct' apprehension of reality," as he indicated in a letter to Raymond Prince in 1965.[12] In seeing the mind's apprehension of reality as a direct experience in which subject and object are initially united, Merton took a position similar to that taken by Heidegger, whom he had been reading in the late 1950s and early 1960s.

Such direct and immediate understanding of reality Merton assumed to have been made possible by the construction of the mind itself and was therefore available, he insisted, even to primitive peoples. Thus, he praised the work of the cave painters and their "contemplative intuition" in portraying the animals in their surroundings, in particular their illumination of the essential being of these animals, their "'deerness,'" for example.[13] In this way, Merton reflected, one came to know not only the deer but the minds that painted them and the similarity of those minds to one's own as well. He thought of the mind's capacity for intuition as a kind of innate memory, a Jungian storehouse of symbols and meanings that were present in the minds of individuals and had historically also been incorporated, not always without distortion, into society and culture.[14] A serious problem arose, he believed, as in contemporary culture, when society and culture lost the sense of the importance of such innate symbolism, inevitably leading to individuals within society ceasing to attend to this fundamental flow of sign and meaning from within.

In this respect Merton saw the role of the artist as especially significant in an age in which, he believed, society had generally lost touch with fundamental ontological realities. In particular, technological culture, which he saw as preoccupied with proximate purposes that had to do with means rather than ends, seemed indifferent to ontological considerations. Nevertheless, he was not at war with science, and marveled at

12. Merton, Dec. 4, 1968, in *The Other Side of the Mountain: The End of the Journey*, 323; Merton, *Honorable Reader*, 42; Merton to Prince, May 22, 1965, in *Hidden Ground of Love*, 495.
13. Merton, Sept. 6, 1965, in *Dancing in the Water of Life*, 291.
14. See Merton, *Conjectures of a Guilty Bystander*, 145.

the intuitive triumphs of science in the case of thinkers such as Einstein. At the same time, for Merton, the psyche, though admittedly primed both by experience and by subsequent reflection about experience, contained an innate and unique predisposition toward an understanding of general truths connected with human nature and its affinity with the rest of being. As evidence of such innate understanding, Merton pointed throughout his life to the convergence of the same ontological and ethical insights produced by individuals and cultures in diverse times and places. The intuitive recognition of the true self and of its innate wisdom for Merton involved a further recognition of the spark of the divine mirror within the self, a mirror that could be seen, he argued, only in the deepest contemplation in which the ego and its preoccupations and anxieties had been temporarily displaced. In Merton's view this inner orientation of the self toward wisdom had been exemplified by Christ, who provided human beings with a living template by which to discern and value the ideally human:

> And if we are to contemplate God at all, this internal image must be re-formed by grace, and then we must enter into this inner sanctuary which is the substance of the soul itself. This passage from the exterior to the interior has nothing to do with concentration or introspection. It is a transit from objectivization to knowledge by intuition and connaturality. The majority of people never enter into this inward self, which is an abode of silence and peace and where the diversified activities of the intellect and will are collected, so to speak, into one intense and smooth and spiritualized activity which far exceeds in its fruitfulness the plodding efforts of reason working on external reality with its analyses and syllogisms.[15]

A vivid instance of the fact that such contemplative activity was directed at experience rather than at conceptual knowledge is present in *The Seven Storey Mountain* in which Merton as a young traveler found himself mystically transported while attending Mass in a Cuban church:

> But what a thing it was, this awareness: it was so intangible, and yet it struck me like a thunderclap. It was a light that was so bright that

15. Merton, "Poetry and Contemplation: A Reappraisal," in *Literary Essays*, 348.

it had no relation to any visible light and so profound and so intimate that it seemed like a neutralization of every lesser experience. . . . The reason why this light was blinding and neutralizing was that there was and could be nothing in it of sense or imagination. When I call it a light that is a metaphor which I am using, long after the fact. But at the moment, another overwhelming thing about this awareness was that it disarmed all images, all metaphors, and cut through the whole skein of species and phantasms with which we naturally do our thinking. It ignored all sense experience in order to strike directly at the heart of truth, as if a sudden and immediate contact had been established between my intellect and the Truth.[16]

In Merton's view the ascent to God could proceed through a positive or negative route of consciousness. Along the mystical *via positiva* the mind searched out and celebrated beings that contained qualities of the divine, not only of the divine nature, the object of Platonic knowledge, but also of the divine presence. In this way the mind ascended through analogy to God, as Saint Thomas Aquinas had done, not only as philosopher but as mystic as well. Proceeding mystically along the *via negativa*, the apophatic route, Merton turned away on a number of occasions from being in general as an inadequate register of the divine, and searched inwardly for the divine spark, as Meister Eckhart had conceived of it, in the human psyche. In *New Seeds of Contemplation* (1962), Merton made it clear that such an intuitive process could lead to a view of the self and of all reality that amounted to a vicarious sharing in the viewpoint of God:

> The most usual entrance to contemplation is through a desert of aridity in which, although you see nothing and feel nothing and apprehend nothing and are conscious only of a certain interior suffering and anxiety, yet you are drawn and held in this darkness and dryness because it is the only place in which you can find any kind of stability and peace. As you progress, you learn to rest in this arid quietude, and the assurance of a comforting and mighty presence at the heart of this experience grows on you more and more, until

16. Merton, *The Seven Storey Mountain*, 284–85.

you gradually realize that it is God revealing Himself to you in a
light that is painful to your nature and to all its faculties, because it
is infinitely above them and because its purity is at war with your
own selfishness and darkness and imperfection.[17]

Considering Merton's writings as a whole, it is evident that he did not
regard the apophatic form of consciousness, the *via negativa*, as a repu-
diation of the creational world—obviously not, since that world was the
basis of the positive path to God, the *via positiva*. As a contemplative he
used both approaches for different kinds of consciousness of God, the
God intimately experienced in creation and the transcendental God
whose being far exceeded analogies that only faintly described divine in-
finity.

It is important not to confuse the intuitive process of contemplation,
as Merton thought of it, in the case of either the *via positiva* or the *via
negativa,* with mere subjectivism or solipsism. He often balked at such
facile assumptions about contemplative experience, as he did in reacting
to the death of his artist friend Victor Hammer. In that case he described
death in general as the absurdity that Camus confronted, a mystery that
offered no clear explanation even to the contemplative. We do not *know,*
he insisted, what happens to the dead, and even the faith of the religious
believer ought to be rooted in our "unknowing."[18] Looking at Merton's
writings as a whole, one can infer that he thought of intuition as like the
sighting of a hilltop in the distance that one could see from afar while
not immediately seeing how to get to it. In order to test the strength of
a particular intuition, Merton assumed that reasoning and evidentiary
methods of various kinds could be used to show whether the original intuition was valid. As an example, quite early in life Merton had had an
intuition that solitude and contemplation were not states that ought to
have been reserved for those in the monastic life but rather that they
were needed by all human beings in order to fulfill and to recognize the
meaning of their lives. Since the early 1950s when Merton made this
view about the importance of solitude known in works such as *Seeds of*

17. Merton, *New Seeds of Contemplation,* 275–76.
18. Merton, July 8, 1967, in *Learning to Love: Exploring Solitude and Freedom,* 260.

Contemplation, readers' attestations as to the validity of his insights about solitude and contemplation have accumulated in many parts of the world. Moreover, in a related area, thinkers such as Carl Jung in books like *The Undiscovered Self* reached conclusions similar to Merton's about the need to acknowledge the unique wisdom of the self and the psyche in a highly technological culture that had become dismissive toward the self. Indeed, Jung claimed that the psyche represented a distinct reality that could not be reduced to physiology or to "anything else."[19] In connection with realities for which evidence was difficult to obtain, Merton viewed the mind as left on its own but with the knowledge that intuition had established its validity in areas where evidence, perhaps of an anecdotal yet persuasive kind, had been forthcoming.

Oddly enough, Merton, rather like the scientist, relied on intuitive understanding to *objectify* knowledge, though he was usually averse to this term because of its Cartesian overtones. Nevertheless, and particularly in the light of his growing interest in Zen Buddhism in the 1960s, he sought to know all things, not analytically but in "complete oneness" with them, as he put it in *Mystics and Zen Masters.*[20] In this way, he added, one's consciousness became the consciousness of all beings, even those beings without intelligence. For this reason he admired Hopkins's idea of inscape and tried to emulate it in his own writing. Through inscape the artist could mentally capture a particular bird, for example, partly from knowledge—and here one recalls Merton the naturalist's studious gathering of information about the plants and animals in his midst—and partly from an intuited identification with the bird. The value perceived stemmed not primarily from the poet's *impression* of a particular bird but rather from the capturing of the bird's ascent through image and sound without interpretive commentary.

The most distinctive characteristic of intuitive consciousness in Merton's opinion was its capacity to resolve multiplicity into oneness, an accomplishment that he associated with the philosophy of Heraclitus, among others. This oneness Merton thought of in terms of wholeness

19. Jung, *The Undiscovered Self,* 46.
20. Merton, *Mystics and Zen Masters,* 245.

by which he meant both its unity and its inclusiveness.[21] For Merton, the unity so obtained involved not only whatever was perceived but also the operation of the mind itself. Thus, he sought ontological intuitions that registered a total response of the mind and the psyche, involving all levels of the mind in a perception of the wholeness in experience. In Merton's eyes wisdom involved not only the horizontal wholeness of unity and inclusiveness but also, as he explained in an essay on William Faulkner, the vertical wholeness, so to speak, of ultimacy:

> In ancient terms, it seeks the "ultimate causes," not simply efficient causes which make things happen, but the ultimate reasons why they happen and the ultimate values which their happening reveals to us. Wisdom is not only speculative, but also practical: that is to say, it is "lived." . . . It proceeds, then, not merely from knowledge *about* ultimate values, but from an actual possession and awareness of these values as incorporated in one's own existence.[22]

The mentioning of ultimate values appears to indicate a process that was at least partly deductive, and this is consistent with Merton's conception of wisdom. He accepted the usefulness of deductive and empirical reasoning as far as they went, leaving room, though, for aspects of wisdom that were less readily dealt with, such as the unconscious motivations that he saw embodied in the archetypes and "symbolic configurations" of the psyche. Furthermore, in the achieving of wisdom Merton argued that fundamental human intuitions needed to be supplemented by those teachers or masters who, having become familiar with the archetypes and symbols of the psyche, could act as instructors or masters to the neophyte, a practice that Merton saw in Eastern religion and regretfully believed had disappeared from Western religion.[23]

Because of his pronounced sense of the dynamic nature of conscious-

21. See Merton, "Herakleitos: A Study," in *The Behavior of Titans*, 79. See Merton, Apr. 9, 1941, in *Run to the Mountain*, 338–39.
22. Merton, "'Baptism in the Forest': Wisdom and Initiation in William Faulkner," in *Literary Essays*, 99.
23. Ibid., 100, 99.

ness, Merton was skeptical about those kinds of consciousnesses, easily found in religious circles, that carefully screened the kinds of thought and experience that were offered to the mind. Similarly, he not infrequently turned against the static quality of much orthodox religious writing and toward the liveliness of the unorthodox and even ostensibly irreligious. Such a view underlay his preference in 1963 for Sartre's *Literature and Existentialism* over Morris West's *Shoes of the Fisherman*. In West's widely read novel about the papacy, Merton saw a glorification of the "status quo" in contrast to Sartre who, although judged inaccurate in his "historical synopsis" and weak in his "pseudo-marxist conclusions," was nevertheless, Merton noted, "powerful and convincing" alongside West.[24]

There were other uses of consciousness about which Merton cautioned, such as self-consciousness, which he termed a futile form of existence.[25] At the same time he eschewed the sort of jealous privacy by which one sought to be conscious of others while shrinking from others' consciousness of oneself, a shrinking that in some cases extended even to God's consciousness of the self. Merton in fact called this reluctance an impediment to spiritual understanding, because it prevented a recognition of the self from the divine point of view, as it were, and thus obscured the discovery of the true self. In *Cables to the Ace* in the late 1960s, he included some provocative lines on this subject:

> Angels again
> Farmers of the mind
> In its flowers and fevers
> Fishers in the blue revolutions of oil
>
> They find me always upside down
> In these reflected glooms
> Lost in the wide rain's
> Foundering accelerations
>
> They walk with me
> Through the shivering scrap-towns
> And clearly show me how to cross

24. Merton, Sept. 20, 1963, in *Dancing in the Water of Life*, 17.
25. Merton, June 20, 1966, in *Learning to Love*, 322–23.

The dubious and elastic
Rail way
To weight weightless
Manuscript burdens

As I become fast freight
A perishing express
To the countries of the dead.[26]

Here Merton wittily visualized himself as a moving train coursing through time and carrying the writings that the angels, messengers of the divine, had leavened with wisdom and thus given weight. Rather than claiming an exceptional value for himself as artist, a matter quite distinct from his belief in the importance of art, Merton playfully and modestly pictured himself as being farmed and harvested by the spiritual power that created him and by the subordinate angelic powers that later attended him. The poem is not, of course, primarily about whether Merton believed that angels existed but rather about his consciousness of himself as used for the good of all of being by a spiritual force that infused the whole of being.

While he placed considerable emphasis on intuitive understanding, Merton was far from unaware of the possibility of self-deception in this respect. His doubts can be seen readily in various writings, but they are especially evident in the journal that he kept on his trip to Asia shortly before he died. Even earlier in the 1960s, however, partly due to his interest in Buddhism, he became especially sensitive to the relativity of perception. An instance occurred in the summer of 1967 when he was struck by the fact that his responsiveness to an article about hunger by Albert Camus seemed to vary in relation to his own state of hunger at the time, an inverse relationship as it happened.[27] Nonetheless, he concluded that a full range of consciousness demanded that one experience hunger even if this led to a weakened consciousness of and somewhat muted articulateness about hunger. Otherwise, one was reduced, he argued, to the *illusory* level of well-fed politicians who made abstract bureaucratic decisions about those who were hungry.

26. Merton, *Cables to the Ace*, in *Collected Poems*, 446.
27. See Merton, July 8, 1967, in *Learning to Love*, 261–62.

The subject of illusion was part of one of the most memorable passages from Merton's journals in the late 1950s, a scene that he revised somewhat for *Conjectures of a Guilty Bystander* in 1966:

> Beauty of sunlight falling on a tall vase of red and white carnations and green leaves on the altar of the novitiate chapel. The light and dark. The darkness of the fresh, crinkled flower: light, warm and red, all around the darkness. The flower is the same color as blood, but it is in no sense whatever "as red as blood." Not at all! It is as red as a carnation. Only that.
>
> This flower, this light, this moment, this silence: *Dominus est.* Eternity. He passes. He remains. We pass. In and out. He passes. We remain. We are nothing. We are everything. He is in us. He is gone from us. He is not here. We are here in Him.
>
> All these things can be said, but why say them?
>
> The flower is itself. The light is itself. The silence is itself. I am myself. All, perhaps, illusion. But no matter, for illusion is the shadow of reality, and reality is the grace and gift that underlies all these lights, these colors, this silence. Underlies? Is that true? They are simply real. They themselves are His gift.[28]

The short imagistic sentences capture the fleeting, tenuous impressions of an evanescent moment. The passage shimmers with perceptual ambiguity as Merton responded to the flowers and light with alternating waves of mystical ecstasy and reflexive caution, finally accepting the fact that he could not know how fully God was present. Of interest in the passage and reminiscent of Wallace Stevens is Merton's acceptance of illusion as the shadow of reality, a Platonic, lesser version but still a version of reality.

The passage is one of the finest Merton ever wrote, stylistically as well as in its suggestive subject matter. In an effort to transcend a purely aesthetic response to the scene, for example, the speaker's imagination is held in check, as can be seen in his reluctance to accept the simile relating the red carnations to blood, an otherwise appropriate symbol for the altar scene. Moreover, the syntax of the passage is taut and separated so

---

28. Merton, *Conjectures of a Guilty Bystander,* 131. See also Merton, Feb. 4, 1958, in *A Search for Solitude,* 164–65.

that the breathless and growing perception of the presence of God is distributed through the sentences rather than being contained in any one of them. Each sentence prepares us in its brevity for the arrival of the next until the energy of the scene has been expended. While buoyantly part of the dynamics of the scene, the imagination moves furtively through it in an attempt to forestall substituting itself for the plenitude of being that is at the center of the experience described.

On his journey to northern India in 1968, Merton became acutely aware of the possibility of illusion in staring at the immense Himalayas. In particular, aware of his own high spiritual expectations about his visit to the region, he cautioned himself against the illusion that a vision lay waiting just out of reach. In a similar vein he drew back from a premature and hasty reading of the Himalayas, which might all too easily be interpreted as a symbol of nature's permanence. In such a deconstructive mood he looked attentively at the mountains until he became aware of the scars left by frequent landslides, which indicated the actual impermanence of the environment. The relativity of his perceptions came home to him suddenly when he observed how the attendant peaks around Mount Kanchenjunga suddenly emerged into majestic prominence when clouds covered the top of Kanchenjunga itself. He concluded that illusion could easily result from a premature perception of a particular scene during which the imagination impetuously imbues the scene with additional or with altered significance. Such was the case, for example, with his visit to the mountainside dwellings of the Tibetan exiles in northern India. While the scene seemed an arbitrary landscape at first, a "rugged, nondescript mountain with a lot of miscellaneous dwellings," the *rimpoches,* or spiritual leaders, each a "reincarnation of a spiritual figure," reorganized the scene in Merton's consciousness into a spiritually intelligible pattern. In the same way, his first impressions of a "somewhat squalid" Bangkok changed on his return to the city following his visit to the much greater poverty and squalor of Calcutta and Pathankot.[29]

29. On Himalayas, see Merton, Nov. 17, 1968, in *Other Side of the Mountain,* 280–81, 282–83; on Tibetan exiles, see Merton, Nov. 5, 1968, in ibid., 254; on Bangkok, see Merton, Dec. 8, 1968, in ibid., 328.

The theme of illusion seemed to Merton to have been part of a dream he had had in which he viewed a dreamed version of Mount Kanchenjunga from the forbidden Tibetan side of the border. He used the incident to theorize that every such mountain had a hidden side and that that side was the "only side worth seeing" because of its unconventionality and because of its engaging of the perceptual apparatus of the imagination. Focusing on the subject of illusion even more intently, Merton, who took a number of photographs of Kanchenjunga, realized that the best photography used illusion, "permitting and encouraging it—especially unconscious and powerful illusions" that would not ordinarily have been brought to one's conscious perceptions of the scene.[30] Perceptual illusion then became in Merton's estimation not an obstacle to intuitive understanding but an enlargement of it, reflecting reality at one end of the subject-object continuum.

A further modification of Merton's conception of intuitive understanding arose from his habit of internal dialogue in which he questioned positions that he himself held. This dialectical approach to understanding seemed to him to issue from God, who in Merton's estimation chose to be revealed in the midst of "conflict and contradiction."[31] Merton's dialogic approach characteristically opened outward to the reader, as anyone familiar with his journals can testify. A precedent for such an involvement of the reader within the circumference of dialogue seemed to him to come from the Bible where the reader found himself or herself not "simply questioning" the Bible but "being questioned by it." Examples of Merton's internal dialectical dialogue are legion. Given his pronounced antipathy to the ascendant technological culture of his time, for example, one notices the many times in which he took himself to task for such apparent oversimplification. In 1956 he characterized his antipathy to technology as a "prejudice." In an unpublished working notebook in 1965 he confessed that he had not explored technological society and its effects on human beings sufficiently, having been too ready to reject that culture, and in that sense he regretted that he had not lived up to his own norms of inclusiveness in considering such an important

30. Merton, Nov. 19, 1968, in ibid., 284.
31. Merton, Jan. 18, 1966, in *Learning to Love*, 354.

cultural reality. In his essay "Symbolism: Communication or Communion?" written in the late 1960s, he argued that the destructive fallout from technology had less to do with technology itself than with the headlong manner in which it was developed and thrust upon society, conceding that in the future a technological society might, if sufficient care were taken, conceivably be a "tranquil and contemplative one."[32]

As opposed to his gradual acceptance of the spiritual roots and force of Marxism, Merton's inner dialogue concerning technology was not simply an evolution of his thought, but was a conflict that stayed with him throughout his writing life. The conflict was grounded in his reluctance, finally, to exclude the possibility of value. In the light of the dialogic element in Merton's writings, given the pacifism that informed works such as his posthumously published novel, *My Argument with the Gestapo* (1969), one cannot help but be surprised by his revisionist position about the Second World War as expressed in his journal in 1961. There, he allowed that, in the case of dictatorship, resistance was not only morally permitted but also required, nonviolently if possible, but if necessary, "violently." In yet another context, given Merton's chronic distrust of formal reasoning because of its sophistic use in supporting evil, for example, a view that he set forth in essays such as "A Devout Meditation in Memory of Adolf Eichmann," in *Raids on the Unspeakable* (1966), he turned around on more than one occasion and urged that one should not distrust reason because of the abuse of it. His habit of internal dialogue was a sign of the openness of his consciousness, an openness that he attributed to being itself as he indicated in *Zen and the Birds of Appetite* in the late 1960s: "The metaphysical intuition of Being is an intuition of a *ground of openness*, indeed of a kind of ontological openness and an infinite generosity which communicates itself to everything that is." As Merton suggested in a letter to Raymond Prince in 1965, such openness in being and, correspondingly, in the consciousness of being made possible an ultimate, nonsolipsistic

---

32. Merton, *Opening the Bible*, 18; Merton, Aug. 22, 1956, in *A Search for Solitude*, 71; Merton, Working Notebook no. 16 (1965), in Merton Collection, Bellarmine University, 53; Merton, "Symbolism: Communication or Communion?" in *Love and Living*, 79.

awareness of the unity of reality that drew together external and internal reality, self and object.[33]

In spite of his strong interest in intuitive understanding, Merton was reluctant to overstate its value, especially alongside that of being. For this reason he warned against a gnostic approach to ontological reflection because this isolated the mind from an existential awareness of being.[34] In Merton's view one looked to religion not primarily because one wanted to know but because one wanted to be. In short, *knowing* was a part of being rather than *being* being a part of knowing.[35] For this reason he distinguished Christian ontology sharply from that of thinkers such as Hegel and Marx, who seemed to him to have apotheosized an abstract future state of humanity rather than having visualized and anticipated actual human beings caught up in the turmoil of history.[36] Such sentiments had always characterized Merton's point of view, even from the days before he entered the religious life. In 1939, in one of the early reviews that he wrote for the *New York Times*, for example, he contrasted Milton and Shakespeare ontologically by observing that Milton too precipitately saw life in moral categories while Shakespeare entered into the lives of his characters, experiencing their full humanity—from which moral meaning, one among many other kinds of meaning, would eventually issue.[37]

In a similar context Merton distinguished between the conceptual tradition of dogma and the concrete and supple, ordinary teaching of the Church, which he described in 1960 as "richer, more living, more nuanced, more detailed, more complete than the formal and extraordinary definitions of theology." Similarly, he reflected in one of his working notebooks in 1967 that if one regarded God primarily as a thinker, then

33. Merton, May 2, 1961, in *Turning toward the World*, 115; Merton, Mar. 27, 1963, in ibid., 307; Merton, *Zen and the Birds of Appetite*, 24–25; Merton to Prince, Dec. 18, 1965, in *Hidden Ground of Love*, 495.

34. Merton, July 9, 1965, in *Dancing in the Water of Life*, 267.

35. See Merton, *Conjectures of a Guilty Bystander*, 10.

36. See Merton, "Christian Humanism," in *Love and Living*, 148.

37. See Merton, "G. Wilson Knight—That Old Dilemma of Good and Evil," in *Literary Essays*, 481–82.

one would look to God for conceptual meaning rather than for the fuller spectrum of meaning that lay embedded in existence.[38] That kind of consciousness, Merton believed, would inevitably lead one to an understanding of God as being itself or, more precisely, the ground or source of all being. Although Merton's bent toward Christian existentialism dominated his thought in the 1960s, there can be no doubt, as commentators such as William Shannon have pointed out, that much of his early prose writing was characterized by conceptual formulations, often with unintended irony on occasions when Merton's subject was ostensibly the *experience* of the contemplative life. He was initially attracted to the conceptual traditions of Catholicism because of his need as a young and disillusioned man for a highly structured cosmology. Once this need had been met, however, he saw the limits of such formulaic thinking and writing, and in a related context he even began to question the pronounced intellectualism of Neoplatonism. Rather than abandoning Neoplatonism, however, he gave it flesh through the intuitions and discourse of embodiment that issued from his increasingly existentialist philosophy.

In a stimulating article, Robert Faricy has suggested that Merton's attraction to Zen Buddhism meant that he had accepted the Buddhist perception that all of being was included within mind, the ultimate reality. While there are some such Platonist elements in Merton's thought, on the whole he went out of his way to prioritize being over thought, as in the case of Zen Buddhism, which he interpreted, in William Shannon's words, as a direct "experience" of life, both of the "unity" of life and of its "existential concreteness." Whatever view one takes of Zen Buddhism, Merton himself described it as possessing a "thoroughgoing existentialism" that brought its adherents into touch with themselves, with others, as well as with ontological reality. In its concentration on being, Zen paralleled Thomist philosophy, which as Etienne Gilson explained in *The Spirit of Mediaeval Philosophy* defined God as "pure being in its

---

38. Merton, May 29, 1960, in *Turning toward the World,* 5; Merton, Nov. 25, 1967, in Working Notebook no. 30 (Sept.–Nov. 1967), in Merton Collection, Bellarmine University.

50   Thomas Merton and the Inclusive Imagination

state of complete fulfillment and realization," a definition to which Merton adhered in *Conjectures of a Guilty Bystander* where he characterized his own existence as a "participation" in the "Being of God."[39]

Calling himself a "Christian existentialist," Merton identified throughout his life with those intellectuals, even Thomists such as Jacques Maritain and Etienne Gilson, who contributed, Merton believed, to an "existentialist Christian perspective."[40] Looking broadly at Merton's attachment to existentialism, one can see that he regarded it as a nexus between consciousness and being. What appealed to him about existentialism was its avoidance of abstraction, its molding of thought to concrete existential realities, and its focus on the present as the matrix of life and experience. All of this complemented his primary conception that life became explicable only by "being lived," as he put it in an essay titled "In Silentio" in 1956. He repeated this theme with accompanying permutations in his essays on art in *Raids on the Unspeakable* in the 1960s, remarking spaciously in his "Message to Poets" that the reason for human existence would be discovered only after all had "walked together" into "contradictions and possibilities."[41]

While Merton's interest in existentialism had been aroused by his reading of Sartre and Camus, he eventually turned to Heidegger for a satisfying philosophical basis of existentialism, having come to Heidegger by way of the Protestant theologian Paul Tillich. Heidegger posited a direct, intuitive apprehension of being that preceded systematic reasoning and that involved an awareness of the world through the medium, so to speak, of one's unreflective, unmediated consciousness of personal existence. In Heidegger's *Being and Time*, for example, the author argued that being could be experienced and perceived without the "explicit concept of the meaning of being having to be already available." For Heidegger, being itself underlay the multiplicity of beings and the

39. Faricy, "Merton and Mysticism of the Mind," 142–43; Shannon, *Thomas Merton's Dark Path*, 200; Merton, *Mystics and Zen Masters*, 232; Gilson, *The Spirit of Mediaeval Philosophy*, 54; Merton, *Conjectures of a Guilty Bystander*, 201.

40. Thomas Merton, "Learning to Live," in *Love and Living*, 4; Merton, *Mystics and Zen Masters*, 270.

41. Merton, "In Silentio," in *Silence in Heaven*, 24; Merton, "Message to Poets," in *Literary Essays*, 371.

totality of life. In addition, he argued as fundamental a consciousness of being that obviated the usual epistemological subject-object division, a feature of existentialism and phenomenology that Merton especially valued. As he put it in *Springs of Contemplation,* a book based upon a series of talks he gave in the late 1960s, without necessarily possessing a definition of being, one was at certain moments "simply overwhelmed" by the "*fact* of being," and from this awareness it was, he added, a short and natural step to an awareness of the ground of being itself.[42]

In addition to these features of Merton's focus on being, in 1965 he described being as a reconciling of the "individual, empirical self" and the world of conceptual abstraction. Thus, existentialism solved for Merton in the philosophical sphere what he had accomplished as an artist in the imaginative and aesthetic sphere, the mediating of the particular and the universal. As has been intimated, it was inevitable that Merton would have been attracted to these converging effects of existentialism. In this respect Hans Küng has been especially illuminating about Heidegger as having conceived of being within a frame that brought being as ontological reality and being as historical reality together, an idea that appealed to Merton with his simultaneous focus on ultimate truth and on the dynamic movement of human experience through time.[43] Furthermore, in religious existentialism Merton saw the filling in of the negative void of directionless freedom implicit in Sartre's writings. For Merton, the prior ontological and epistemological void of Christian existentialism involved the shedding of ephemeral realities in favor of more ultimate ones and thus resembled in some respects the apophatic tradition of Christian mysticism.[44] Balanced against the existentialist void that refused to define things prior to existence and experience was the unifying and lustrous view of being that Merton found in Saint Thomas Aquinas, who, like the existentialists, emphasized existence and act rather than a priori conceptualizing. In an early poem on

42. Heidegger, *Being and Time,* 6; Merton, *Springs of Contemplation,* 15.
43. Merton, preface to Japanese translation of *Seeds of Contemplation,* in *Honorable Reader,* 89; Küng, *The Incarnation of God: An Introduction to Hegel's Theological Thought as Prolegomena to a Future Christology,* 391–92, 394.
44. See Merton, *Mystics and Zen Masters,* 269.

Saint Thomas Aquinas in *A Man in the Divided Sea* (1946), Merton observed a seamless union of being and mind, matter and form, in which
"matter lay as light as snow / On the strong Apennine of form." In the
philosophy of Saint Thomas Aquinas he noted with approval a turning
toward the world and away from pure intellectualism. Aquinas, he maintained, returned to the "realities that the symbols were intended to sig-
nify."[45] In a similar way he summed up the philosophical perspective of
Saint Francis of Assisi, who was, as has been suggested, a great influence
on Merton, in suggesting that for Francis God was synonymous with
the "isness" of everyday reality.

Although Merton's christological consciousness was still apparent in
the writings that occupied him in the last decade of his life, as George
Kilcourse has demonstrated in his book, *Ace of Freedoms: Thomas Merton's Christ*, on the whole and especially in the light of his intensified interest in Zen Buddhism, his awareness of God tended to become relatively more ontological and impersonal in that later period. Aldous
Huxley in *Ends and Means*, which Merton acknowledged as a major influence on his thinking as a young man, predicted such an evolution of
consciousness among those who were contemplatives:

> The biography of most of the first-class Christian mystics is curi-
> ously similar. Brought up to believe in the personality of the triune
> God and in the existence and ubiquitous presence of other divine
> persons, such as the Virgin and the saints, they begin their mysti-
> cal career by entering, as they suppose, into relations with super-
> natural personalities. Then, as they advance further along the path
> . . . they find that their visions disappear, that their awareness of a
> personality fades, that the emotional outpourings which were ap-
> propriate when they seemed to be in the presence of a person, be-
> come utterly inappropriate and finally give place to a state in which
> there is no emotion at all.[46]

In some ways Merton does seem to have traveled along the road that
Huxley described. His early poetry, for instance, is peopled with the fig-

45. Merton, "St. Thomas Aquinas," in *Collected Poems*, 99; Merton, *Conjectures of a
Guilty Bystander*, 185.
46. Huxley, *Ends and Means*, 290.

ures of his religion, whereas the later work seems in contrast relatively impersonal and philosophical. Even Merton's tender feelings toward Mary, the mother of Jesus, become transformed in the later work into the poetic but more impersonal language of the "Hagia Sophia." His vision of being in the later period of his life certainly conveys emotion, but, and here one can agree with Robert Faricy, the elevated feelings are rather cerebrally spiritual. At the same time, in the later writings Merton's intuitive contact with God has a strong affective dimension, although that affective quality is directed toward the more ontological and existential aspects of God—"radical being" and "actuality."[47] This overall shift in direction and focus may have been somewhat hidden by the fact that in celebrating being in this way Merton clung in his journals and poetry to the salient shapes, colors, and sounds of being, especially those of the natural world.

As has been suggested, what made being so lustrous for Merton was the positive ethical value that he associated with it, drawn in particular from Thomist philosophy. In a recorded talk that he gave on Saint Thomas Aquinas at the Abbey of Gethsemani in Kentucky in the 1960s, he stipulated that, for Aquinas, being and goodness were synonymous, that in proportion as a thing existed, in that proportion was it good. Merton went so far as to suggest that even in ostensibly evil people there was a preponderance of good inherent in their very existence.[48] He was not unaware of the burden of evil and suffering that was a part of existence. He addressed this matter in his journal in 1949, for example, observing that the suffering of Job had not been answered rationally within the biblical text. Instead, Job's solution was "concrete," a "vision of God" that relied on the providential character of God. In his later years Merton focused less anthropomorphically on God as merciful and more on being—with the divine mercy being assimilated into what Merton regarded as the beneficence of being. In this context he identified with what he regarded as Zen Buddhism's attempt to reach an unself-conscious

---

47. See Faricy, "Merton and Mysticism of the Mind"; Merton, "Seven Words," in *Love and Living*, 111.

48. See Merton, "St. Thomas Aquinas and the Goodness of All Being," audiotape no. 90-B, in Merton Collection, Bellarmine University.

awareness of the ground of being wherein one recovered a primordial state of consciousness. When possessed of such consciousness, he registered his awareness of being as felicitously good, noting in one of the talks given in the late 1960s that came to constitute *Springs of Contemplation* that at the source or ground of being, being and love were synonymous.[49]

While Merton never abandoned the concept of God as transcendent and in that way separate from creation, increasingly as he moved through the 1960s he rejected any notion of the divine that in any way resembled deism, focusing instead on the divine immanence in being. For this reason he warmed to the ideas of Teilhard de Chardin, who postulated a providential, divine current in evolution without thereby, however, reducing divinity to the process of evolution itself.[50] Rather than seeing God as the end point of existence, though, Merton thought of God as the unifying center of existence, from which position being could be eschatologically oriented yet made accessible in its fullness within the boundaries of the present moment. In this light one can understand the enormous importance that he attributed to contemplation with its focus on the present.

In 1951, relatively early in his life as a writer, Merton saw the writing that he had been doing as at worst a threat to the contemplative life and at best merely an aid to his primary vocation to the contemplative life. By the mid-1960s, however, he had come to regard his writing not only as involving the pursuit of consciousness but also as his way of participating in being.[51] In part, this reflected his awareness that his writing was going out into the world and no doubt altering the lives of some of his readers. In part, though, this perception also derived from his expanding awareness of just how much of life came down to consciousness, or, in the existentialist terms that he came to favor, how much of

---

49. Merton, Sept. 3, 1949, in *Entering the Silence: Becoming a Monk and Writer,* 366–67; see Merton, *Mystics and Zen Masters,* 224; Merton, *Springs of Contemplation,* 16.

50. See Merton, "The Universe as Epiphany," in *Love and Living,* 176.

51. Merton, Mar. 4, 1951, in *Entering the Silence,* 453. See also "Poetry and the Contemplative Life." Merton, Apr. 14, 1966, in *Learning to Love,* app. C, "A Postscript" [371].

being was constituted by consciousness. Here, though, one must distinguish between consciousness in a conceptual sense and consciousness as a fundamental awareness of existence, prior to reason or reflection or even the forming of impressions. Such consciousness, which words such as *enlightenment* simply do not sufficiently cover, Merton regarded as so intimately attached to being as to breathe its very air. Nonetheless, Merton's plunge into social criticism in the 1960s in many influential books and essays revealed his conviction that his focus on being had ethical implications involving, for example, ecology and peace, which could and needed to be addressed on the level of the particular. At the basis of such thinking was his conviction that a consciousness of the splendor of being required one to defend being. The fact that he perceived his solitude threatened by the widespread reaction to his social criticism in the 1960s did not in his mind invalidate that criticism. It was nevertheless ironic that the success of Merton's social criticism in the 1960s imperiled the contemplative silence that made the kind of social criticism he created possible in the first place.

Some of Merton's readers might argue that his jealous guarding of his solitude, which in turn enabled his celebration of consciousness and being, was a tribute to the power of artificial circumstances. Who, in the ordinary course of things, it might be added, other than protagonists in a novel by Henry James, perhaps, had the ample time required to devote to the pursuit of such rarified consciousness? Merton was quite aware that, although his monastic life encompassed physical privation, it made possible luxuries of time and consciousness that were beyond the reach of most people. On the other hand, given his relative seclusion, he was capable of astute insight into the suffocatingly materialistic and morally rudderless society in which most of his contemporaries lived. By way of example, in the course of his lifetime he became acutely aware that Western society had become demandingly hyperactive, even in its so-called leisure time, and as an alternative he advocated periods of solitude and stillness. Always conscious of the inner freedom of human beings, however, Merton encouraged his readers to risk altering their lives through the pursuit of contemplative solitude while at the same time recognizing on their behalf how difficult this might be. He heard the clamor that rang around them himself, both through his reading—and he was surprisingly up-to-date in this respect—and through his own search for silence within the bustling enterprise of his monastery in the 1950s. He heard it also within the fractious and distracting institutional struggles within his church in the 1960s. Amid the din, however, he insisted, was the great dome of being—beatifically immersed in silence.

3

Solitude and the Self

On the threshold of his monastic life in the early 1940s, Merton felt himself drawn into a silence and a solitude that appeared to him like a fortress. Such was the effect of an evocative passage in *The Seven Storey Mountain* in which he described first seeing the Abbey of Gethsemani in Kentucky:

> I looked at the rolling country, and at the pale ribbon of road in front of us, stretching out as grey as lead in the light of the moon. Then suddenly I saw a steeple that shone like silver in the moon-light, growing into sight from behind a rounded knoll. The tires sang on the empty road, and, breathless, I looked at the monastery that was revealed before me as we came over the rise. At the end of an avenue of trees was a big rectangular block of buildings, all dark, with a church crowned by a tower and a steeple and a cross: and the steeple was as bright as platinum and the whole place was as quiet as midnight and lost in the all-absorbing silence and solitude of the fields. Behind the monastery was a dark curtain of woods, and over to the west was a wooded valley, and behind that a rampart of wooded hills, a barrier and a defence against the world.[1]

The passage reveals Merton's power as a describer. Capturing the tint and intensity of each dramatized moment of perception, he leads the eye

---

1. Merton, *The Seven Storey Mountain*, 320.

measuredly through the images so that the sequential aspects of the scene appear not a moment before they should in the sustained atmosphere of expectation. Moreover, those aspects of the scene that do come forward quickly sink back into the darkness from which they had emerged as the young man in the taxi moves in an increasingly heightened state of expectation toward the fulfillment of his young life's journey.

While this well-known passage from *The Seven Storey Mountain* may be taken as a sign of Merton's desire to retreat from the mainstream of American society, it was followed by an equally evocative passage in which he qualified the sort of solitude that he encountered at Gethsemani. In that subsequent passage Merton describes himself thrown out of sleep in the middle of the night by monastery bells that "were flying out of the tower in the high, astounding darkness," bells that drew him, half-asleep, into a procession of those who were headed for the great monastery church in order to say the night office. Groping his way in darkness toward the interior of the church, Merton was met there by a "silence with people moving in it" that was "ten times more gripping than it had been in my own empty room."[2] The silence is seen as more "gripping" because it was communal in spite of its projection of many separate souls ascending to God. Thus, the inclusion of the two silences—that found in the privacy of Merton's room and the subsequent scene of communal silence in the church—adds up to a more complete picture of contemplative silence than would be apparent if one had only the first scene of Merton's arrival at the monastery to deal with. Both pools of silence were important to Merton from the very beginning of his monastic life.

Nevertheless, by 1947 he wrote to Mark Van Doren that he was consumed by a thirst for an even greater solitude than he had obtained, a reflection perhaps of the lack of privacy that the Trappists' dormitory lifestyle at Gethsemani involved. In his early years in the monastery Merton found himself blissfully taken up by the life of prayer and detached from many of the activities that had interested him beforehand, including writing. Although it was a silent activity, writing, even writing about the monastic life, distracted the contemplative, Merton believed, from

2. Ibid., 322–23.

the union of the self with God. In *The Waters of Siloe*, one of a number of writing tasks assigned to him by his abbot in the 1940s, Merton affirmed the "peace of the spiritual stratosphere" in which he believed the distractions and preoccupations of ordinary life were distant from the prayerful unity with God that he experienced at the center of his soul. By 1949, however, he had modified his position somewhat, rejecting, for example, the sort of false solitude, as he put it in his journal, that excluded society, a point that he stressed as well in *Seeds of Contemplation*, which was published in the same year.[3] The solitude he experienced was not absolute, and would inevitably and ironically be interrupted by his attempt as a writer to share its richness with others. In fact, this presented him with a dilemma with which he had to struggle throughout his life: the conflict within him between the solitary contemplative and the writer. He learned to live with the dilemma as the emblem of his own nature, but this did not stem his troubled awareness of its contradictoriness. At the same time, he maintained consistently that solitude led paradoxically to an experiencing of life in its "fullness" in contrast to what he called the "common life."[4] It was not just that solitude and the contemplation that it afforded added to the sum of life's experiences but rather that the common life itself was thereby transformed into a state connected to what Merton thought of ontologically as the heart of being.

One can glean an appreciation of Merton's attachment to solitude in the late 1940s from his poem "Song," which appeared in *The Tears of the Blind Lions* (1949):

> When rain, (sings light) rain has devoured my house
> And wind wades through my trees,
> The cedars fawn upon the storm with their huge paws.
> Silence is louder than a cyclone
> In the rude door, my shelter.
> And there I eat my air alone
> With pure and solitary songs

---

3. Merton to Van Doren, Nov. 5, 1947, in *Road to Joy*, 21–22; Merton, *Waters of Siloe*, xxviii; see Merton, *Seeds of Contemplation*, 42. See also Merton, June 19, 1949, in *Entering the Silence*, 326.

4. Merton, May 28, 1965, in *Dancing in the Water of Life*, 251.

> While others sit in conference.
> Their windows grieve, and soon frown
> And glass begins to wrinkle with a multitude of water
> Till I no longer see their speech
> And they no longer know my theater.[5]

Secluded in his rough shed, temporarily on his own, Merton reflected, not unkindly, on the strain of communal living, leading him to project toward his fellow monks a somewhat artificial self, his "theater," as he put it, in contrast to his "pure" moments of joy in solitude.

At various points in his life Merton acknowledged that his thirst for solitude issued from a deep-seated need for privacy, a need that he ascribed on one occasion in 1961 to his English background. In spite of his many contacts with those beyond the monastery, which are reflected in his voluminous correspondence, it is well known that he disliked unexpected intrusions upon his privacy—especially after he had moved into his hermitage in the 1960s. His need for solitude was critically tested in the 1960s when his social essays drew the attention of many who wanted to meet him, but it was especially tested in his romantic relationship with the young nurse, M., in 1966. Even at the emotional peak of that relationship, Merton found himself pulling against it in the name of solitude, describing himself in his journal as a "free" and "wild" being, like the deer in the woods near his hermitage.[6] The philosophy of solitude that Merton had developed grew out of the necessities of his own being, arising from the well of experience, as it were, a sequence that appealed to Merton with his existentialist viewpoint.

What Merton discovered in his periods of solitude was that when his privacy was protected, he paradoxically relaxed and warmed in his attitude toward his fellow human beings, acquiring a "compassionate knowledge of the goodness" of others, as he put it in *Thoughts in Solitude* in the late 1950s. While this observation might strike some readers as disingenuous, Merton's approach appealed to a population that, sand-

5. Merton, "Song," in *Collected Poems*, 197.
6. Merton, Jan. 8, 1961, in *Turning toward the World*, 86; Merton, "A Midsummer Diary for M.," June 23, 1966, in *Learning to Love*, 342.

wiched within an increasingly congested, technological culture, saw little recognition there for the life of the self. Having been separated from
this culture for a decade, Merton was able in his writings to report on
the effects that this separation had had on him. Among other things the
experience had, he claimed, allowed him to regain what he called his
"normal human balance."[7] For Merton, silence and solitude created a
bubble that the self could occupy. In this way the self could slowly learn
to do without or at least to counterbalance those externally produced
mirrors of itself that choked out the shy, tentative shoots sent forth by
the self.

In 1966, in a letter to Erich Fromm, Merton recognized that his need
for solitude had been in part related to the friction that resulted from the
routines of institutional living. Having been somewhat muted by his
youthful joy in the monastery in the 1940s and in particular by his warm
respect for his abbot, Dom Frederic Dunne, this friction became increasingly evident in the 1950s and 1960s when he concluded bleakly
that there was little to be looked for from church officialdom. What particularly galled Merton was the tacit undervaluing of solitude both from
the higher echelons of the mainstream Church and from inside his own
order. At a deeper level, though, in an essay titled "The Solitary Life,"
which was published in 1960, he reflected perplexedly on his relationship to his fellow monks, focusing on what he called the "terrible irony"
of striving for solitude while living in a community. In that ostensibly
contradictory situation, he observed, even when surrounded by the car-
ing solicitude of others, tensions arose from the very regularity and what
Merton called the "automatic mechanisms" of collective life.[8] In such a
situation he found refuge in the fixed discourse of the liturgy simply because it opened out into the transcendental, and offered a way out of the
mundane relationships that were an inevitable part of a cenobitic way of
life. More important, the sacred language and music, heirs to the ages,
allowed Merton to move out of conventional time and space and in that

---

7. Merton, *Thoughts in Solitude*, 119; Merton, June 4, 1963, in *Turning toward the World*, 327.

8. Merton to Fromm, Oct. 13, 1966, in *Hidden Ground of Love*, 324; Merton, "The Solitary Life," in *The Monastic Journey*, 161.

way to recognize the solitude and true selves of his fellow monks, thereby making possible a renewal of his relationship with them.

Once Merton had come to terms with his dual vocation as monk and artist, there were two principal effects of solitude that he came especially to value: the departure from the prevailing sounds and images of contemporary culture in the West and, second, the creative work, especially the poetry, that issued from solitude and the contemplative discernment that solitude made possible. In connection with his withdrawal from secular society, Merton argued that this too had been fortuitous in allowing for a separation of "reality from illusion."[9] In this way the mind could intuitively focus on aspects of reality that would be invisible in society at large, aspects that could be approached in intuitive "flashes" when the mind was intently trained on the perception of being.[10] Such is the theme of a poem written in the early 1960s in *Emblems of a Season of Fury* titled "Song: If You Seek. . . ." The poem is a soliloquy in which solitude declares that it precedes the self into an "emptiness" where there arises the possibility of an intuitive leap. This leap Merton presented as a sidestepping of the customary useful dialectics of reasoning, an ascent into a holistic ontological awareness, a "flash / Beyond 'yes,' beyond 'no.'"[11]

What distinguishes Merton's thinking about contemplative solitude was his insistence that solitude was an act and not merely a condition or state. Otherwise, he argued, it simply became a form of passive existence, what he characterized as a kind of "permanent coma."[12] The act involved the uniting of mind and body in a temporary fusion, thereby enabling the contemplative to concentrate on the richness of being shared by all parts of the self. Merton thought of solitude as a dynamic and fluid aspect of his life, making possible major transitions in ideas and convictions and still more important changes in the composition and focus of his identity.[13] As he indicated in a letter to Mark Van Doren in 1948, he was reluctant to accept the static description of his identity in terms

9. Merton, Dec. 8, 1950, in *Entering the Silence,* 446.
10. See Merton, "Some Personal Notes," Mar. 6, 1966, in *Learning to Love,* 367.
11. Merton, "Song: If You Seek . . . ," in *Collected Poems,* 340.
12. Merton, "Part of a Midsummer Diary for M.," June 20, 1966, in *Learning to Love,* 321.
13. See Merton, June 4, 1963, in *Turning toward the World,* 327–28.

of particular roles such as poet, monk, or hermit. In this connection he made it evident throughout his life that he required fresh injections of ideas, impressions, and information in order to grow. There had to be clean water, he confided to Miguel Grinberg in 1966, for the "spirit to drink." Furthermore, he wanted to grow as a person in relationship to his time, not in order to emulate that time but rather to recognize its distinctive viewpoint. Otherwise, he would not be able to communicate with those who were his contemporaries. Thus, on one occasion he distinguished between the foreignness of Dante's static, cosmic consciousness, as he came to think of it, and the consciousness exhibited by Camus, which conveyed a restless modernity.[14]

Pushing the dimensions of contemplative solitude even further, Merton maintained that the consciousness generated therein had to be related back to being rather than being cultivated as a spiritual quest in itself.[15] At times this took the form of an apophatic experience as can be seen in a journal entry that he made in the spring of 1968. The entry reflected a time in Merton's life when he believed that Gethsemani no longer provided sufficient solitude, and so he had decided to visit Alaska and northern California as possible alternative sites for a hermitage. While staying in the redwood area of northern California, he wrote that he wanted to linger by the ocean for a couple of months, that he needed the "silence" and the "emptying" that this would bring.[16] By emptying, Merton meant not only shedding the cares and activities of ordinary life but, more important, abandoning the stake that the ego felt in these cares and activities. This ostensibly isolating experience did not necessarily, he argued, desensitize one to the needs of others, but rather allowed the self to see other human beings from a viewpoint through which one hoped to discover what their and one's own *real* needs were. One of these needs, a need that Merton believed was embedded in the human psyche, was the need for inner freedom, a need that could be felt,

14. Merton to Van Doren, Mar. 30, 1948, in *Road to Joy,* 22; Merton to Grinberg, Oct. 28, 1966, in *Courage for Truth,* 204; Merton, Oct. 4, 1966, in *Learning to Love,* 144–45.

15. Merton, May 6, 1968, in *Other Side of the Mountain,* 96.

16. Merton, May 21, 1968, in ibid., 120.

he believed, only when there was no longer a disposition in the self to satisfy the needs of the ego. He pointed to the Desert Fathers of ancient Egypt and Syria as having done without the ordinaries of life in order to gain the independence that allowed them to find this inner freedom. Separated from the world around them, they had, Merton noted, nothing to conform to except the divine voice deep within their psyches, calling them to become their true selves.[17]

Having thus arrived at such inner freedom, those who followed the path to solitude would feel themselves suddenly and unexpectedly a part of and in harmony with the rest of being. Such is the theme, for example, of Merton's elaborate and exquisitely crafted poem "Elias—Variations on a Theme," which was published in *The Strange Islands* in 1957:

> The free man is not alone as busy men are
> But as birds are. The free man sings
> Alone as universes do. Built
> Upon his own inscrutable pattern
> Clear, unmistakable, not invented by himself alone
> Or for himself, but for the universe also.[18]

Merton's distinction in the poem between the loneliness of a life lived in the collective mirror and the heightened consciousness of being that accompanied the solitary life was part of the intuitive harvest produced by his own solitude. In such solitude he experienced his connection with nature and with the cosmos in such a way as to strengthen his psychic foothold in the world. He could follow this experience of being to the highest level, thereby silhouetting merely social relationships as contrastingly small. As anyone familiar with Merton's social writings can attest, this was not the result of a dismissive view of society since the good of society became the subject of a number of impassioned essays and poems by him in the 1960s. Rather, he evolved his way toward an inclusive view of society in which social relationships were perceived through an ontological lens, thus allowing one to see society in a fuller and therefore truer light.

17. Merton, "The Wisdom of the Desert," in *The Wisdom of the Desert*, 6.
18. Merton, "Elias—Variations on a Theme," in *Collected Poems*, 244–45.

When Merton said, as he did on a number of occasions, that his solitude increased his sympathy for others, he referred not only to his compassion toward them but also to his felt union with them. This union was not only the result of his prolific writing, through which he drew others into dialogue, but more profoundly through his searching out in that writing the solitudes of those who were reading him. That this was Merton's strategy as a contemplative he indicated in the choice of a title in 1967 for one of his published journals, *The Vow of Conversation*. He was in fact creating a community of those who had learned to escape the collective mirror, even temporarily, and so unite with the undiscovered self that he had attempted to cultivate both in himself and in his readers. The community of solitaries included, in Merton's view, not only those who had ventured upon contemplative solitude in a formal manner but also many others, including William Faulkner, whose novel *The Wild Palms* he characterized as a portrayal of the "cosmic, existential solitude" of human beings in the *"complete"* sense.[19] Merton thus saw himself as standing in the midst of a society of solitaries whose conception of the self stood in sharp distinction to that of the society around them and who were united through this understanding. In this way, he believed, solitude would eventually lead to a reconstitution of the self, a saner and more whole self than that which had existed. What that self contained was what Merton repeatedly referred to as sapiential understanding or wisdom, a consciousness of the innate ontological riches of the psyche and of the self.

The value of solitude lay especially in the silence that accompanied it, and for this reason solitude in Merton was often pictured against scenes of nature. Nature drew the self outward, so to speak, enchanted by the beauty that lay before it. This initial act of movement outward, first experienced in childhood, drew the self to sympathize with something beyond its own needs and desires, and thus prepared it to respond empathetically to other human beings and creatures and finally to the source of life itself. Silence for a contemplative such as Merton did not necessarily mean literal silence but rather the turning off of the flow of sound from the culture at large, a flow that had become overwhelming and tox-

19. Merton, "Faulkner Meditations: *The Wild Palms*," in *Literary Essays*, 517.

ic, as Merton demonstrated throughout his long satiric poem *Cables to the Ace*. On the other hand, the sounds of nature, the sounds of birds and of the wind, not only did not threaten the inner silence of contemplation but quite often nourished it. A remarkable thing about Merton, given his enormous output as a writer, was that for him language was merely a transitional instrument, a "half-world," as he referred to it, which in being shaped yet also restrained could lead the self to other and greater realities within the larger and more meaningful silence of being.[20] He conveyed this perception in a poem titled "In Silence," which was included in *The Strange Islands:*

> Be still
> Listen to the stones of the wall.
> Be silent, they try
> To speak your
>
> Name. . . .
>
>   Do not
> Think of what you are
> Still less of
> What you may one day be.
> Rather
> Be what you are (but who?) be
> The unthinkable one
> You do not know. . . .

So addressed by silence, the self responds:

>   . . . The whole
> World is secretly on fire. The stones
> Burn, even the stones
> They burn me. How can a man be still or
> Listen to all things burning? How can he dare
> To sit with them when
> All their silence
> Is on fire?[21]

20. Merton, Jan. 11, 1950, in *Entering the Silence*, 398.
21. Merton, "In Silence," in *Collected Poems*, 280–81.

The poem's minimalist form conveys its restrained attitude to language, which on any occasion was likely in Merton's view to serve a writer's self-indulgence. Here, though, the minimalism, which is present in the phrasing and in the shortened lines, shows how language can coexist with silence in the sort of half-life he referred to in the poem whereby the mind is able to connive with language in order to transcend it. The imagery of the stones is powerfully revealing in this respect. Inert and silent at first, the stones catch fire in the silent observer, who is surrounded by silence until the stones burst into flame in an energy that captures the mind's enlivening, transforming perceptions. For Merton the moment is not only psychological and imaginative but also spiritual and ontological, since the stones' catching fire is an emblem of the unfathomable vitality of being, a reality that the mind, bathed in silence and solitude, can occasionally glimpse.

As he developed his ideas about solitude, Merton became convinced that solitude not only provided the detachment and inner freedom that could accommodate ontological insight but could facilitate as well the sort of critical skepticism and irony that informed perceptive social criticism.[22] In fact, this is what happened in Merton's own case as he moved from the formally religious writing of his early period to the social criticism of the 1960s. Thus, paradoxically, the solitude that had drawn Merton away from society led him back to it as a social critic, not for the ultimate purpose of dividing but of uniting those who through racial discrimination or armed conflict or poverty had already been separated from other human beings. Thus, in prose works such as *Seeds of Destruction* and *Conjectures of a Guilty Bystander*, and through the poems in *Emblems of a Season of Fury*, *Cables to the Ace*, and *The Geography of Lograire*, Merton drove home his conviction that his solitude belonged not only to God but to society as well.[23] In this way he distinguished the solitude that underlay his social criticism from the laissez-faire individualism that he associated with industrial societies and their accompanying myths—such as that depicted in Defoe's novel *Robinson Crusoe*. Given the contemplative's latently compassionate orientation toward others,

22. See Merton to Mery-Lu Sananes and Jaime Lopez-Sanz, Mar. 7, 1966, in *Road to Joy*, 339.
23. Merton, Dec. 13, 1960, in *Turning toward the World*, 74.

the effect of solitude was in Merton's view to silhouette through contrast the suffering brought about by the kind of social organization that induced fragmentation and alienation. Thus, solitude became a means of enlarging consciousness about the experience and value of human existence by providing a vantage point not easily available within a society flooded with images and sounds and messages that gave no hint of any alternative life for the self. Although the life of solitude in Merton's case involved a calling to the religious life, in fact he more than once suggested that religious organizations frequently overlooked or marginalized the value of solitude. Whether in ordinary or in the religious life, however, in Merton's view the path of solitude, which he advocated for all, enabled one to achieve an external, independent vantage point from which to view society. In addition to this benefit there was always the possibility of discovering, through patient listening from within, the self's true needs and hopes. This in turn, he maintained, could confer an unforeseen, magisterial sense of one's own being and an otherwise difficult-to-achieve openness to the being of others.

Although Merton spent a lot of time as a writer in attempting to illuminate the importance and range of consciousness, he resisted identifying the self with consciousness.[24] He was concerned about the possibility of confusing the self with self-consciousness, as limiting in its own way, he thought, as identifying the self with the ego. This was an important issue for someone such as Merton who, as a writer, addressed the self and his own self as his principal subject. Although his idea of the self in some ways resembled Jung's conception of the self, as both Anne E. Carr and Robert Waldron have suggested, it reached beyond Jung in its ontological significance. In this connection, Carr has observed that Merton's genius lay in his "fusion of religious or metaphorical discourse and psychological, experiential language in a holistic symbolic vision that reveals how any pattern or system falls short of the mysterious uniqueness of the person." Attempting through the writing of fiction to create "some new, objective, separate person" outside himself had not worked, Merton wrote in his journal in 1939. Furthermore, as if following self-consciousness into even higher registers, throughout his life he

24. See Merton, "Some Personal Notes," Jan. 20, 1966, in *Learning to Love*, 355.

used his journal as a way of trying to understand himself—as in the romantic relationship with M. in 1966. In this connection he had always been fascinated by Saint Augustine's discussion of memory in the *Confessions* in which the author pictured memory as a "belly" in which the experiences of the self could be stored and then retrieved without necessarily reviving the intensity or duress that had accompanied the original experience, something analogous, it would seem, to Wordsworth's emotion recollected in tranquillity.[25] One of Merton's great gifts as a writer was his ability to bring the face of the past back with vividness and feeling and with a sense of immediacy that made it seem at one with his present flow of consciousness. In this way the reader catches a glimpse of Merton's self as it so shuttles back and forth between past and present where it is both narrator and interpreter of experience, recalling interpretation of the past even while modifying and surpassing this interpretation in the light of presently held views. Although this may appear Proustian, Merton went out of his way to distinguish this presentation of the self from the sort of thing he saw Proust doing or Rilke, for that matter, about whose poetry he was otherwise very appreciative. He tried to distinguish what he was attempting by saying that he reached beyond memory and imagination, beyond dreams even, to heretofore unvisited spaces of what he called "deeper meditation."[26] In this manner he tried to indicate that his subject was the ontological self, that which transcended the psychological and even the spiritual.

In this respect Merton felt that he was closer to writers such as Faulkner and Camus, who had manifested, he thought, a strong ontological bent. As an example of this characteristic, part of their and his own consciousness as writers, he believed, involved an acceptance of death, not merely stoically, but rather in such a way that the self might be liberated from one of its chief oppressors. The fear of death, he had concluded, lashed the self to the pursuit of externals in a relentless search for security. A further impediment to the healthy emergence of the self

25. Carr, *Search for Wisdom and Spirit*, 130; Merton, Dec. 20, 1939, in *Run to the Mountain*, 118; Merton, Sept. 4, 1966, in *Learning to Love*, 122; see Saint Augustine, *The Confessions of St. Augustine*, 216–17.
26. Merton, Oct. 3, 1967, in *Learning to Love*, 298.

in Merton's view was the tendency of highly structured institutional societies to mint the selves of the citizens within it by projecting socially desirable images of the self. In an important essay on symbolism written in the late 1960s, he argued that when human beings were reduced to or confined within the boundaries of their empirical selves they came to feel excluded from themselves, separated from the roots of their nature as human beings and "condemned to spiritual death by thirst and starvation in a wilderness of externals."[27]

Pushed to a certain point, Merton observed in his well-known essay "Rain and the Rhinoceros," individuals might go through life never having experienced themselves as real, only seeing and experiencing themselves through the collective mirror. The problem with such an external definition of the self in Merton's view was not simply the tension between the self and society but rather a problem that had to do with a more fundamental epistemological stalemate: the objectification of the self. The problem was one that had haunted the romantic writers and reached back to the origin of Cartesian awareness. It had to do with the destructive effects on the self of self-consciousness, effects that Merton focused on in the following line from section 84 of his long poem *Cables to the Ace:* "Once you become aware of yourself as seeker, you are lost." In a sense self-objectification was one of the difficulties that stood in the way of Merton's unrestricted embrace of Zen in the 1960s. In connection with Zen Buddhism, Merton's friend Daisetz Suzuki maintained that a state of enlightenment was reached when the mind was "devoid of all its possible contents except itself." After the mid-1960s Merton embraced this sort of union of the subjective and the objective, interpreting such "objectivity" as a variation of apophatic or kenotic mysticism. One of his most radical statements about the union of the self and the nonself in the 1960s occurred in an essay titled "Seven Words" in which he declared that the world was not outside of but rather inside the self: "We *are* the world," he concluded.[28] In a sense this perception

27. Merton, "Symbolism: Communication or Communion?" in *Love and Living,* 65.
28. See Merton, "Rain and the Rhinoceros," in *Raids on the Unspeakable,* 15–16; Merton, *Cables to the Ace,* in *Collected Poems,* 452; Suzuki, *Mysticism,* 28; Merton, "Seven Words," in *Love and Living,* 120.

of unity produced a potential division in Merton's conception of the self, stemming from his dual allegiance to a personalist conception of the self rooted in Christian philosophy and to an emphasis, derived from mystics such as Eckhart, on being, an emphasis that helped to attract him to Buddhist ontology.

In the writings of the 1960s one can see the tension created by Merton's straddling of these two rather different ontological worlds in the long series of ruminations on the contemplative life titled "The Inner Experience." In this detailed examination of the contemplative life, Merton separated the evil done by the self from the "good ground of the soul."[29] While such a distinction might appear to have driven a wedge between the quotidian and the ontological self, Merton's continued belief in the value of the organic, affective self was trenchantly expressed in his dramatization of the conflict between the self and technology in section 66 of *Cables to the Ace:*

> Science when the air is right says "Yes"
> And all the bubbles in the head repeat "Yes"
> Even the corpuscles romp "Yes."
>
> But lowdown
> At the bottom of deep water
> Deeper than Anna Livia Plurabelle
> Or any other river
> Some nameless rebel
> A Mister Houdini or somebody with fingers
> Slips the technical knots
> Pops the bubbles in the head
> Runs the vote backwards
> And turns the bloody cooler
> All the way
> OFF.[30]

Here Merton explored the elements of the self through the sexual substratum, which is conveyed through an allusion to James Joyce's ebul-

29. Merton, "The Inner Experience: Christian Contemplation," 215.
30. Merton, *Cables to the Ace,* in *Collected Poems,* 436.

lient language ("Anna Livia Plurabelle"). From that point in the poem he moves into a mysterious area, an area occupied by an emergent self apparently immune from technological manipulation. This can be seen in the subversive and apparently irrational act of turning off the socially pacifying air conditioner, an act attributed to "Mister Houdini," Merton's playful persona for the true self.

Similarly, in "With the World in My Bloodstream," one of the posthumously published poems included in the *Eighteen Poems* dedicated to M., Merton documented his unintended involvement as a patient in modern medical technology following back surgery. Ironically, the apparently beneficial surgery led to a temporary accommodation to the "invented air / And for the technical community of men." Set against his submission to this aspect of technological culture, however, was the "spark" within, the German mystic Meister Eckhart's term, it will be remembered, for the mind of the divine in the soul:

> Only the spark is now true
> Dancing in the empty room
> All around overhead
> While the frail body of Christ
> Sweats in a technical bed
> I am Christ's lost cell
> His childhood and desert age
> His descent into hell.[31]

Merton's postsurgical, groggy indebtedness not only to modern medicine but also to the larger world of technological euphoria that surrounded it left him with a sense of his body having abandoned the other and most important part of him: the inner self that clung surrealistically to life. For this reason, he identified in the poem with the largely unknown life that in the biblical account Christ lived in the desert and in the descent into hell, a perfect example to human beings of the terrifying submission of the self to God in the darkness. Against such a powerful projection of the brilliance of science as the surgery had been, Mer-

---

31. Merton, "With the World in My Bloodstream," in ibid., 617.

ton might simply have submitted to a separated, perhaps layered view of the self, rescuing his spiritual dimension, as it were, by cutting it loose. Such was not his idea of the self, however, as can be seen in "The Inner Experience" in which he makes it abundantly clear that the true self was not a *part* of our being, like a "motor in a car," but rather "our entire substantial reality itself, on its highest and most personal and most existential level." It was, he added, "our spiritual life when it is most alive."[32] Merton regarded the true self, then, not as something one possessed but rather as a way of existing in the fullest possible sense.

By the 1960s he tended to see this fullness of life as the offshoot of what was *natural* to human beings rather than as what resulted from an ascetic disciplining of the self. In this matter Merton was Rousseau-esque. In 1959, for example, he accepted the view that the original tendency toward sin or moral evil was in all likelihood not inherited from one individual—as in the Book of Genesis—but rather passed on to the individual by society. Also Rousseauesque was Merton's belief in an inner self, a "naked" self that existed prior to and apart from socialization and that was in his words "ultimate" and "indestructible."[33] Merton's affirmation of the natural self is evident in a talk he gave in Alaska in the months before his death in 1968 in which he recounted the life and death of a fellow monk at Gethsemani. Father Stephen, he explained, had been an eccentric man with a passion for gardening. This tendency in his nature had been thwarted, however, by his abbot, who decreed that Father Stephen should restrain his love of gardening in order to discipline himself and in this way attain a higher spiritual state. When a new abbot took office, Father Stephen was given permission, Merton continued, to garden as much as he liked, and did so until his death. Merton's description of that death is full of warmth and humor:

> On the feast of St. Francis about three years ago, he was coming in from his garden about dinner time and he went into another little garden and lay down on the ground under a tree, near a statue of

32. Merton, "The Inner Experience: Notes on Contemplation," 5.
33. Merton, Nov. 8, 1959, in *Search for Solitude*, 341; Merton, "Learning to Live," in *Love and Living*, 5.

Our Lady, and someone walked by and thought, "Whatever is he doing now?" and Father Stephen looked up at him and waved and lay down and died. The next day was his funeral and the birds were singing and the sun was bright and it was as though the whole of nature was right in there with Father Stephen.[34]

Noting the coincidental naturalness of the setting of Father Stephen's death, including the details of the feast of Saint Francis and the singing birds, Merton consummated his narrative theme of the goodness of the natural self.

An acceptance of their natural selves was necessary, Merton was convinced, for human beings to be fully themselves in a spiritual sense. Conscious of the fact that many of his religious associates might have reservations about Rilke's nonreligious, psychological study of the gospel story of the prodigal son, Merton nevertheless argued that Rilke had revealed important psychological truths that should be accepted as the basis of any further spiritual extrapolation of truth: "Why not recognize what is ours," he reflected in connection with Rilke's narrative, "and start from there?"[35] While some might see Merton's view here as simply a restating of the Thomist principle that grace builds on nature, what is distinctive is the essential *goodness* that he attributed to the natural self. At the same time, he saw this natural self as a platform that could lead to further transformation, to the formation of a self, for example, that was patterned on a christological model.[36] In Merton's view this new self not only would bear a resemblance to Christ but would paradoxically do so in a thoroughly individual manner, as he indicated in a talk that he gave in the 1960s on William Faulkner's story "The Bear."[37]

Because of his belief in the goodness of the natural self, Merton had in some way to account for the unconscious. Here he distinguished between the "psychosomatic" unconscious, which he perceived as rooted in the "biological substratum," and the ontological unconscious, which he

34. Merton, "The Life That Unifies," in *Thomas Merton in Alaska*, 148–49.

35. Merton, *Dancing in the Water of Life*, 346. This entry was part of a sequence titled "Some Personal Notes" written toward the end of 1965.

36. See George Kilcourse, *Ace of Freedoms: Thomas Merton's Christ.*

37. Merton, "The Bear," Credence Cassette no. AA 2079, n.d.

equated with what mystics such as Eckhart called the ground of the soul.[38] In making the distinction, Merton intended not to separate the self into parts but rather to indicate levels of activity to which the whole self might be directed. Thus, in reflecting in 1957 on how he might have written his earlier work *The Ascent to Truth* if he were writing it then, he said that he would have included more of a discussion of the psychological aspects of mysticism, including the "unconscious drives." In the 1960s in "The Inner Experience," he did, however, distinguish between the potentially pathological aspects of the unconscious, which he ascribed to the exterior self and associated with Freudian pathology, and the spark of the inner self, the voice of God imprinted in the psyche to orient it spiritually. For Merton, while the spiritual inner self might not affect an entrenched pathology that had a physiological cause, it could certainly address a pathology that had a psychological root. While Merton came to respect Freud's originality in describing the pathology of the self, he disagreed with what he perceived as Freud's mechanistic approach, as had Jung.[39] Nevertheless, he appears to have accepted that mechanistic analyses had their place when applied to mechanistic phenomena.

Nonetheless, Merton was obviously fascinated by some of the areas of the subconscious explored by Freud and by Freud's stratification of consciousness. He was especially interested in dreams, and recounted a number of his own dreams in his journals. In dreaming, Merton believed, as had Freud, that the subconscious spoke to the understanding.[40] Because of his wariness about the reductiveness of analytical discourse, however, Merton usually narrated his dreams without much further comment. Typically, his dream narratives suggest that he saw in dreams a wide range of subconscious activity, including the procession of Jungian archetypes. In a dream that he had in 1958, he encountered a young, virginal Jewish girl named Proverb. In a persuasive exploration

38. Merton, *Faith and Violence*, 112.

39. Merton, preface to the French edition of *The Ascent to Truth*, in *Honorable Reader*, 28; Merton, "The Inner Experience: Society and the Inner Self," 126; Merton, Oct. 3, 1941, in *Run to the Mountain*, 423.

40. Merton, Apr. 6, 1951, in *Entering the Silence*, 454.

of Jungianism in Merton's writings, Robert Waldron has suggested that the girl symbolized Merton's "anima" and that when she embraced him with "'virginal passion'" they became "unified" as "one man/woman." While Merton himself outlined the allegorical meaning of the dream as representing his love of holy wisdom, there are further unaccounted nuances that one is tempted to explore. For example, if it is true that the dream symbolized his love of wisdom, which is given the female form that it would later receive in his prose poem "Hagia Sophia," nevertheless, the drama of a young woman lovingly looking at him is clearly something different and less simply allegorical.[41] While Merton perceived this dream as allegorical, his approach to his dreams as observer was characteristically open-ended, and as narrator he tended to submit to the integrity of his dreams as universes of being immensely richer than any possible explications of them.

In Merton's writings there are times when the subconscious and the unconscious fused with the mystical, as in his early poem "After the Night Office—Gethsemani Abbey," a poem from *A Man in the Divided Sea* (1946) that Patrick O'Connell has ably explicated.[42] After a night of intense, prayerful union with God, Merton describes himself and his fellow monks as returning to the "windows" of their

> deep abode of peace,
> Emerging at our conscious doors
> We find our souls all soaked in grace, like Gideon's fleece.[43]

While the process of the night's prayerful concentration is suitably linked to the action of God, a divine intervention that is amplified by the allusion to the miraculous story of Gideon in the Book of Judges, nonetheless, the clear implication of the phrase "our conscious doors" is that Merton had earlier met blissfully with God in a subconscious area of the self.

---

41. Waldron, *Thomas Merton in Search of His Soul: A Jungian Perspective*, 99; see Merton, Feb. 28 and Mar. 4, 1958, in *Search for Solitude*, 176.

42. See O'Connell, "Thomas Merton's Wake-Up Calls: Aubades and Monastic Dawn Poems from *A Man in the Divided Sea*," 152–56.

43. Merton, "After the Night Office—Gethsemani Abbey," in *Collected Poems*, 109.

In section 86 of *Cables to the Ace,* Merton quoted Meister Eckhart in describing humanity as a "wilderness," again a word with pronounced natural connotations. Implicit in this description and in the anecdote about Father Stephen mentioned earlier is a respect, one might say a Blakean respect, for the essential ontological freedom of the self. Thus, in one of the talks included in *Springs of Contemplation,* Merton characterized Martin Luther sympathetically as one who, having followed all of the rules punctiliously required of an Augustinian monk, realized at some point that, in Merton's words, "you don't have to do all these things. You may or you may not, but you don't have to. If you do, it's not bad, there's nothing wrong with it. But don't base your security on observances. . . . However, if it's going to upset somebody, skip it. It's a matter of freedom."[44] Merton was undoubtedly reflecting his own sense of liberation here, which had grown appreciably following his living full-time in a hermitage. Typically and existentially, he used the perceptions gained from that experience to modify his idea of the self in a way that he believed would free others from forces that obscured a perception of the ontological richness of the self, whether these others were living on their own or in community.

Merton had been attracted to the question of the self and freedom by Etienne Gilson, who had argued in *The Spirit of Mediaeval Philosophy* that medieval Christian philosophers had embraced Aristotle's conclusion that human beings possessed a "spontaneous will" to achieve their "natural end"—happiness. Merton contrasted Gilson's view, with which he remained in agreement throughout his life, with what he regarded as the prevailing contemporary view of freedom that was centered on desire and longing. This view he regarded as a travesty of human freedom and especially of the decision-making matrix of freedom.[45] His emphasis on this dimension of freedom is connected with his valuing of existentialism. We are, so Merton and the existentialists contended, what we have chosen to be. While some might find Merton's belief in volitional

44. Merton, *Cables to the Ace,* in *Collected Poems,* 453; Merton, *Springs of Contemplation,* 191.

45. Gilson, *The Spirit of Mediaeval Philosophy,* 305; see Merton, *Conjectures of a Guilty Bystander,* 301.

freedom anachronistic, others, such as the Harvard biologist Edward O. Wilson, have offered a pragmatic support for Merton's conception of freedom. Because, Wilson contends, the self cannot be fully known, its belief in its own freedom is biologically fortunate, opening it to new possibilities of adaptation and survival. In Merton's reckoning the presence of a divine spark in the soul was the root of its fundamental ontological liberty, a liberty that if exercised, as he put it in *Seeds of Contemplation* (1949), would nourish the self, establishing its identity in the most profound sense possible. The fact that the exercise of moral liberty, even given the best intentions, in some circumstances produced ill effects did not daunt Merton, who argued that such an outcome was an inevitable risk and that, nevertheless, the ideal of freedom was "perhaps the deepest and most crucial need" of human beings.[46]

Merton's thinking about the self and freedom extended ultimately into the contemplative's unity with the divine through which the self and its creator came together in mutual recognition without there being a sacrificing of the identity of either. In an essay on Erich Fromm in a collection titled *Faith and Violence* (1968), he reiterated his view that there were two major arenas for the divine presence: the cosmic, in which case the self had to go out of itself to reach God, and the immanent, in which case the self had to look within and there discover the "truth and transcendent value" of the *"ordinary self."* In this connection Anne E. Carr has observed that especially in the later Merton, one encounters his discovery of the "original affirmation given in one's limited, relational, created being." It is in this latter context that he spoke of "sacred man" in his poem "Gloss on the Sin of Ixion," in *Emblems of a Season of Fury* (1963). Similarly, in his 1960s essay "Symbolism: Communication or Communion?" Merton declared that the sacredness of human beings consisted in the fact that the truth they sought lay primarily within themselves.[47]

46. See Wilson, *Consilience: The Unity of Knowledge*, 131–32; Merton, *Seeds of Contemplation*, 17; Merton, *Conjectures of a Guilty Bystander*, 77.

47. Thomas Merton, "A Note on *The Psychological Causes of War*, by Erich Fromm," in *Faith and Violence*, 114; Carr, *Search for Wisdom and Spirit*, 126; Merton, "Gloss on the Sin of Ixion," in *Collected Poems*, 314; Merton, "Symbolism: Communication or Communion?" in *Love and Living*, 69.

It was in his early writings that Merton had stressed the transcendence of God, a transcendence that reached infinitely beyond the self and was ostensibly therefore linked to apophatic contemplation. Nevertheless, throughout his life he recognized that speaking of the soul as annihilated by the energy created by the presence of God, as some mystics had done, was largely metaphorical and indicative of a state in which one temporarily lost the sense of having a separate existence. At the fundamental level of creation—the level of the inherited psyche—Merton regarded human intelligence as a participation in the intelligence of God. Mystical contemplation took this participation one large step further in giving the self the experience of the presence of the divine. Such an experience lay within the circumference of the human yet took the self beyond the perimeter of ordinary human experience. In the inner temple of the self, as it were, the divine, in Merton's view, not only recognized itself through seeing its own creation but also, fortuitously, revealed itself to the mirror or self in which it appeared. He added that all of this had to be conveyed through metaphorical language since it involved the description of an event that was ineffable. One cannot help but see the parallel here to Plato's conception in the *Phaedo*—a work that Merton loved—of the soul as the mirror of the divine.[48]

The mention of Plato underscores part of the polarity in Merton's conception of the self that breathed the air of the absolute as well as that of the Heraclitean world of growth and movement. In this connection Anne E. Carr has observed that in considering Merton's conception of the self, there would seem to have occurred a shift from the "hidden self, preconceived by God, to that of the self's continual and responsive *creation* or re-creation of itself in changing personal and historical contexts."[49] Carr's is an attractive paradigm of Merton's development, stretching from his eager search for cognitive absolutes in the 1940s to his later appreciation of the fluctuations of the self afloat on the tide of history and of culture. The later Merton in fact perceived the absolute as existentially hovering within being and within the perceiving self, an ontological gyroscope, as it were, through which the self could plunge into

48. See Plato, "Phaedo," in *The Portable Plato*, 225.
49. Carr, *Search for Wisdom and Spirit*, 130.

diverse worlds of observation and thought while keeping its inner eye, so to speak, on being and on the author of being. So stabilized, he became more and more outgoing in his conception of the self and more and more comprehensive about how much of his own self was worthy of attention, including the most quotidian details of his existence. If he evolved an existentialist view of the self that gave off new light based upon his changing experience like the lucent tail of a comet, it is also true that he saw this light as part of a surging, cosmic creative energy in which he participated and whose vitality and movement he had in his early writings perceived too abstractly and with perhaps too much stillness.

Merton's emphasis on the ontological and psychological importance of the self in some significant respects recalls Carl Jung's claim that within modern technological nations the individual self occupies a merely marginal place. This was especially unfortunate, according to Jung, since the concrete existential self was the "true and authentic carrier of reality," in contrast to abstract and scientific descriptions of it.[50] For Merton, the concrete existential self was a preeminent source of reality in addition to being capable of adding reality to other things through the transforming power of the imagination and the exercise of moral freedom. This perception would appear to have been the import of his poem "Elias—Variations on a Theme":

> Under the blunt pine
> Elias becomes his own geography
> (Supposing geography to be necessary at all),
> Elias becomes his own wild bird, with God in the center,
> His own wide field which nobody owns,
> His own pattern, surrounding the Spirit
> By which he is himself surrounded:
>
> For the free man's road has neither beginning nor end.[51]

The implication of these lines is that the ordinary human being's "road" has a rather predictable beginning and end. Instead of such a linear plod-

50. See Jung, *The Undiscovered Self,* 113–14.
51. Merton, "Elias—Variations on a Theme," in *Collected Poems,* 245.

ding, Merton imaginatively visualized the self as hovering in time and space, indeed mastering them with its chosen directions, yet being simultaneously steadied ontologically by a consciousness of God at the "center" of its geography.

There is a similarly lyrical and triumphant presentation of the self in the prologue to *The Geography of Lograire* in the late 1960s:

> To have felt
> All my old grounds
> Forgotten world
> All along
> Dream places
> Words in my feet
> Explain the air of all
> Feel it under (me)
> Stand
> Stand in the unspoken
> A cool street
> An air of legs
> An air of visions
>
> *Geography.*
> *I am all (here)*
> *There!*[52]

In this poem all of the constituents of Merton's self are gathered and interfused, as can be seen in the arresting image of words in his feet. As a result of this reintegration of the self, the self could begin to dominate the space that it materially inhabited in addition to learning to navigate the expanse of time. While the poem incorporated a vision of the ideal, for Merton the poetic celebration of the self, as for Whitman, was more than a solipsistic escape from the deadening view of technological culture. Rather, it was an ontological awakening to the riches of being within the compass of the self that technological culture with its lack of interest in ontology had essentially overlooked. Inasmuch as it did attend

52. Merton, *Geography of Lograire*, in *Collected Poems*, 497–98.

to the self, Merton noted, technological culture presented a picture of the self based on what he called *"velleity,"* or desire.[53] This was in order to create a self well adapted to the sort of homogeneous consumer culture that had in the modern period become so clearly coordinated with technological culture. In this way, Merton believed, contemporary Western society had succeeded in overshadowing and controlling the self even while failing to understand it.

53. Merton, *Conjectures of a Guilty Bystander,* 303.

4

Nature and Time

In part because of Saint Francis of Assisi's legendary attachment to nature, Merton once told a correspondent that there was not a saint whom he admired more.[1] Nonetheless, there were occasions in his early years in the monastery when, imbued with ascetic ideals, Merton became self-conscious about natural things in the widest possible sense, wondering at the seeming absurdity of a person being "sanctified," for example, by something he "naturally likes."[2] At the same time, Catholic philosophy and theology, in contrast to Calvinism, permitted a love of nature, since nature led one to think of the Creator. Merton was obviously drawn to the monastic life at Gethsemani in part because of the forested and hilly Kentucky setting, but in addition he appreciated the salubrious effects of a lifestyle that combined manual and intellectual work, as he explained to Rosemary Radford Ruether in 1967. While he had been attracted in the 1940s by the silence that attended the work of the monks in the fields, he became alarmed at times by the technological updating of the monastic farm and cheese works in the 1950s under Dom James Fox. He seems to have reached a state of ambivalence about the matter by the time he wrote *Conjectures of a Guilty Bystander* in 1966, arguing that if technological innovation had been required, it had not come with-

1. Merton to Anthony Bannon, Feb. 12, 1966, in *Witness to Freedom*, 164.
2. Merton, Feb. 2, 1949, in *Entering the Silence*, 276.

out a cost in terms of the solitude for which the monastic life had been established.[3]

Contemplative theology used the "vision of God in nature" as a preamble to a supernatural vision of God, as Merton observed in *Bread in the Wilderness* in 1953. Indeed, in an apophatic view of nature in *Thoughts in Solitude* in the late 1950s, he portrayed nature as useful in emptying the mind of distracting thoughts and images and therefore preparing it for the contemplation of God. This was a relatively restrained and tepid approach to nature in comparison with the radiance that it possessed even in some of Merton's earliest writings. His explication in *The Ascent of Truth* in the early 1950s, for example, that nature stimulated an intuitive perception of the divine was central to his thinking throughout his life, in spite of his rather uncharacteristically analytical language in that book.[4] Furthermore, the journals and poems produced a different view of nature from the more flattened view found in much of his expository writing during the early years—as can be seen in this extract from his journal in the late fall of 1948:

> Today, unless I am mistaken, is the feast of Bl. John Ruysbroeck—
> or would be if he had one. The morning sky behind the new horse-
> barn was as splendid as his writing. A thousand small high clouds
> went flying majestically like ice-floes, all golden and crimson and
> saffron, with clean blue and aquamarine behind them, and shades
> of orange and red and mauve down by the surface of the land where
> the hills are just visible in a pearl haze and the ground was steel-
> white with frost—every blade of grass as stiff as wire.[5]

Merton's capturing of the delicate, evanescent hues of this winter scene indicates something other than an emptying of the mind in preparation for contemplation of the divine. His aesthetic pleasure in looking out at the world is everywhere evident and affirmed. More than leading the mind upward to God, this exquisite scene led him to an appreciation of

3. Merton to Ruether, Mar. 9, 1967, in *Hidden Ground of Love,* 506; see Merton, *Conjectures of a Guilty Bystander,* 16.
4. Merton, *Thoughts in Solitude,* 111; Merton, *The Ascent to Truth,* 27.
5. Merton, Dec. 2, 1948, in *Entering the Silence,* 248.

the divine art that was the natural world. If Merton had always remained vigilant about the possibility of being called a pantheist, he was simultaneously aware of God as both immanent in and transcending nature. Moreover, that he used these scenes of nature as occasions for contemplation is evident here in his contextualizing of the scene—the flow of meaning back and forth between the beauty of soul of the medieval mystic John Ruysbroeck and the beauty of the natural foreground. The juxtaposition stimulates a crosscurrent of impressions that makes the icy scene holier than it would otherwise appear and the saint's presence more tinted with natural coloring than would otherwise be the case. The effect does not seem to be the result of a constructed collage, as in, say, a poem by Ezra Pound, but rather sprang from Merton's spontaneous openness to the suggestiveness of his immediate surroundings.

Just as he placed a high value on the inner freedom of the self, so too, in a significant link with romanticism, did Merton associate nature with freedom. Writing in his journal in 1952, he observed that every wave of the sea was free: "Every river on earth proclaims its own liberty." The reason was that the "independent trees own nothing and are owned by no one and they lift up their leafy hands in freedom." Another example was his vivid description of a hawk's flight in *Conjectures of a Guilty Bystander* in which the bird is seen "flying in freedom." What Merton meant by freedom was a Rousseauesque recognition of the ostensible grace and freedom of nature. In addition, he celebrated the instinctive energy of nature as an emblem of freedom, as can be seen in the spring landscape of an early poem in *Figures for an Apocalypse* (1947) in which the "huge bulls" were portrayed roaming in their pens and singing like "trains." Merton looked to nature to freshen his perceptions, aware that no two moments witnessed in a natural landscape would be the same. In 1964 he recorded such changes frequently, as in his view of the hills around him, hills that had become dark and "etched out with snow, standing in obscurity and in a kind of spaciousness" he had "never seen before."[6] Such perceptions not only registered the virtually illimitable

6. Merton, entry for the Octave of Corpus Christi, June 1952, in ibid., 474–75; Merton, *Conjectures of a Guilty Bystander*, 224; Merton, "Spring: Monastery Farm," in *Collected Poems*, 169; Merton, Jan. 1, 1964, in *Dancing in the Water of Life*, 52.

beauty of the creational world around him, but also awakened the power of his own imagination by which he hoped to see into the heart of things.

A paradoxical aspect of nature's value for Merton had to do with its imperfection and mortality. In 1950 on a day trip to Louisville he became fascinated by a junk wagon he saw there that later surfaced in his imagination with unexpected exoticism, like something "precious once seen in the Orient." He saw the wagon a few times on trips to the city, and then dreamt about it, hearing in the dream the bells of the mules that pulled the wagon, which was inexplicably held together by green boards in "marvelous disorder." In some respects Merton's impression of the junk wagon is reminiscent of Wordsworth's pleasure in seeing the cottages of the Lake District that seemed to grow out of their rugged surroundings. As with the scene of the junk wagon, Merton's comfort in the presence of natural decay is also evident in his poem "Elias—Variations on a Theme" in which he came to feel at home on the monastery grounds in a crumbling trailer with "wet, smashed wheels" and a "rotten tree" near it.[7] There is more here than Merton's resistance to the nondecaying properties of many of the products manufactured by modern technology, though this was undoubtedly part of his attitude toward the trailer and the rotten tree. He believed that his closeness to nature, where things died all the time, made the thought of death more natural and therefore more acceptable than it was in highly socialized environments. Until one reached this kind of acceptance, he believed, the self could never develop, and would forever be the prey of whatever manipulative forces in society played on one's fear of mortality. Putting the matter in a different form and on a higher plane, he wrote that only when our "activity proceeds out of the ground in which we have consented to be dissolved" would it reach others in "true communion."[8]

Although Merton, like Blake, refused to divinize nature, he did write

7. Merton, Dec. 13, 1950, in *Entering the Silence,* 447; see Wordsworth, *Wordsworth's Guide to the Lakes,* 62; Merton, "Elias—Variations on a Theme," in *Collected Poems,* 241–42. See Patrick O'Connell, "The Geography of Solitude: Thomas Merton's 'Elias—Variations on a Theme.'"
8. Merton, "Love and Solitude," in *Love and Living,* 23.

to a correspondent in 1964 that he meditated "best" in the woods around him.[9] In part, this was because of a kindred awareness that enabled him to see the natural elements around him, as Saint Francis of Assisi had done, as "brother and sister."[10] On another occasion he described two crows perched in an oak tree beyond his gate as part of a "menage, a liturgy, a fellowship of sorts," a consortium uniting himself, nature, and God.[11] Given such consciousness, he could praise the refusal of Hindus to eat the animals around them because of their feeling of communion with the creatures in their midst, which was their way, as Merton put it, of participating in the "ontological mystery of being."[12]

At times, nature's "truth" and resplendence drew Merton temporarily away from the formal texts of his religion, as can be seen in this beautifully etched sequence of scenes from his journal in 1963:

> Cold at first, the hermitage dark in the moonlight . . . a fire in the grate (and how beautifully firelight shines through the lattice-blocks and all through the house at night!). Then the sunrise, enormous yolk of energy spreading and spreading as if to take over the sky. After that the ceremonies of the birds feeding in the dewy grass, and the meadowlark feeding and singing. Then the quiet, totally silent, day, warm mid morning under the climbing sun. It was hard to say psalms: one's attention was totally absorbed by the great arc of the sky and the trees and hills and grass and all things in them. How absolutely true, and how central a truth, that we are purely and simply *part of nature*, though we are the part which recognizes God.[13]

Although in this scene Merton had become rapt in the quiet display of the rising day and thus could not give himself to the ritualistic saying of the Psalms, he was clearly not at odds with the liturgies and prayers of his religion. Rather, he was struck by the power with which nature held him

9. Merton to Etta Gullick, May 22, 1964, in *Hidden Ground of Love*, 367.
10. Merton, Feb. 27, 1950, in *Entering the Silence*, 412.
11. Merton, Feb. 13, 1968, in *Other Side of the Mountain*, 56.
12. See Merton, "Symbolism: Communication or Communion?" in *Love and Living*, 71–72.
13. Merton, Apr. 13, 1963, in *Turning toward the World*, 312.

and by the subsequent realization that he was a part of nature, not simply in an abstract, scientific sense but existentially as well. Indeed, rather like Wallace Stevens, he was aware that in engaging contemplatively with nature, the mind projected an image of itself onto nature, thereby paradoxically opening up a new source of reality and self-knowledge. Expressing his attraction to the *Duino Elegies* of Rilke in 1965, he appeared to accept the sort of interfusion of consciousness and nature that one finds in Rilke, even if he found Rilke somewhat narcissistic at times. Epistemologically, Merton seemed unperturbed by this sort of interfusion, even if he had some reservations about the consequent difficulty in comprehending Rilke's poetry. Fundamentally, the mind and nature in Merton formed a continuum based upon a resemblance, or what Whitman in a similar frame of mind called a similitude found in the realization of a sharing in being.

Alongside his interest in nature, about which he resolved to school himself as an amateur naturalist in the 1940s and 1950s, Merton gradually registered an increasingly detached relationship to the official pronouncements of organized religion, which seemed to him contrastingly tedious and insipid at times. On one occasion in 1963, for example, he noted that some aspects of the Church struck him as oddly *"secular"* alongside the "sacred" spring season that had begun to take shape around him. Moreover, in a reflection that was closer to Wordsworth than to Blake, he wrote two years later that nature constituted a "beginning of revelation." In a similar vein, writing to Marco Pallis in 1965, he dismissed as unsatisfactory and "misleading" the division between the ideas of the natural and the supernatural in traditional religious discourse. Confiding to Margaret Randall in 1967 that for him the woods were "life," he came to think of nature as having a cleansing and thus a quasi-sacramental effect.[14] By 1967 his consciousness of the penetration of nature by the divine was so seamless that the making of strong distinctions based on the superior ontological status of the sacraments over nature

14. Merton, Apr. 16, 1963, in ibid., 313; Merton, Aug. 12, 1965, in *Dancing in the Water of Life,* 279; Merton to Pallis, Easter 1965, in *Hidden Ground of Love,* 470; Merton to Randall, June 6, 1967, in *Courage for Truth,* 220; see Merton, Apr. 22, 1951, in *Entering the Silence,* 457.

would have struck him as pedantic. This was not only because Merton had veered somewhat closer to pantheism, especially given his attraction to Buddhism in the 1960s, but primarily because he viewed the presence of God within the world as an overridingly powerful reality that over-shadowed such distinctions, even if it did not invalidate them.

There is a memorable sense of this consciousness in Merton's poem "Song for Nobody," which was included in the *Emblems of a Season of Fury* in 1963:

> A yellow flower
> (Light and spirit)
> Sings by itself
> For nobody.
>
> A golden spirit
> (Light and emptiness)
> Sings without a word
> By itself.
>
> Let no one touch this gentle sun
> In whose dark eye
> Someone is awake.[15]

While the image of the singing, solitary flower conveys the sense of ex-ternal nature in a way that reminds one of Wordsworth, the most star-tling and original lines in the poem have to do with the appearance of the dark eye of the flower in which "someone is awake." Merton's aware-ness of a consciousness underlying and animating nature here attained an almost Gothic intensity.

In the mid-1960s Merton pushed his portrayal of the sacredness of nature almost to the limit in two pieces of poetic prose in *Raids on the Unspeakable*, "Atlas and the Fatman" and "The Early Legend: Notes for a Cosmic Meditation." In introductory notes to *Raids on the Unspeak-able*, he was careful to point out that his lyrical presentation of Atlas, a mythic personification of the Atlas Mountains of North Africa, was not

---

15. Merton, "Song for Nobody," in *Collected Poems*, 337.

to be mistaken for a world soul but was rather a titan, representative of the natural rhythms and goodness of nature. In "Atlas and the Fatman," the natural world, personified by Atlas, is steeped in a magisterial silence that accompanies a natural harmony and order vastly superior to the claims and even the aims of modern technological culture. A similar motif is present in "The Early Legend: Notes for a Cosmic Meditation" in which nature, suffused with a superhuman, beneficent intelligence, guides the procession of natural events from a heart that lay "at the bottom of the sea."[16] The essay reveals a romantic primitivism to which Merton always responded in other writers such as William Faulkner, who set his great story "The Bear" in a landscape in which human beings were in direct, intuitive contact with nature.

In a manner that recalls American romantic writers such as Emerson and Thoreau, Merton thought of nature emblematically as a text by which the mind could read ultimate reality. Thus, there is a good deal of imagery in his writing having to do with nature addressing itself to a compatible human understanding. In his essay "Rain and the Rhinoceros," there is the following illustrative reflection:

> The night became very dark. The rain surrounded the whole cabin with its enormous virginal myth, a whole world of meaning, of secrecy, of silence, of rumor. Think of it: all that speech pouring down, selling nothing, judging nobody, drenching the thick mulch of dead leaves, soaking the trees, filling the gullies and crannies of the wood with water, washing out the places where men have stripped the hillside! What a thing it is to sit absolutely alone, in the forest, at night, cherished by this wonderful, unintelligible, perfectly innocent speech, the most comforting speech in the world, the talk that rain makes by itself all over the ridges, and the talk of the watercourses everywhere in the hollows![17]

In contrast to the ancient pastoral myth, nature is here not sympathetically attuned to the desires of human beings. On the other hand, it does

16. Merton, "The Early Legend: Notes for a Cosmic Meditation," in *Raids on the Unspeakable*, 127.
17. Merton, "Rain and the Rhinoceros," in *Raids on the Unspeakable*, 9–10.

speak a language that, even if "unintelligible," is meaningful at a deeper level than human language. Its meaning has to do not only with the supernal beauty of creation and therefore of the Creator but also with an autonomous world outside of human consciousness to which human consciousness can and must respond in order to understand the full spectrum of reality in which it is suspended.

Such scenes are ubiquitous in Merton's writing, as in his 1965 evanescent description of a flycatcher tracing in flight a "sudden, indecipherable ideogram" against the "void of mist." In 1966 in the preface to the Japanese translation of *Thoughts in Solitude,* he declared, echoing Saint Bernard of Clairvaux, that there was nothing that he could say about the solitary life of meditation that had not been "said better by the wind in the pine trees," adding that he had attempted in the book to echo the voice of the rain, though not the wind, which inexpressibly opened onto a "deeper" silence in which one might encounter the "Hearer" who is "No-Hearer."[18] The intuiting of such a mysterious hearer in nature and the motif of the wind in the pine trees recall Wallace Stevens's poem "The Snow Man." While Stevens's poem is impressionistic and epistemologically uncertain, however, Merton's evocative statement is ontological, pointing toward an accessible, ultimate reality.

Though language fell short in the communication with nature, Merton saw his relationship with nature as reciprocal, wondering in his journal in 1968, for example, how photos that he took of some old logs with "strange abstract patterns" in them would turn out.[19] He thought of the photographs as a cooperative effort on the part of both himself and nature in producing the pattern that the photographs would reveal, a combination of the natural scene and his interpretation of it in taking the photograph. Even when absolutely mute and still, nature could communicate, and did so in a number of Merton's poems, as in the following stanzas from the poem "Love Winter When the Plant Says Nothing," which was included in *Emblems of a Season of Fury* in 1963:

18. Merton, June 12, 1965, in *Dancing in the Water of Life,* 255–56; Merton, preface to the Japanese translation of *Thoughts in Solitude,* in *Honorable Reader,* 111.
19. Merton, May 21, 1968, in *Other Side of the Mountain,* 119.

> Secret
> Vegetal words,
> Unlettered water,
> Daily zero. . . .
>
> Fire, turn inward
> To your weak fort,
> To a burly infant spot,
> A house of nothing.[20]

The wintry inexpressiveness of the plant becomes an emblem of the deepest reaches of the soul where a small fire burns within even when the outer self had sunk into solitude. Nature here is portrayed as both emblem and model in its beckoning of the mind to contemplation.

Although Merton linked nature as creation to a latent, divine intelligence, he also associated it with the unconscious, as in the following Easter-morning scene in his journal in 1965:

> I got up and said the old office of Lauds, and there was a wood thrush singing fourth-tone mysteries in the deep ringing pine wood (the "unconscious" wood) behind the hermitage. (The "unconscious" wood has a long moment of perfect clarity at dawn, and from being dark and confused, lit from the east it is all clarity, all distinct, seen to be a place of silence and peace with its own order in disorder—the fallen trees don't matter, they are part of it!)[21]

Even though the trees were not felled naturally but instead had been cut by Merton's neighbor, he here viewed them as part of a natural cycle, like the natural rotation of night and day. Similarly, although the wood thrush sang with a pitch that reminded him of liturgical chants with which he was familiar, the emphasis is on the unconsciousness of nature, its representing of that vast part of being that is not consciousness, both in the cosmos generally and in the self. In particular, the scene symbolized the floating of the observer's consciousness in the unconsciousness of nature, a beacon for Merton toward the kind of unity he

20. Merton, "Love Winter When the Plant Says Nothing," in *Collected Poems*, 353.
21. Merton, Apr. 18, 1965, in *Dancing in the Water of Life*, 231.

sought in mystical contemplation. The connection between his belief in the latent immanence of God in nature and the role of nature as the unconscious lay in his perception that the unconscious was a reminder of a creational dimension of existence that lay beyond and that preceded human initiative.

In a sophisticated essay on nature titled "The Wild Places," he traced the Western romantic mythology of nature to the burgeoning growth of urbanization. In terms of American culture he contrasted the American romantics' love of nature with that of the Puritans, who saw it as a fallen and evil world and therefore exploitable. Merton acknowledged especially the role of Thoreau, whose hermitic life in the woods he regarded as a forerunner of his own, in connecting nature with ontological awareness. In particular, he repeated Thoreau's caution that the destruction of nature would inevitably lead to the destruction of human beings, who would thereby have lost a vital contact needed for their psychic survival. Such an apprehension underlay his lifelong antipathy to technological culture, which he saw as hubristically having detached itself from the value of the natural world both in itself and as a dimension of human existence. Putting this another way, he wrote to Carlton Smith in 1967 that technological culture was "dangerously indifferent to authentic human values" and "naively" preoccupied with efficacy as an "end in itself." As if to illustrate the point that he could be positive about technological culture, on flying to Asia in 1968 he remarked upon the seclusion and tranquillity that flying made possible. At the same time, in an earlier entry made while flying to Alaska, he had described the "big shining masses" of the jet engines as standing out "fiercely blue-black" against the cloud, sealing this observation with a bleak quotation from *The Tibetan Book of the Dead* about the coming of a "dull blue light from the brute world."[22] This Yeatsian sense of foreboding was certainly close to the heart of Merton's thinking about technology.

In a sardonic passage he addressed the problem of technology and nature in his extended poetic sequence *Cables to the Ace* in the late 1960s:

22. See Merton, "The Wild Places," 39–40; Merton to Smith, Apr. 9, 1967, in *Hidden Ground of Love*, 558; on flying to Asia, Merton, Oct. 15, 1968, in *Other Side of the Mountain*, 209; on flying to Alaska, Merton, Sept. 17, 1968, in ibid., 181.

Will my rat ever recover?
Will he call again
Ringing the septal region
That earthly
Paradise in the head
Two millimeters away
From my sinus infection?

Political man must learn
To work the pleasure button
And cut off the controlling rat
Science is very near but the morbid
Animal might always win.[23]

On one level Merton here darkly considered the contrast between the atavistic, animal nature of human beings and their smoothly programmed behavior in the age of technology. On a deeper level, however, there is the sinister implication that human beings were passing from an animalistic level of behavior to a technologically conditioned state without ever having evolved into full human beings.

In Merton's judgment, while human beings were a part of nature, they were that very distinctive part that was "conscious of God."[24] This consciousness aligned human beings with the rest of nature, not in a purely instinctive manner but in an ever expanding understanding of the ontological significance of human beings and of the rest of the natural world. It was precisely here that Merton considered technological culture deficient and at the very least premature in its attempted transformation of a natural into a technological world. Merton's cautionary view in this matter was not a rejection of particular advances in, say, medical science; rather, he was alarmed at the headlong rush of technology over nature without due consideration, both ecologically and ontologically, of the present value of the existing world. Support for such a skeptical view of technological ascendancy has come from thinkers such as Carl Jung and more recently Edward O. Wilson, who has looked at the matter

23. Merton, *Cables to the Ace*, in *Collected Poems*, 409.
24. Merton, *Conjectures of a Guilty Bystander*, 268.

from the point of view of evolutionary biology. Wilson observed sober-
ly that there had as yet been no technology produced that could sustain
life as the earth could and that there was no prospect of such technology becoming available. This was also, he added, the conclusion of two
biologists who had participated in the Biosphere 2 project: "'Earth remains the only known home that can sustain life. . . . To believe otherwise is to risk reducing Earth to a wasteland, and humanity to a threatened species.'"[25]

In spite of his attraction to nature both in itself and as an emblem of
the self in its relationship to the cosmos, Merton was aware of the random violence of nature. This is evident in his anguish at the news of the
drowning of his beloved aunt Kit in the stormy waters between the north
and south islands of New Zealand in 1968. In trying to reconcile the
death of this good woman with his belief in a loving God, Merton concluded that God shared his pain at the accidental death of his aunt at
the hands of nature. Still, there remained a "stark absence" of all "relat-
edness," Merton believed, between the "quiet, gentle, unselfish courage"
of his aunt's life and her "dreadful, violent" death. Merton seems romantically at odds here with traditional Catholic philosophy and theology that regard nature as a neutral element, possessing both beauty and
violence among other attributes, but having no moral standing. One can
see the same sort of romanticism in his reaction to the Darwinian aspects of nature. This came out particularly in his correspondence with
Czeslaw Milosz, who accused him of ignoring the suffering brought
about by nature. Merton answered that he and nature were "very good
friends" and that although he was perfectly aware of the predatory aspects of nature, he did not attribute evil to nature, reserving that for human beings.[26] In this instance Merton *was* on solid Catholic philosophical and theological ground. In a subsequent reflection about the
exchange with Milosz, however, he construed the matter in a novel way
in arguing that one's attitude toward nature was simply an extension of
one's attitude toward oneself and toward others, concluding that human

25. Wilson, *Consilience,* 306.
26. Merton, Apr. 25, 1968, in *Other Side of the Mountain,* 85; see Merton to Milosz,
May 6, 1960, in *Courage for Truth,* 65–66.

beings were "free to be at peace" with themselves, with one another, and "also with nature." Similarly, Merton confided to Dorothy Day in 1961 that he believed the nature of human beings to be essentially more non-violent than not.[27]

The most vivid instance of Merton's sublimation of the Darwinian aspects of nature occurred relatively early in his life as a monk and writer in 1950. After having seen a hawk swoop down into a school of starlings, taking one of the birds, he described his emotions, subsequently recollected in tranquillity:

> I tried to pray, afterward. But the hawk was eating the bird. And I thought of that flight, coming down like a bullet from the sky behind me and over my roof, the sure aim with which he hit this one bird, as though he had picked it out a mile away. For a moment I envied the Lords of the Middle Ages, who had their falcons, and I thought of the Arabs with their fast horses, hawking on the desert's edge, and I also understood the terrible fact that some men love war. But in the end I think that hawk is to be studied by saints and contemplatives because he knows his business.[28]

While the reference to men loving war might seem to cloud the issue of the relative moral standing of human beings versus nature, Merton here alluded to a sort of amoral love of war, like a love of sport, by a human being unaware, like the hawk killing the starling, of its moral dimension. He came close in the passage, as Blake had done, to closing the gap between the lamb and the tiger in his acceptance of the scene as an expression of nature's power. The passage is one of the most memorable from Merton's journals not only because of its momentous themes but also because of its stylistic and especially its dramatic trenchancy. Set in pictorial juxtaposition are the startled monk with his mind floating in a contemplative serenity and the hawk whose urgent flight reveals the dynamics of predation. Caught by surprise, the monk stares, transfixed by

27. Merton, Conjectures of a Guilty Bystander, 124; Merton to Day, Dec. 20, 1961, in Hidden Ground of Love, 143.

28. Merton, Feb. 10, 1950, in Entering the Silence, 408. The incident is also described in The Sign of Jonas, 274–75.

the beauty and power of the hawk, whose nature, even if it does not express the monk himself, does express in some mysterious way the monk's and the hawk's creator. Unable to fully resolve the incipient questions that lie below the surface of the passage, Merton nevertheless sinks into a kind of awe and a relief that he should have been loved by such a God.

Later in life Merton reacted somewhat similarly to the sight of diamondback rattlesnakes in New Mexico that were "too beautiful, too alive, too much themselves" to be seen as evil or even terrifying. Again, he came close here to regarding the power of nature as a neutral force, in this respect reflecting both Thomist philosophy and Blake. In the unfallen world in Blake, according to Northrop Frye, the creative energy of God included "twisting the sinews of the tiger's heart." Here one is reminded of Merton's notes about Blake in a course taken at Columbia in the late 1930s in which he understood Blake's Christ to have epitomized both the lamb and the tiger. In this way Merton can be said to have perceived nature romantically but with a romanticism buttressed by the theology of the Incarnation. In fact, Merton set forth such a hybrid view in a letter to Dorothy Day in 1961 in which he said that the state of nature itself had been turned toward goodness by Christ's participation in matter. In this context one comes to understand how Merton modified Catholic philosophy and theology in the light of his romantic assumptions. At times this modified vision of nature becomes sublimely compassionate, as in Merton's perception of God's empathetic suffering due to the pain endured by both human beings and animals.[29] The apparent contradiction of God identifying with the suffering of animals while having created the conditions that produced that suffering Merton accepted as an opportunity for moral development, a response to pain that led fortuitously to the birth of pity. At the same time, perhaps because he was essentially a joyful person, Merton tended to place suffering at the margin of his thinking, and in this respect he may be said to have overlooked a major aspect of Buddhist thought with which in many other respects he was in accord.

29. Merton, May 22, 1968, in *Other Side of the Mountain,* 108; Frye, *Fearful Symmetry,* 71; see Merton, "Romanticism," n.p.; Merton to Day, Dec. 20, 1961, in *Hidden Ground of Love,* 142; Merton to Jeanette Yakel, Mar. 21, 1967, in *Road to Joy,* 347.

Having believed his place to be at the "teeming heart of natural families," as Merton put it in *Cables to the Ace*, he exhibited a strong ecological consciousness throughout his life at the Abbey of Gethsemani. In a small personal monograph dedicated to Merton, Brother Patrick Hart, Merton's longtime friend and colleague, has said that Merton was always concerned about natural conservation. With his inclusive vision he saw that ecological consciousness was not a particular application of consciousness but rather the effusion of a generalized awareness of the world. As he wrote in 1962 after reading Rachel Carson's book *The Silent Spring*, human beings were in the process of destroying nature because they had already been destroying themselves, "spiritually, morally, and in every way," adding that this was "all part of the same sickness."[30] In this sense Merton envisioned not merely a physical ecology but also a "mental ecology," a "living balance of spirits," as he put it in his own case, in this "corner of woods."[31] He included in his ecological zone not only nature but the mind as well, not only the birds but also the writings of Tertullian, Chuang Tzu, and Isaiah in a synthesis that interlaced tendrils of mind, body, and nature. With this comprehensive consciousness Merton was able to see not only the importance of ecological consciousness to the survival of the planet but also the psychological and spiritual value to human beings of a balanced, nonexploitative relationship to nature. At this level of perception, Merton argued in his accomplished study *The Ascent to Truth*, an ultimate ecological spiral would likely include God. In this ultimate scenario he recalled the role of natural contemplation in mystical theology whereby the mind arose toward a perception of the *nature* of God as the epitome of all that is good.

For Merton, time, like nature, was a part of the goodness of the created world and of its Creator. One can see the interaction of nature and time in the lyrical conclusion to *New Seeds of Contemplation* (1962): "For the world and time are the dance of the Lord in emptiness. The silence

30. Hart, *Thomas Merton: First and Last Memories*, n.p.; Merton, Dec. 11, 1962, in *Turning toward the World*, 274.
31. Merton, *Dancing in the Water of Life*, 239. This passage formed part of the original draft of Merton's well-known essay "Day of a Stranger," which was written in May 1965.

of the spheres is the music of a wedding feast. . . . [N]o despair of ours can alter the reality of things, or stain the joy of the cosmic dance which is always there. Indeed, we are in the midst of it, and it is in the midst of us, for it beats in our very blood, whether we want it to or not."[32]

As with almost everything else about Merton, his idea of time was eclectic, drawn from a wide variety of philosophical, religious, and literary sources. In part, with its attachment to intuition and to consciousness, Merton's idea of time resembled that developed by the French philosopher Henri Bergson, with whose thought he was familiar. For Bergson, especially as expressed in *Duration and Simultaneity* in 1922, time was intimately connected with intuitive consciousness that, unlike rational consciousness, could link the separate moments of experience into a necklace of unfolding motion and meaning, which Bergson called duration. For Bergson, and for Merton, physics converted time into separate measurable points that obscured its underlying unity. While not disputing that time involved a succession of moments and changes, Bergson posited a unifying continuum that endured within and throughout succession and change. Similarly, in his early journal *Run to the Mountain,* Merton presented time as a durational continuity, observing that in time we "follow an action from its beginning to its end—from the time it is insensibly born out of some other action, until it is insensibly lost in another action with a different meaning still."[33]

It was in Merton's rejection of time as an abstraction that he seems most to have separated himself from thinkers such as Saint Thomas Aquinas, with whom in some other respects he considered himself in harmony, having described himself in a 1968 essay on Blake, for example, as one who still clung to some central aspects of Scholastic philosophy. For Saint Thomas Aquinas, the mind came to a knowledge of things by abstracting ideas of them from images. Merton's emphasis on intuitive as opposed to rational, deductive knowledge, which might seem to place him closer to Kant than to Aquinas, found an echo, if indeed not an influence, in the writings of his friend Jacques Maritain, a Thomist with an unusual respect for intuitive understanding. In 1967 in

32. Merton, *New Seeds of Contemplation,* 297.
33. Merton, Oct. 15, 1939, in *Run to the Mountain,* 53.

his lecture on the Easter service in Faulkner's *Sound and the Fury*, Merton indicated that he had read and appreciated Maritain's *Creative Intuition in Art and Poetry* (1953). For Maritain, art had its origin in the intuitive, "preconceptual" life of the intellect that permitted a fusion of the artist's intuitive knowledge of the self and the external world, a process that in the finest art gave rise to a "flash of reality."[34] Like Merton, Maritain argued that artistic intuition was not directed toward "essences" detached from "concrete reality" but rather toward "concrete existence" as "connatural" to the soul. In particular, the destination of the artist was durational, the presentation of a "complex of concrete and individual reality" captured in the "total unicity of its passage in time." For both Merton and Maritain, such creative intuition stretched toward an "infinite reality" seen to be present and "engaged" in any "singular existing thing." Similarly, as Merton put it in his lecture on *The Sound and the Fury*, one could eventually move through the experiential concreteness of the aesthetic, moral, and liturgical to an "intuition of the ultimate values of life, of the Absolute Ground of life, or even of the invisible Godhead."[35]

For Merton, intuitive consciousness dictated an unequal valuing of passages of time based upon their perceived significance, a significance that derived from relationships.[36] Typically in Merton's writings, especially in his poetry and journals, selected moments of action and perception were expanded to reveal their significance. An example can be found in the evocative early poem "The Reader," in *The Tears of the Blind Lions* (1949), in which, preparing to read aloud from the lives of the saints at mealtime, Merton heard his fellow monks approaching: "With robes as voluble as water. / I do not see them but I hear their waves." The image both captured and expanded the particulars of the moment by imagistically melting the usual boundaries of the material world, thereby predisposing the reader toward an awareness of the spiritual. It

34. Merton, "Blake and the New Theology," in *Literary Essays*, 9; Saint Thomas Aquinas, *Summa Theologiae: A Concise Translation*, 1a:85:1; Maritain, *Creative Intuition in Art and Poetry*, 4, 115.

35. Maritain, *Creative Intuition*, 126; Merton, "'Baptism in the Forest,'" in *Literary Essays*, 101.

36. Merton, June 3, 1963, in *Turning toward the World*, 326.

was in the uniting of the moment with durational continuity, a continuity that here stretched to the infinite, that Merton expressed both his mysticism and his romanticism. The passage also indicates the way in which the literary impressionist in Merton led him to use space, here present in the ocean-wave imagery, to dilate the moment. In addition to particular moments being so singled out, particular sections of Merton's life could also gather unusual significance, as in the reflection in his journal in 1941 that his years in France in the late 1920s seemed retrospectively to have been his "whole life." By the same token, durational consciousness allowed one to see not just the subjectively interpreted life but also the real life, cumulatively arrived at, part of a chain, as he put it, in which one's past experiences shaped one's present life.[37]

For Merton, memory was crucial in forming the continuity of consciousness that in turn corresponded to a perceived external unfolding of history or time. In this respect, as a romantic writer, he was especially attracted to the power of memory in rescuing the otherwise lost fragments of experience and of time. In an entry in his journal (now published as *Run to the Mountain*) in the autumn of 1939, he wondered: "What is this terrific importance that memory seems to have for me?" In the same journal Merton reflected insightfully in reply to this question about the relationship between time and the gestation of an idea in consciousness: "We think we possess some idea," he observed, and then, by a series of accidents, through a long "desert of difficulties," we come upon little "scraps of intuition" that are finally integrated into the "same old idea" that had been germinating in consciousness. In this way, Merton wrote, we are really "living that idea, working it out in our lives." He noted that fragments of time and consciousness were sometimes brought together by moments of intuitive insight that gave rise to a perception of the "truth" of things in a "flash" and with an impression of "wholeness."[38] In Merton's writings the mind's struggle against the dissolution of the past, either through forgetfulness or through an inability to piece the past together, was only occasionally successful, but these moments

37. Merton, "The Reader," in *Collected Poems*, 202; Merton, Mar. 23, 1941, in *Run to the Mountain*, 328; see Merton, July 21, 1962, in *Turning toward the World*, 232.
38. Merton, Oct. 15, 1939, in *Run to the Mountain*, 58, 339.

of success represented a triumph over the attrition of fragmentation and the erasure of continuity.

At least as significant as memory to Merton was the role of the imagination not simply in recording the unfolding of events but in revealing the curved unfolding of time's meaning as well. If memory recovered the past, albeit selectively, then imagination was a faculty "deeper than memory," as he put it in 1939, in its transformation of perceived fact into significance. At the same time he regarded the operation of memory and imagination as overlapping. Imagination made the relevance of reconstructed past experience to the meaning of the present apparent, and that reconstruction, particularly in art, depended upon the reciprocal working of both memory and imagination. Merton praised the poetry of Edwin Muir, for example, for reconciling the world of the present with that of the past, adding that in the artistic imagination, the heroes of Homer and the biblical patriarchs coexisted with each other in the contemporary artist's imagination in a way that illuminated the "crises" of the artist's own life and culture. In this way the unifying force of the imagination united the past and present fragments of experience in a durational continuum that in the best art illuminated the direction taken by not only an individual life but also a cultural period or optimally the whole human community through great stretches of time. In Merton's view the greatest artists were those who, like Edwin Muir, were teleologically aware of the beginning and the end of things so that the moments selected for the artist's subject were shot through with a full understanding of a durational path that provided both direction and meaning. Duration inevitably involved the linear development of events, and for Merton this depended at some point on the articulation of the significance of the passing moments of experience, even when these moments seemed quite mundane. Speculating about the usefulness of recording ordinary moments of experience in his journal, he concluded that whether or not these entries would have any lasting value for anyone else, they had at least clarified the content of his daily life by transmuting this content into unfolding "words and sentences," thereby giving them a durational narrative and syntactic form, as opposed to their formless existence in the mind.[39]

39. Ibid., 57; Merton, "True Legendary Sound," in *Literary Essays*, 33; Merton, Oct. 1, 1939, in *Run to the Mountain*, 35.

In some respects, Merton believed, art resembled the intersection of the divine and the human in religion. Speaking of Fra Angelico's painting of Saint Anthony, for example, he pointed out that the action in the picture, though drawn from the past, had as a work of art "no past and no future." Furthermore, although it captured a frame of movement, it did not itself move, and was thus both in and out of time. The painting would, like Keats's Grecian urn, presumably, always be in the viewer's present, "not remembered, not hoped for," but "continually *there*."[40] Because of the capacity of art to funnel past memories and future hopes into the present, it was always for Merton a human activity that, like religious liturgy, could saturate the present with enlarged possibilities for action and meaning.

In Merton's writings one of the distinctive differences between memory and imagination was the access that the imagination provided not only to the past but to the present and future as well where alternate patterns of duration could be discerned. Frequently, he spoke of the ability of artists, particularly, since their imaginations were so incandescent, to anticipate the future prophetically, not necessarily through foretelling, though he was not averse to this in his own writings, but more characteristically through their ability to grasp the "momentous predictions hidden in everyday life," as he put it in his well-known essay "Message to Poets." One of his great gifts as a writer lay in his ability to intuitively perceive the distress and alienation felt by the human spirit in a Western culture that dismissed a potentially nourishing solitude, for example, as demeaning and antisocial. In Merton's view, what was remarkable about the artist's grasp of these hidden grains of reality was that often the artist did not become aware of what he or she discerned until the work of art had been produced, an occurrence that he described as a "spontaneous explosion" of the artist's hopes.[41] Such a situation seemed to him analogous to religion, where the fluidity of the relationship of past, present, and future could often be paradoxical as the soul groped toward meaning and fulfillment. *The Seven Storey Mountain* is filled with such fluid movements of time and consciousness whereby in moving toward his future as a Trappist monk, for example, he found himself excavating his past for early signs of his having been on such a journey.

---

40. Merton, Oct. 15, 1939, in *Run to the Mountain*, 53.
41. Merton, "Message to Poets," in *Raids on the Unspeakable*, 159, 155.

In Merton's view the reality of time derived from God as the provider of time. His emphasis on the acceptance of time as a reality beyond consciousness as well as within consciousness recalls the philosopher George Grant's observation that in pretechnological society people did not think that they "made the world valuable" but rather thought that they "participated in its goodness." Similarly, Merton cautioned against the tendency of human beings to see time as a mere projection of their own desires and obsessions and thereby inevitably impose a "paralysis" on time that would "ruin the world," as he put it strongly in his essay "Herakleitos: A Study." In order to highlight the independence of time from human origin, if not from human consciousness, he tended to visualize time in images drawn from the natural world. In his essay "Atlas and the Fatman," he juxtaposed natural time, symbolized by Atlas, with technological time, indicating in this instance the shallowness and illusoriness of that time that had been appropriated by the human ego: "We made believe," the speaker in the essay declares, "that it was six o'clock. We made believe that it was midnight. Atlas must have deigned to smile on our efforts." While Atlas speaks in a musical idiom, a harmonious version of the rhythm of time, he is aware of human beings listening not to his music, that of the created world of nature, but rather to "clock and cannon," a dissonance that alliteratively links clock time directly with technology and with destruction. Both the clock and technology, here the technology of war, distanced human beings from the created world and hence from the author of reality. Similarly, in *Opening the Bible,* in a discussion of Dilsey's intimation of time in Faulkner's novel *The Sound and the Fury,* Merton observed that Dilsey's superior and realistic perception of time was to be measured not by the clock but by the process of living and of "organic growth." At the same time, although Merton regarded nature as valuable in allowing us to transcend the prison of either the individual or the collective ego, nature was not deemed to be equivalent to God. Rather, nature, exemplified by the rhythm of the seasons, he had explained in *Seasons of Celebration* (1955), was finally capable of reminding us by its cycle of renewal and death that "death" was the "end of all."[42]

42. Grant, *Time as History,* 44–45; Merton, "Herakleitos: A Study," in *The Behavior*

Thematically incorporated into Merton's conception of time was an attitude of acceptance not only of the independently created reality of time but also of the superiority of a *natural* maturation throughout time. In *Opening the Bible,* which was written in the late 1960s, Merton urged that one should accept the natural rate of the maturation of things and of consciousness without attempting to force either into a premature development, awaiting the time, not passively, but not aggressively either, when the fruit was "finally ripe." In a lecture on Faulkner in 1967, which was later titled "Time and Unburdening and the Recollection of the Lamb: The Easter Service in Faulkner's *The Sound and the Fury,*" he observed that the Bible was concerned with time's *fullness,* with the time for an "event to happen, the time for an emotion *to be felt,* the time for a harvest or for the celebration of a harvest." Time's purpose, from Merton's point of view, was to enable growth and transformation, the fruitfulness that change could accomplish. In human lives the curve of growth allowed for the connecting of the fragments of time into a unity of purpose that would ideally bring the soul's ripening into line with the pattern desired by the divine mind. In Merton, there are two parallel lines of duration, one embedded in human consciousness, the other in the divine mind. The drama of a human life thus involved a potential but by no means certain maturation through which these two lines might and ideally would converge. As Patrick O'Connell noted in his analysis of Merton's poem "Elias—Variations on a Theme," the "task of human freedom in Merton's writings was to actualize, to incarnate, the true self eternally known and loved by God."[43] A dramatic example of this aspect of Merton's thinking can be seen in his early poem "On the Anniversary of My Baptism," in which after perceiving his birth in a Catholic town in the Pyrenees as having providentially "marked" him for the "cloister," he then imagined the divine hand preparing the waters of his baptism:

---

of Titans, 82; Merton, "Atlas and the Fatman," in *Raids on the Unspeakable,* 92, 101; Merton, *Opening the Bible,* 48; Merton, *Seasons of Celebration,* 50.

43. Merton, *Opening the Bible,* 49; Merton, "Time and Unburdening and the Recollection of the Lamb: The Easter Service in Faulkner's *The Sound and the Fury,*" in *Literary Essays,* 500; O'Connell, "Geography of Solitude," 183–84.

> The day You made the waters,
> And dragged them down from the dividing islands
> And made them spring with fish,
> You planned to bless the brine out of the seas
> That were to be my death.[44]

The death mentioned here is presumably that of the old self, a theological precondition for baptism. The passage captures the dimensions of the curve of duration, which here involved not only the intersection of the forward motion that brought Merton from childhood to his monastic calling, together with his subsequent memory of that development, but also the mind of God itself, imagining from before his birth Merton's life with its own future-looking curve of duration, a stunning act of divine hope and of the divine embracing of time.

In Faulkner's novel *The Sound and the Fury*, Jason Compson, Merton contended, attempted to force everything, including time. In Merton's view Jason had much in common with modern technocrats in that both regarded time as an enemy, interfering with the sovereignty of the mind over the world. The Christian, on the other hand, should not, Merton wrote in *Seasons of Celebration* (1965), see time as an antagonist but rather should accept the attrition of time, including the death in which that attrition inevitably culminated. Christian worship, he continued, was "at peace with time because the departure of time need not frighten the Christian" whose life had passed through time "'hidden'" in God.[45] Merton visualized life not as a process of attrition and subsequent release but rather as a drama whose outcome was centered on the present. Unlike Proust, he declared that he was interested in time not only because it illuminated the womb of the past but also because it revealed the *present* and particularly those choices embedded in the present that had been generated by the past.[46] The relationship of the present to durational time marked the apogee of Merton's conception of time—as enacted in religious liturgy, for example. In the liturgy, he wrote, the pres-

---

44. Merton, "On the Anniversary of My Baptism," in *Collected Poems*, 157.
45. Merton, *Seasons of Celebration*, 47.
46. See Merton, Oct. 15, 1939, in *Run to the Mountain*, 57.

ent moment had something of the "character of eternity" in which all reality was present at once. In this way were reconciled and intertwined both the "universal" and the "personal" aspects of time. For Merton, the liturgy revealed the fullness that was implicit, yet also hidden, in time. By being open to the fullness of life present in the liturgical act, the participant in the liturgy was suspended in the intersection between time and eternity, whose form was not that of a sudden catapult into the future but rather that of an expansion of the possibilities of the present. These possibilities included what Merton with his romantic conception of nature thought of as a "primordial," "archetypal," and "sacred" band of time that subsisted within the "heart of secular time."[47]

He discussed the contrast between secular and liturgical time in the previously mentioned lecture on the Easter service in Faulkner's *Sound and the Fury*. In that essay he defined the impact of the Reverend Mr. Shegog's Easter homily in the following way: "*[N]ow* he is simply saying not only what they know, *but what is present among them!* Now: he is *re-creating* in them their realization of the great truth: *Jesus lives!* . . . The Word of God breaks into time, into the community of *the chosen,* into those who belong to God. It reveals the beginning and the ending: *at once!* It reveals the *meaninglessness* of time and the *full meaning* of time."[48]

In an early poem written in the 1940s, "A Mysterious Song in the Spring of the Year," Merton depicted the intersection of the finite and the infinite in the present moment as an access to eternal energy made possible by the contemplative soul's ability to slip angularly between the hands of the clock. Similarly, in the Easter service in *The Sound and the Fury*, he commented on Dilsey's transcendence in a rare moment of such intertwining as seeing both the beginning and the ending of her own, of the Compson family's, and of humanity's struggle through time. In Merton's view Jason Compson, who identified with contemporary technological culture, lived entirely "by clock time, by telegrams, telephones, timetables," thereby making it difficult for him to measure what was "real, significant, full of meaning." Clock time, Merton added, could not

47. Merton, *Seasons of Celebration*, 56, 47.
48. Merton: "Time and Unburdening," in *Literary Essays*, 512.

permit one to live in "expectation, anticipation, fullness" and thus was severed from the durational curve of growth and maturation that alone conferred meaning.[49]

From Merton's vantage point the problem with Jason Compson's and with the technocrat's perception of time was that it reduced time to an abstraction symbolizing a succession of moments believed to be inherently useless in themselves unless driven by the intentions of the individual or the collective ego. In his "Message to Poets," Merton wrote: "As for the technological Platos who think they now run the world we live in, they imagine they can tempt us with banalities and abstractions." Similarly, in his essay on the Easter service in Faulkner's *Sound and the Fury*, he remarked that for the most part in contemporary Western culture there was no real experience of time, since our relation to time was "wholly linear" and "wholly abstract."[50] In Merton's view the rational intellect with its dependency on abstraction obscured our perception of the concrete unfolding of time in nature and in the involuntary "natural" parts of the self. This excessive reliance on abstraction robbed human beings of their experiential knowledge of time, a knowledge that artists particularly attempted to provide.

Since Merton valued the existential, creational aspects of his existence as channels toward the infinite, he was reluctant, even reactionary, in responding to technological culture, which characteristically altered time by wanting to speed it up. In an evocative poem titled "Night-Flowering Cactus," Merton focused on the hidden, nocturnal life of nature in an effort to highlight time in nature as a paradigm of the role of a non-rational self-abandonment and acceptance that were involved in genuine maturation. The exquisitely beautiful flower, which is unseen on the one night on which it blooms, reflected an existence that belonged "neither to night nor day," as Merton put it:

> I neither show my truth nor conceal it
> My innocence is descried dimly

49. Merton, "A Mysterious Song in the Spring of the Year," in *Collected Poems*, 160; Merton, "Time and Unburdening," in *Literary Essays*, 513, 500.

50. Merton, "Message to Poets," in *Raids on the Unspeakable*, 161; Merton, "Time and Unburdening," in *Literary Essays*, 499.

> Only by divine gift
> As a white cavern without explanation.[51]

The imaginative trope of the flower as a spiritually kenotic white cavern silhouetted the limits of rational understanding. Moreover, to attempt to explain the strangeness of the cactus's flowering would have been to subsume it within the same sort of intellectual abstractness to which the technocrat was prone. Merton insisted on a respect for the transcendental mystery at the base of things in order to prevent the mind from foreclosing hastily on reality. The point of the mystery was not to celebrate mystery itself but rather to keep the mind attentive and open to further reflection and growth in its own durational unfolding. All of this was emphasized in a beautiful passage from his early journal *Run to the Mountain,* in which he mused that in the time of Advent "sweetness" fell from the "skies of Time's darkness like a radiance" that was "just beyond our vision."[52]

Time, from the vantage point of technological culture, on the other hand, Merton believed, was a tabula rasa regarded with both frustration and contempt, an obstacle in the way of human progress. In Merton's writings this contempt for time was expressed in his peripatetic poem "Kandy Express," which was composed in 1968:

> We rush blindly
> In a runaway train
> Through the great estates
> Headlong to the sea.
> That same sea which Queen Victoria
> By a miracle of steam
> Changed into sodawater.[53]

This portrait of English colonialism revealed a blindness to the scale of time and nature that predated the coming of the English to Ceylon, now Sri Lanka, a land whose beauty and majesty Merton as a railway travel-

---

51. Merton, "Night-Flowering Cactus," in *Collected Poems,* 351–52.
52. Merton, Nov. 29, 1941, in *Run to the Mountain,* 459.
53. Merton, "Kandy Express," in *Collected Poems,* 721.

er depicted as having devolved into racially segregated social clubs with their whiskey and soda water. The abstractness of the English view of India and Ceylon was ironically paralleled in Merton's view by what he perceived as an analogous tendency in the great French Jesuit paleontologist Teilhard de Chardin, whose optimistic evolutionism seemed to him to overlook the concreteness, and especially the moral turpitude, of history. Teilhard's "scientific mystique," as he put it in an essay on Camus's *Plague*, did not "delay overlong to worry about the death of a few thousands here and there." Merton's model of time required a fine balance between the concrete and the abstract, the still and the moving, as when in rejecting a too abstract idea of time, he declared biblical time to be refreshingly and realistically concrete in the way in which it grounded itself in narrative events.[54]

Although Merton's idea of time was durational, he did not necessarily see time as a *smooth* curvature of unfolding. On the one hand history was dynamic because of the friction between the divine intention and the egocentricity of individuals. On the other hand, he found himself identifying with the pre-Christian, ostensibly pantheistic vision of Heraclitus. In "Herakleitos: A Study" in *The Behavior of Titans* (1961), Merton supported the Heraclitean view of the cosmos as a "'conflict' of opposites" that was in fact a "stable and dynamic harmony." In this essay Merton interwove the Christian and romantic strands of his view of history by presenting Heraclitus as a Greek philosopher whose dynamic view of history was compatible with Christianity. Was Christ, who "came to cast fire on the earth," Merton wondered, "perhaps akin to the Fire of which Herakleitos spoke?" Where Bergson had portrayed duration as the "fiery path" traced by a shooting star, Merton provided a nexus between the Heraclitean image of fire and durational time in the image of the infusion of the eternal into the present moment as a "seed of fire."[55]

In thinking about time Merton found himself drawn to certain gen-

54. Merton, "*The Plague* of Albert Camus: A Commentary and Introduction," in *Literary Essays*, 217; Merton, *Opening the Bible*, 49.
55. Merton, "Herakleitos: A Study," in *Behavior of Titans*, 82, 91; Bergson, *Duration and Simultaneity with Reference to Einstein's Theory*, 50; Merton, *The Sign of Jonas*, 361.

eral aspects of Einstein's thought, especially the idea that the universe had "no center and no limits," as he put it in a letter to Ernesto Cardenal in 1963. One consequence of Einstein's theory of relativity that appealed to Merton's imagination was that time and space were viewed no longer as separate, independent entities but rather as related to each other in a four-dimensional continuum of space-time. Any such overcoming of barriers always appealed to Merton, especially when part of a dynamic cosmology. This did not mean that he began to see the cosmos as dominated by process. In his essay "Blake and the New Theology," which was published in 1968, he went out of his way to say that he regarded God and the universe as driven by *act* rather than process, a distinction that seemed to him to intensify the dynamic character of the universe. Merton's alternating view of time as both act and process presents the reader with something of a problem, since the durational flow of time would seem to point to process rather than to act. What reconciled these elements in Merton's thought was his perception that the divine act of creation fused time to the eternal so that the incomplete, durational movement through experience was somehow shot through with the fullness, decisiveness, and instantaneity of the eternal. In Merton's writings the signs of the eternal within the finite were in the intuitive mind and consciousness as well as to some extent, as has been suggested, in nature. He was attracted to the presence of the numinous in intuitive consciousness and in nature not just because of his belief in the Incarnation but also because as a romantic he believed in the essential goodness of the inner self, what he called the "deep transcendent self," and of nature.[56]

Merton's religious imagery often incorporated a fluid and dynamic quality while it was also anchored in absolute meanings that steadied the movement of the images through space and time. Such an image was that of the old trailer at the monastery, a place of solitude and contemplation for Merton that figures in his poem "Elias—Variations on a Theme." The trailer is enigmatic in that, while it stood still, it yet moved "faster and faster," a paradox based not only on Christian teleology but

56. Merton to Cardenal, [1963], in *Courage for Truth*, 143; Merton, "Blake and the New Theology," in *Literary Essays*, 9; Merton, *New Seeds of Contemplation*, 7.

also on Einstein's modernist view that a moving object may appear to be still or to move at various speeds depending on one's vantage point.[57] While Merton imaginatively embraced the shifting dynamics of perception implied in Einstein's theory, he believed that these diverse perspectives were all aligned and steadied by their relationship to God, the generative yet stabilizing force in his turning world.

In a talk given during his trip to Alaska in 1968, he set forth an important distinction between the contemplative view of time—a meeting of the eternal and the temporal in the present—and a prophetic view of time in which, looking at the sweep of past, present, and future, one saw salvation *history* advancing. In Merton's view the contemplative could not detach himself or herself from history even if contemplation itself involved a nonhistorical focusing of the mind. Thus, as he put it in an essay in *Seeds of Destruction* in 1964, he regarded the contemplative as not free *from* time but free *in* time. In Merton's final published journal, *The Other Side of the Mountain,* he described the achieved state of contemplation as an escape from the ordinary consciousness of time into a "*'temps vierge,'*" a separate "space" in which, however, the process of contemplation itself viewed in the past would nevertheless develop and reflect its relationship to time.[58]

A respect for the historicity of time gave Merton among other things an indelible sense of the uniqueness of the moment, as can be see in the following evocative extract from *Conjectures of a Guilty Bystander:* "A sweet summer afternoon. Cool breezes and a clear sky. This day will not come again. The young bulls lie under a tree in the corner of their field. Quiet afternoon. Blue hills. Day lilies nod in the wind. This day will not come again."[59] The uniqueness and stillness of the moment described are portrayed as in a tension with the durational flow of time that is oriented toward the unfolding of a process or action. The tension is revealed to have been only superficial, however, as each pole of this bifocal view of time is valued, indeed is *saved,* through the use of memory, as in Words-

57. Merton, "Elias—Variations on a Theme," in *Collected Poems,* 242.
58. Merton, "This Is God's Work," in *Thomas Merton in Alaska,* 79; see Merton, *Seeds of Destruction,* xiv; Merton, Nov. 7, 1968, in *The Other Side of the Mountain,* 262.
59. Merton, *Conjectures of a Guilty Bystander,* 34.

worth. What made the tension especially fruitful in Merton's eyes, however, was the intensity that it gave to the present through which the present became the privileged focus for traffic from the past and future.

In terms of the prophetic view of time, Merton had a sense of the present period of history as climactic, a time in durational terms of "finality and of fulfillment." In writing to Daniel Berrigan in November 1961, in the midst of the cold war, he believed that the end might well have been at hand: "*[V]enit nox,*" he wrote, "maybe the total *nox.*" The apocalyptic edge in Merton's writing derived from his sense that he lived in an age of two radical, superimposed eschatologies, that of "secular anxieties and hopes, and that of revealed fulfillment," as he put it in his essay "The Time of the End Is the Time of No Room," in *Raids on the Unspeakable.* While Merton listed a number of different crises faced by contemporary culture, including ontological emptiness, an oppressive, predatory commerce, and a tendency toward self-breeding technological warfare, in the prologue to *Raids on the Unspeakable* he summed up the primary danger faced by contemporary people as that of "dehumanization."[60] Ironically, though, he believed that there was one major advantage to the attack against human dignity posed by the modern world: contemporary perils and horrors might alert human beings to the eschatological choices that lay before them and might otherwise be overlooked in a more benign-looking secular culture. Merton's view here was somewhat analogous to that of Flannery O'Connor, whose grotesque characters were meant to shake the sleeping reader into an awareness of the unsuspected, apocalyptic stakes that were involved in human experience.

Similarly, in Merton's view, Christians over time had lost the sense of drama felt by the early Christians who lived, he noted, in the imminent expectation of the return of Christ. This expectation, he argued in *Zen and the Birds of Appetite* (1968), freed the early Christians from conventionality so that they were more easily aware of and detached from the

---

60. Merton, "The Time of the End Is the Time of No Room," in *Raids on the Unspeakable,* 65; Merton to Berrigan, Nov. 10, 1961, in *Hidden Ground of Love,* 71; Merton, "Time of the End," in *Raids on the Unspeakable,* 65; Merton, prologue to *Raids on the Unspeakable,* 3.

usual pressures and constraints of living. Over time, though, he added, because of the impact of Hellenistic philosophy with its dominant rationality, Christianity became experienced "'statically'" rather than "'dynamically.'" The eschatological dimension of Christianity also distinguished it, Merton recognized, from Buddhism. Like Blake, he focused on the eschatological as an aspect of the present. In an essay titled "Seven Words," which he wrote in the late 1960s, there was this question: "Who would want a joy," he questioned, "that he could never get rid of? Eternal life, on the other hand, has nothing in it which would be better if it were ended. The very concept of an end is no longer relevant, for the goal is attained. There is, then, no more goal, there is no end. All is present and all is actual."[61] Beginning with an implied allusion to Keats's jaded lovers in the "Ode on a Grecian Urn," Merton rejected the preference of desire over experience in favor of an eschatological present that met and indeed surpassed all desire.

Paradoxically, Merton held the view that Marxism, at least as set forth by Marx, was as much a part of a biblical eschatology as of a secular one, having been strongly influenced by what Merton called the traditional idealism of "Judaeo-Christian messianism." For Merton, history, either at the present time or at some time in the future, was moving inexorably toward a final accounting in which in biblical duration the "injustice of oppressors" would be punished and those they oppressed would "receive their just reward." Differing with Marx, he believed that the problem with a secular view of history was that it was likely to be centered on the past, a rut into which human beings inevitably returned in a fruitless search for meaning. In an essay titled "Faulkner and His Critics," he interpreted Faulkner's early fiction, that which preceded *The Sound and the Fury*, as caught in this sort of Spenglerian stasis, a "closed universe of cyclic and tragic involvements." The difference, he argued, between the intervention of Christ into history and that of other heroes hinged upon the difference in their effects on time. As he put it in *Seasons of Celebration* (1965), Christ's redemptive action was not merely a "past historical fact with a juridical effect on individual souls" but also an act that con-

61. Merton, *Zen and the Birds of Appetite*, 18–19; Merton, "Seven Words," in *Love and Living*, 104.

tinued to permeate the present with meaning and choices that offered the possibility of hope for the future, an escape from the Spenglerian cycles of history with their repetitive dead ends.[62]

While Merton perceived the past as frozen in what he called "necessity," he regarded the forward movement of history as more than that of a "blind life force." The animating spirit of history was the "free and loving will" of God, the divine imagination that, Merton wrote, "thought each moment of my existence before I was," and engraved the image of this divine thought on the heart of every human being where it was especially readable in moments of solitude. The ontological choices between secular and religious eschatology Merton presented in terms of the notion of *crises* in *Conjectures of a Guilty Bystander* (1966), crises of choice that loomed for human beings whether or not they were aware of them either as individuals or as a culture. Pondering the historical crisis faced by the Christians in the Roman Empire who were overwhelmed by the barbarian invasions, Merton reflected that if Christians had been "good enough," either then or now, the barbarians could not have helped becoming Christians. While Merton's vision darkened appreciably in the 1960s, he prophesied eloquently in *Raids on the Unspeakable* that in spite of the massing armies in the contemporary world, the "eschatological banquet" would not be that of the birds on the bodies of the slain but the "feast of the living," the "summons of The Great Joy," the "cry of deliverance."[63]

Merton's idea of time was integral with those romantic elements of his thought that involved an ontological consciousness of and longing for the unity of all things. About the surge of reverence for the idea of unity, however, that most orthodox of Catholic apologists, G. K. Chesterton, had some insightful, cautionary words in an essay titled "What Is Right with the World" (1910):

> There has crept into our thoughts, through a thousand small openings, a curious and unnatural idea. I mean the idea that unity is it-

62. Merton, *Opening the Bible*, 42, 41; Merton, "Faulkner and His Critics," in *Literary Essays*, 120; Merton, *Seasons of Celebration*, 48.

63. Merton, Dec. 3, 1940, in *Run to the Mountain*, 269; Merton, Jan. 4, 1940, in ibid., 127; Merton, "Time of the End," in *Raids on the Unspeakable*, 74.

self a good thing; that there is something high and spiritual about things being blended and absorbed into each other. . . . Now union in itself is not a noble thing. Love is a noble thing; but love is not union. Nay, it is rather a vivid sense of separation and identity. Maudlin, inferior love poetry does, indeed, talk of lovers being "one soul," just as maudlin, inferior religious poetry talks of being lost in God; but the best poetry does not. When Dante meets Beatrice, he feels his distance from her, not his proximity; and all the greatest saints have felt their lowness, not their highness, in the moment of ecstasy. . . . Division and variety are essential to praise. . . . There is nothing specially right about mere contact and coalescence.[64]

While Chesterton, with his penchant for antithesis and paradox, exaggerated the ways in which love was not synonymous with unity, he did call attention to one of the ways in which Christianity and romanticism were different. For Christians, unity is something that must be earned through piety and the practicing of virtue prior to a final judgment that in the Christian view awaits all. While the romantic in Merton led him to suppress the note of a final, separating judgment and to instead register his own longing for the unity of all being, he was not completely romantic in that he grounded his conception of reality in the external world and in a God whom he saw as existing separately from as well as in the world. At the same time, as has been suggested, he was elsewhere in his writings acutely conscious of the sanctity of creation, especially within the hidden and shy recesses of the self and in the beauty of nature. For Merton, as for Emerson and Whitman, such alternating currents in the spiritual life were signs not of contradiction but of inclusiveness. Typically, for most of his life, when led to choose a pantheistic model of time, as in the above-quoted essay on Blake, he resisted, opting instead for a transcendentalist model. But on the whole he preferred not to choose. For a contemplative like himself, time intersected with the eternal both within the mansion of consciousness and within the created world where the face of God could still be recognized.

The nexus for the interweaving of nature and time in Merton's

64. Chesterton, "What Is Right with the World," in *A G. K. Chesterton Anthology*, 346.

thought was his romantic emphasis on the organic. Recalling Merton's term as the master of novices from 1955 to 1965, Brother Patrick Hart remembered especially his leading of work parties to plant trees and his great pleasure at the growing things around him—including the young novices in his care. What Merton's respect for the organic led to was a recognition that he did not want to return nostalgically to an earlier period of his life, such as that in the 1940s, which was marked by a youthful ascetic fervor.[65] The continuity of the self, sustained by memory and imagination, offset Merton's anxiety about losing the past. Moreover, his organic view of experience allowed for change and movement, indeed encouraged it, while holding on to what he called the "center" in his life that over time he would approach from different directions.[66] The principle of movement was an inner freedom in the self that transcended desire and that in its highest moments could be offered to others through his writing. Ironically, because of his commitment to growth, Merton was hesitant about the very tranquillity that he had gone to the monastery to find, believing, more intensely than ever toward the end of his life, in the need for "change and transformation."[67]

Intellectually, Merton turned, over the course of his writing life, increasingly away from the cast of certitude that surrounded Catholic culture in the 1940s and 1950s toward an organic model of truth that in many respects resembled John Henry Newman's. So strong was his commitment to growth and change that he told a group of women from a religious order in the late 1960s that when dealing with the young they had better choose even a potentially imprudent spirituality over a safer, dead one.[68] As a Christian humanist Merton objected to an a priori view of history that some used prescriptively and proscriptively in order to direct the lives of those in their care, an approach that avoided creative changes that did not fit the existing model. A profound creativity, Merton contended, had generated the Cistercian architecture of the twelfth century that grew out of its time in contrast to what he judged to be a

---

65. Hart, *Thomas Merton*, n.p.; see Merton, Dec. 11, 1958, in *Search for Solitude*, 237.
66. See Merton, Jan. 25, 1964, in *Dancing in the Water of Life*, 67.
67. Merton, May 30, 1968, in *Other Side of the Mountain*, 113.
68. Merton, *Springs of Contemplation*, 126.

somewhat artificial search for new forms within the Cistercian community in the 1960s.[69] The genuineness of the process of growth depended utterly on time, as he put it in "Rain and the Rhinoceros," arguing in an ironic reversal of a well-known psalm that contemporary human beings needed a time to be "unborn" within the social womb prior to being born as themselves.[70]

As has been suggested, in Merton's view part of the foundation needed for an organic approach to thought and experience was an acceptance of death. Without this, he maintained, life could be lived only in an infantile fashion, harnessed to a categorical imperative for survival.[71] By analogy Merton applied the same principle to the self and to culture, and for this reason he was attracted, at least in some respects, to the evolutionary model of the world set forth in Teilhard de Chardin's theology. Reading Teilhard de Chardin led Merton to an objectified view of religion as itself the result of evolution, a predictable turn of thought for someone like himself who had grown increasingly uncomfortable with the fixed, triumphalist model of Christianity that had prevailed during his early years as a monk. As Emerson had embraced evolution in the nineteenth century for its cognitive unifying of being, so too did Merton in the twentieth. He was wary of technological culture because of its destructive impact on nature and because of what he regarded as its disregard for those aspects of wisdom that were emblematically present in nature. Nevertheless, as has been suggested, he was not at odds with science itself. The evolutionary model was one that, while tied to empirical evidence, nonetheless reached imaginatively into ontological reality with a vision that freshened yet again his consciousness of and passion for being.

69. See Merton, Dec. 28, 1947, in *Entering the Silence*, 150–51.
70. Merton, "Rain and the Rhinoceros," in *Raids on the Unspeakable*, 17.
71. See Merton, "Seven Words," in *Love and Living*, 101.

5

Paradise and the Child's Vision

Inspired no doubt in part by Blake's attempt, through his engraving and writing, to restore a golden age, a primordial state from which human beings had fallen into a degraded and fragmented state, Merton customarily avoided what he thought of as the dark Augustinian or Calvinistic viewpoint of sin. He was equally doubtful, however, about what in a letter to the novelist Julien Green he called a "casual naturalism and naive optimism." Nevertheless, he also seemed doubtful about any theology of suffering that was strongly tied to the idea of punishment.[1] One of the important liberating features of Merton's approach to reconstituting consciousness along paradisal lines was the removal of the distinction between the sacred and the secular, since, from Merton's point of view, the upholders of the sacred had, in the West at any rate, given themselves over to institutionalism. As he put it in an important essay on William Faulkner written in the late 1960s: "In spite of all the talk of believers about breaking down the limits between the sacred and the secular, one still feels that there is a very obsessive insistence that one's whole experience of life has to be dominated *from without* by a system of acquired beliefs and attitudes and that every other experience has first . . . to be tested by this system of beliefs." Regarding the note of resistance in Merton's writing elicited by his sensitivity to institutional op-

---

1. Merton to Green, Sept. 22, 1966, in *Courage for Truth,* 273; Merton, *Conjectures of a Guilty Bystander,* 127.

pressiveness, George Woodcock has observed that there was a tension in Merton between a "quintessential vision" of the "original idea" of the monastery, the idea of a withdrawal from society, and the "routine" monasticism that had become institutionalized and had therefore put itself at risk of compromising its ideals by in some respects imitating the world from which it had separated itself.[2]

Whereas evil was generally associated by Merton with the stridency of collective consciousness, images of evil in a more fundamental, theological sense are not lacking in his writings, especially in the early writings. An example occurs in his poem "Dry Places," which was included in *The Tears of the Blind Lions* (1949). In that poem the "skinny father of hate rolls in his dust" in a desert landscape radically different from the contemplative paradise perceived by the ancient Desert Fathers. In the sinister desert in Merton's poem, the survivors resolve to "wring a few green blades / From the floor of this valley" in memory of the "legend of the world's childhood" when "all God's larks called out to Him / In their wild orchard." While in Merton's early writings paradise was often a biblical one, he later came to locate the seat of paradise in the psyche. Within the self, in Merton's view, dwelt the most precious of paradisal gifts, a fundamental inner freedom, particularly freedom from the demands of the ego, a freedom that, once attained, Merton lyrically referred to in 1965 as a "paradise tree."[3]

Merton's appreciation for such inner freedom had developed considerably by the mid-1960s from the rather rigid, religiously orthodox idea of freedom that one encounters in works such as *The Seven Storey Mountain* and in the early books of poetry. In these writings from the 1940s, freedom involved the joyful exercise of the spirit within a providential cosmology and an ecclesiastical tradition whose defining characteristic was certainty. Later, Merton focused more on the self than the Church and on the freedom of the self in its intimate relationship with God. In much of the early work, couched in the language of Catholic theologi-

2. Merton, "'Baptism in the Forest," in *Literary Essays*, 97; Woodcock, *Thomas Merton: Monk and Poet*, 185.

3. Merton, "Dry Places," in *Collected Poems*, 216–17; Merton, May 1965, in *Dancing in the Water of Life*, 242.

cal texts of the period, the path to paradise was conceived as a struggle one underwent through a suppression of desire and a release from the wheel of attachment to the things of this world. In 1967, a year before his death, Merton was inclined to imagine paradise in quite different terms. In reading Kafka's *Trial,* for example, with its intense depiction of the effects of guilt, he defined innocence in his journal as not having to prepare a justifying answer for others, for "if you already have an answer prepared you are already guilty."[4] The change in Merton's way of speaking about innocence and guilt was not so much a sign of his having abandoned the Thomism and asceticism that had guided his writing of works such as *The Ascent to Truth;* rather, it was a sign of his having adopted a freedom in his view of the world that transcended either attachment to or detachment from that world, including the Church.

Even as a young man, before entering the monastery, Merton had adopted the Thomist view of evil as a deficiency of good with the corollary that everything that existed was good by virtue of its very existence. Some years later, in the early 1950s, Merton maintained in *The Ascent to Truth* that human beings were "naturally" inclined to good rather than evil. Enlarging on this view, writing in his journal in the spring of 1958, he noted that he did not ordinarily observe signs of culpable evil in human beings, not because evil did not exist but because it was overshadowed by an innocence that prevented sin and evil from being perceived as decisive and "important." Similarly, in a talk given to novices at the Abbey of Gethsemani in the 1960s, Merton observed that human beings could not make their *nature* evil even if they were capable of doing evil things. With even more boldness, theologically speaking, he emphasized the importance of Teilhard de Chardin, the Jesuit paleontologist, who in tracing the hand of God in the process of evolution affirmed the "'holiness of matter.'"[5] Indeed, in the 1960s, as is shown in his remarkable, free translations of Heraclitus, Merton came to regard the moral division of reality into good and evil as a limitation of human understanding:

4. Merton, June 26, 1967, in *Learning to Love,* 255.

5. Merton, May 2, 1939, in *Run to the Mountain,* 3; Merton, *The Ascent to Truth,* 7; Merton, Mar. 19, 1958, in *Search for Solitude,* 183; Merton, recorded talk to novices, "St. Thomas Aquinas and the Goodness of All Being," Tape 90-B-1, Merton Collection, Bellarmine University; Merton, June 26, 1965, in *Dancing in the Water of Life,* 260.

> To God all things are good and fair and right,
> But men hold some things wrong, and some right.
> Good and ill are one.[6]

Merton's rationale for his belief in the goodness of humanity stemmed from his view that the doctrine of original sin, of an innate tendency toward evil, had to take into account the uneasiness that human beings generally felt in doing evil, a sign that they were at odds with the essential goodness of their own natures, as it were.[7]

Merton did not mean to discount the reality of evil; in fact, he once described Christianity as being empty of meaning without its belief in the fall of human beings from a remembered and conceivable paradisal state.[8] At the same time he pointed to an underlying and steadfast tendency toward goodness based upon the evidence in the world of the goodness of its Creator, the signature of God on the world. In addition, there was the sublime transformation of the idea of the human effected by the life of Christ. Not all human beings, as Merton was well aware, shared his paradisal consciousness of the immense capacity for good locked within the human psyche. As with so much in Merton, here too the question came down to a matter of perception and consciousness, not in place of but as a prior condition to behavior. Reflecting on the relation between perception and paradise in the 1950s, he used the analogy of a pane of glass in order to compare fallen perception to Edenic perception:

> The corruption of cosmic symbolism can be understood by a simple comparison. It was like what happens to a window when a room ceases to receive light from the outside. As long as it is daylight, we see through our windowpane. When night comes, we can still see through it, if there is no light inside our room. When our lights go on, then we only see ourselves and our own room reflected in the pane. Adam in Eden could see through creation as through a win-

6. Merton, "The Legacy of Herakleitos," in *Behavior of Titans*, 102.
7. Merton, *Conjectures of a Guilty Bystander*, 72.
8. Merton, "Blake and the New Theology," in *Literary Essays*, 10.

dow. God shone through the windowpane as bright as the light of the sun.[9]

While the phrasing to some extent echoed the theological language of Merton's early years in the monastery, his image of a transparency of being as a paradisal vision reflected an idea that would hold up through his later writings. Matter was viewed not as an intractable enemy to be overcome but rather as a medium that one could value for making possible a recognition of the spiritual dimension of being.

Under the influence of Buddhism and rather like Thoreau, who thought of God as culminating in the "present moment," Merton came to think of existence as paradisal in a present and immediate sense. In *Zen and the Birds of Appetite* in the late 1960s, for example, he described paradise as a state or place on Earth that belonged to the present rather than to the future, a state in which human beings had been "originally created to live on earth." In such a state or place could be found the "lost innocence" and the "emptiness and purity of heart" that were now internalized in the self as a consciousness of inner and outer unity. In an ecstatic sequence in *Conjectures of a Guilty Bystander*, he exclaimed that paradise was all around us and that the biblical sword over our fallen world had been removed though we had not yet realized it.[10]

Merton regarded the Fall, or the world of experience as Blake called it, as a separation of the cosmos into parts that longed for a restoration of their primordial unity. Similarly, in an essay titled "From Pilgrimage to Crusade," which he wrote in 1964, he declared bardically that we were all "pieces of the paradise isle." Here, he modified the emotional tenor of the drama of fragmentation that he believed had characterized human behavior historically by indicating that the separated pieces retained something of their holistic origins. He attempted to make clear that the paradisal was something that participated in the ordinary reality of the world and that the numinous incandescence thereby given off

9. Merton, *Bread in the Wilderness*, 61.

10. Thoreau, *Walden*, 96–97; Merton, *Zen and the Birds of Appetite*, 116–17; Merton, *Conjectures of a Guilty Bystander*, 118.

could be seen at fortuitous moments not only by religious visionaries and artists but also by any number of other human beings. Merton did not proceed as far as Blake in proclaiming a divine humanity, but he did believe that God was present in human beings without, however, being identical to them. For this reason, he concluded, paradise was "always present within us."[11] Increasingly, as he turned toward Buddhism in the 1960s, he focused on paradise as truth or reality rather than as the conventional paradise of Christian eschatology. Moved to tears as a young man by the perception of divine mercy, he nevertheless turned in his later years, as Wordsworth had done, to philosophical consciousness. The effect of this was to place even suffering within a more ontological and less theological context in which it figured as experience and therefore as a participation in the fullness of being.

An aspect of the primordial that especially appealed to Merton, as it had, he realized, to Thoreau, was that of simplicity. This can be seen in a radiant and beautifully constructed passage from Merton's journals in the winter of 1965:

> Wonderful clear water pouring strongly out of a cleft in the mossy rock. I drank from it in my cupped hands and suddenly realized it was years, perhaps twenty-five or thirty years, since I had tasted such water: absolutely pure and clear, and sweet with the freshness of untouched water, no chemicals!! I looked up at the clear sky and the tops of the leafless trees shining in the sun and it was a moment of angelic lucidity. Said Tierce with great joy, overflowing joy, as if the land and woods and spring were all praising God through me. Again their sense of angelic transparency of everything, and of pure, simple and total light. The word that comes closest to pointing to it is simple. It was all simple. But a simplicity to which one seems to aspire, only seldom to attain it. A simplicity that is, and has, and says everything just because it is simple.[12]

The observation that the moment "says everything" offers a clue as to what Merton meant by simplicity, a quality of fullness whereby all the

11. Merton, "From Pilgrimage to Crusade," in *Mystics and Zen Masters,* 112; Merton, *Zen and the Birds of Appetite,* 137.

12. Merton, Jan. 6, 1965, in *Dancing in the Water of Life,* 187.

parts of the depicted experience—the sensations, thoughts, and emotions—were in harmony with one another.

Among the writers to whom Merton was attracted because of their paradisal themes was Chuang Tzu, some of whose Taoist writings he translated. In Chuang Tzu, Merton became especially aware of the indivisibility of paradisal consciousness, an indivisibility that became possible only once one had shed the self-awareness that separated the mind from the object of its attention. The abandoning of Cartesian awareness was a constant problem for someone like Merton who sought extended consciousness, just as it had been a problem for the romantics in the nineteenth century. Thus, rather like Keats in the "Ode to a Nightingale," he celebrated the self-forgetfulness that allowed him to unite with the whole of being. Incidental to this extension of himself into the whole of being was his growing awareness of the underlying unity of the spiritual and philosophical writers he was consulting. For this reason it seemed to him that the thought of Zen Buddhism unexpectedly resembled that of the Desert Fathers of the fourth century, and these in turn paradoxically dovetailed in Merton's thinking with the writings of Chuang Tzu, Heraclitus, and Meister Eckhart. Increasingly, he perceived a singleness of being projected in this blended consciousness, and understood the unity of these diverse thinkers and writers to have been in part the offshoot of his own receptive, reconciling intelligence.

The primordial ontology that underlay Merton's paradisal consciousness can be found in many corners of his writing. He admired, for example, Albert Camus's advocating what he called a "primordial humanism, the seeds of which are implanted" in human nature. With a similar atavistic orientation, Merton, in an informal talk given in Calcutta in the fall of 1968, argued that what human beings had most to recover was their original unity and that that recovery was achievable in what they still retained of their original state as human beings.[13] For Merton, the primordial return in time could be accomplished not only through the sort of detachment from society exhibited by the Desert Fathers but also

13. Merton, "Terror and the Absurd: Violence and Nonviolence in Albert Camus," in *Literary Essays*, 232; Merton, "Thomas Merton's View of Monasticism," in *Asian Journal*, app. 3, p. 308.

through a voyage into the self in order to discover the "paradisal inner sacred space" where the original, "archetypal" human being dwelt in "peace and in God."[14] The searching of the self for one's original face meant leaving behind the trophies of the ego and its history. Similarly, one let slip away the "piled-up garments of thought" that were extraneous to the self and to its essential being.[15] Although Merton understood the self to include the cultural envelope that had in part shaped it, he wanted to get back to a point before that cultural history began so as to exclude as much as possible the historical, and especially the collective, imprinting on the self. At that *point vierge*, as he thought of it, a paradisal consciousness could emerge from a "confused primordial dark night."[16] The new consciousness would be what Merton thought of as holy wisdom, the Creator's engraving on the psyche of a longing for unity and for completeness that would open out into the "center of all created being."[17] Indeed, it was the completeness or wholeness of Merton's idea of the primordial that was more important in his mind than the primordial itself. Commenting on the poetry of Louis Zukofsky, for example, he observed that Zukofsky's poems, which he saw as exquisitely attuned to the significance of wholeness, could be understood only against the background of "silence and warmth that is the ground and the whole." Putting the matter differently and even more strongly, in "The Inner Experience" he described the passage about Eden in Genesis as a symbolic account of humanity's fall from *unity*.[18]

The recovery of a sense of living in paradise, in Merton's view, historically involved a confrontation with those for whom the idea of paradise was a closed chapter. Thus, his paradisal consciousness was regarded as ingenuous because it clashed with the ontological pessimism of Western religion, a habit of perception that he spent his whole life trying to overcome. As an example, in his important long poem *The Geography of Lograire* (1969), the Ranters, a sect in seventeenth-century

14. Merton, May 14, 1967, in *Learning to Love*, 235.
15. Merton, Jan. 20, 1963, in *Turning toward the World*, 291.
16. Merton, "Hagia Sophia," in *Collected Poems*, 366.
17. Merton, "Learning to Live," in *Love and Living*, 9.
18. Merton, "Louis Zukofsky—the Paradise Ear," in *Literary Essays*, 131; Merton, "The Inner Experience: Christian Contemplation," 201.

England, were depicted as associated with a paradisal vision that caused them to be persecuted. One of the Ranters, Jacob Bauthemly, states his belief that "'God is in all creatures, / Man and Beast, Fish and Fowle,'" while others teach that there is neither "heaven nor hell / But what is in man" and that God does not hate. "'Not even sin?'" queried those prosecuting the Ranters prior to sentencing and maiming. An affront to the established religion of seventeenth-century England, the Ranters, with whose paradisal vision Merton clearly identified, proclaimed an eschatology in which there would be a "'generall Restauration wherein all men shall be reconciled to God and saved.'"[19]

While Merton appeared to adhere, at least nominally, to the theological idea of the Fall as a temporal event, even if enclosed in a symbolic and mythic form in the Genesis narrative, nevertheless in the 1960s he tended to interpret the doctrine of the Fall as an ontological statement about an innate conflict between an inner orientation toward unity and a blind flight from unity. In the poem "Origen," which he had prepared for publication in a new collection shortly before the time of his death, he recalled the rejection of Origen by the early Church due to Origen's prediction of the repentance and final forgiveness of all of the damned. Merton's poetic reflections about Origen's eventual restoration are moving and tender:

> In the end, the medieval West
> Would not renounce him. All antagonists,
> Bernards and Abelards together, met in this
> One madness for the sweet poison
> Of compassion in this man
> Who thought he heard all beings
> From stars to stones, angels to elements, alive
> Crying for the Redeemer with a live grief.[20]

Merton's awareness of the heterodoxy of Origen's theological position about the fate of the damned is evident in the poem but as a fainter note

---

19. Merton, *Geography of Lograire*, in *Collected Poems*, 522, 524, 520.
20. Merton, "Origen," in *Collected Poems*, 641.

in a warm tribute to Origen's robust vision of a divine mercy that would finally encompass all.

Apart from the psychological and social disorder brought about by human blindness, Merton's paradisal vision also had to reckon with yet another fragmenting element in human history and myth: the apparently autonomous and at times destructive world of nature. He relied on the myth of Prometheus to address the issue of a perceived faulty legacy of nature, including human nature, and the deterministic implications of that inheritance. With his eye on the modern inclination to brush the Creator out of the picture, he portrayed modern Promethean re-creators of the world as ironically attempting to steal the fire of their own spiritual freedom, that which had already been given to them by God. In Merton's paradisal view of things, the riches of God's largesse are everywhere apparent. Having come to the Abbey of Gethsemani in the early 1940s, he was struck by the natural paradise that surrounded him, a place of abundant beauty in which tulips opened their divinely created "chalices" to the bees of spring. Enchanted by his new Kentucky surroundings, he perceived the monastic world in which he had immersed himself as a paradise in both an earthly and a heavenly sense, the earthly paradise encompassing a "perfect community" that was both physically self-sustaining and spiritually and psychologically revitalizing.[21] Merton's consciousness of living in a paradise thinned out in the 1950s, but was renewed during his gradual move into his hermitage in the early 1960s. From that vantage point he looked out with the sense of having an overview in every sense of the word and as one who, looking around him, witnessed a "sea of paradise." In spite of his frequently stated identification with mystics such as Saint John of the Cross who are associated with apophatic consciousness, Merton's life, especially as recorded in his journals, appears to have been more frequently characterized by a heightened awareness of the brimming cup of existence, of nature in particular, as in the following scene recorded in the early 1960s: "Receiving an honor: A very small gold-winged moth came and settled on the back of my hand, and sat there, so light I could not feel it. I wondered at the

21. Merton, Apr. 10, 1941, in *Run to the Mountain*, 347; Merton, Apr. 8, 1941, in ibid., 336.

beauty and delicacy of this being—so delicately made, with mottled golden wings. So perfect. I wonder if there is even a name for it. I never saw such a thing before. It would not go away, until, needing my hand, I blew it lightly into the woods."[22] Merton was here engaged by the originality of the moth's appearance and the intimacy and harmony of its behavior. The phrasing of the passage with its short, breathless sentences, its ample use of short *i* sounds, and its seamless flow of language deftly captures the moment's hushed rarity.

Merton's paradisal consciousness in the 1960s arose in contexts other than nature—in the liturgy, for example. According to visitors, Merton's saying of Mass in his hermitage was a joyous occasion for him, flanked by his treasured icons, particularly that of Elias. In concert with nature, which, like the liturgy, activated his transforming imagination, the effect at such golden moments was to leave him with the impression that all things had a "heavenly existence." On other occasions he was aware of regarding nature with a literal eye whereby the beauty of the woods, fields, and flowers was perceived as "good, but not heavenly."[23] The fortuitous moments of paradisal consciousness, then, were considerably more than a grateful perception of the beauty and goodness of the world. As with Blake, for Merton, the font of the imagination, seen as a means of attaining a direct, ontological insight into being, awakened the mind at certain times to what, although frequently overlooked, was always and everywhere present.

Even within the strictures of the apophatic approach to mysticism, Merton could attain paradisal vision, although paradise in these circumstances paradoxically presented itself as a desert. An early setting of Merton's desert-paradisal theme occurred in the poem "The Flight into Egypt," in which in an otherwise rather conventional poem the unexpected image of the "singing desert" stands out luminously from the text.[24] A further glimmering of Merton's apophatic paradisal vision occurs in the poem "The Fall," published in *Emblems of a Season of Fury* in

22. Merton, May 21, 1963, in *Turning toward the World*, 322; Merton, June 5, 1963, in ibid., 328.
23. Merton, Apr. 24, 1964, in *Dancing in the Water of Life*, 99.
24. Merton, "The Flight into Egypt," in *Collected Poems*, 28.

1963. In that poem the speaker observes that only nameless beings could be at home in the universe:

> They bear with them in the center of nowhere the
>   unborn flower of nothing:
> This is the paradise tree. It must remain unseen until
>   words end and arguments are silent.[25]

Historically, as George H. Williams has pointed out, the desert inhabited by the fourth-century Desert Fathers was perceived as a wilderness, even if the modern conception of a wilderness generally implies a more verdant landscape. For Merton, though, the desert was a place where the self could look out and look within without being distracted by visual or audible clutter. In *Thoughts in Solitude* in the late 1950s, for example, he argued that the desert gained its particular value for the contemplative from the fact that it had little value to anyone else and so enabled the mind to concentrate on God as the epitome of being.[26] A variation on the theme of the desert as paradise in Merton's writings occurs in the "Kane Relief Expedition" section of *The Geography of Lograire,* which was set in the frozen desert of the Canadian Arctic:

> Morning came at last
> The storm over we sighted
> Quiet mountains green and
> Silver Edens
> Walls of an
> Empty country. . . .
> Then whales came
> And played around us all day.[27]

Rather like Robert Frost's bare November days, the empty landscape leads the mind into imaginative movement, taking it beyond the satisfactions of the outer to those of the inner eye.

---

25. Merton, "The Fall," in *Collected Poems,* 355.
26. See Williams, *Wilderness and Paradise in Christian Thought,* 132. Merton was familiar with Williams's book. Merton, *Thoughts in Solitude,* 18.
27. Merton, *Geography of Lograire,* in *Collected Poems,* 525–26.

There is more than Frost's or Emerson's transcendentalism at work in Merton's desert-paradise motif, though. A clue can be found in a letter that a correspondent from a California religious order wrote in 1968 in which she summed up a talk that Merton had given on his circuitous journey to Asia. In summary he told the group that a desert became a paradise when it was accepted as a desert and not resisted or fled from because of its being a desert. Here one encounters the other side of Merton's contemplative thought, his acceptance of suffering—which does not, however, imply that he pursued it. Merton's paradisal conception of suffering linked up in his mind with the idea of the desert as void and waste, which suffering might seem to be. He considered the matter in his ironic long poem *Cables to the Ace* in the late 1960s: "Desert and void. The Uncreated is waste and emptiness to the creature . . . yet from this poverty springs *everything*. . . . Everything comes from this desert Nothing. Everything wants to return to it and cannot." As with suffering, the void of the desert could draw one back, as the flora of the created world did, to origins. Thus, the asceticism of the monastic life, though far short of grave suffering in Merton's account of it, emptied the world seen by the eye, and made possible what he called a new creation in which one's right relationship to being was restored. Relating asceticism to nature in a letter to Rosemary Radford Ruether in 1967, he was careful to point out that monastic asceticism implied a rejection not of the beauty of the natural world but rather of the materialism historically present in society at large. Significantly, in a letter to a correspondent in 1959, he described himself as being happy "with the novices and with the woods and with the desert," an indication of his readiness to alternate the woods and monastic asceticism as paradisal species.[28]

While Merton came to adopt a paradisal vision as an ontological framing of experience, he felt the presence of paradise around him only at privileged moments. One of these moments occurred in the spring of 1959 when he had gone for a medical appointment. At the corner of Fourth and Walnut Streets in downtown Louisville, which now bears a

28. Unpublished report of Merton's meeting with the sisters of Our Lady of Redwood Monastery, White Thorn, Calif., 1968, Merton Collection, Bellarmine University; Merton, *Cables to the Ace,* in *Collected Poems,* 452; Merton to Ruether, Mar. 9, 1967, in *Hidden Ground of Love,* 504; Merton to Sister Anita [Wasserman], Apr. 9, 1959, in *Witness to Freedom,* 187.

plaque in commemoration of the incident, he suddenly felt his union with all of the human beings around him and the consequent dropping away of his monastic separation, not from the world but from other human beings. The episode is contained in his journal, recently published as *A Search for Solitude*, as well as in the revised and expanded version of the original journal published as *Conjectures of a Guilty Bystander* in 1966. A comparison of the two texts is instructive in indicating the growing freedom and intensity of Merton's paradisal consciousness in the period between the two publications. In the first version, although Merton was ecstatic over his feelings of joyful unity with those around him, he was also inhibited by a self-conscious reflection concerning the women around him on the sidewalk, although he noted with a celibate relief that they had not been women of exceptional beauty.[29] Shedding this rather awkward reflection in the revised version some years later, he amplified and deepened the narrative of this epiphanic event:

> Then it was as if I suddenly saw the secret beauty of their hearts, the depths of their hearts where neither sin nor desire nor self-knowledge can reach, the core of their reality, the person that each one is in God's eyes. If only they could all see themselves as they really *are*. If only we could see each other that way all the time. There would be no more war, no more hatred, no more cruelty, no more greed. . . . I suppose the big problem would be that we would fall down and worship each other.[30]

The lavishness of Merton's language here is an indication of how open his spiritual landscape had become by the mid-1960s, even when, as in this passage, he appeared to tread on questionable theological ground with the image of human beings worshiping one another. Paradise, whether said to be so or not by theology, was at hand at Walnut and Fourth. While one might readily see the difference in the two versions of Merton's experience as a development, it is important to see in what that development consisted: that it was primarily a development in Merton's ecstatic assumption of a strong inner freedom. Indeed, as has been

---

29. Merton, Mar. 19, 1958, in *Search for Solitude*, 182.
30. Merton, *Conjectures of a Guilty Bystander*, 142.

intimated, the recapturing of such a freedom was a salient part of what Merton meant by paradisal vision: "Paradise," he noted in the 1960s, was the "radical self in its uninhibited freedom."[31]

Working outward from this maturation, he modified and inevitably enlarged the scope of his idea of paradise based upon his perception of paradisal consciousness in others. When these encounters involved those who were not part of his own faith, he nonetheless frequently recognized in them a genuine element of truth that in turn allowed him, gratefully, to expand his own thinking in a way that might not have occurred from within his own tradition. He valued the "mysticism" reflected in Boris Pasternak's writings, for example, as "more pagan" and "more primitive" and therefore fresher than that found in his own contemplative traditions.[32] His attraction to the primordial in Pasternak's paradisal consciousness was related to a quality of "wonder" in Pasternak's writing as an artist and as a "paradise man" that awakened Merton to the pristine beginnings of human consciousness. There, before the jadedness brought by knowledge and familiarity gained a foothold, one would feel an appropriate awe at the astonishing multiplicity of being.[33] In addition to the paradise perceived by the artist was the insightful work of some of the Fathers of the Church, such as Origen and Gregory of Nyssa, who in the early centuries of Christianity perceived in the Scriptures the ingredients of a paradisal vision, albeit within a theological setting. More and more, however, Merton was imaginatively stirred in the latter part of his life by the pre-Christian, indeed by the precivilized, "original, cosmic revelation" of artists such as Pasternak and by their evocation of a timeless "inward, spiritual world." He described the openness of this world as a "living, transcendental and mysterious history of individual human beings" in the "indescribable interweaving of their destinies" in contrast to the transcribed "formal, and illusory, history of states and empires."[34] By this Merton did not mean that political and social history were inherently unreal but rather that, as with Keats's

---

31. Merton, "Learning to Live," in *Love and Living*, 8.
32. Merton, "The Pasternak Affair," in *Disputed Questions*, 13.
33. Merton, Nov. 22, 1967, in *Other Side of the Mountain*, 15.
34. Merton, "The Pasternak Affair," in *Disputed Questions*, 17–18.

citadel in "Ode on a Grecian Urn," they derived their chief significance from being part of a universal and permanent reality. In Merton's view the paradise that Pasternak reflected in his writing was that of the self, that self that had become the spinning light at the center of Merton's conception of paradise. This was not the self as ego but the self as the transparency of being, as he put it in "The Fall" in *Emblems of a Season of Fury:*

> There is no where in you a paradise that is no place
>   and there
> You do not enter except without a story.
>
> To enter there is to become unnameable.[35]

Rather than seeing this poem as a portrayal about the ascetic extinction of personality, it should be seen, if one is to see it as Merton saw it, as a depiction of the existential expansion of the self through an enlarged consciousness of and participation in the manifold richness of being.

As has been intimated, a particular locus of paradisal consciousness in any culture, Merton believed, was the artist. This was because the artist possessed what he termed an "ingrained innocence." By innocence Merton understood, following the thought of Jacques Maritain, an ontological, as distinct from a moral, innocence. In this connection, in discussing the poetry of Edwin Muir, he declared that the poet's giving of names to things through his or her imagination and linguistic virtuosity was a "primordial metaphysical" act of the mind that was part of the "Edenic office" of the artist. Similarly, in discussing the playful though abstruse poetry of Louis Zukofsky, he believed that he had once again recovered paradise through a freshening of consciousness brought about through the originality of the artist's vision and use of language. Art also integrated worlds that had been separated through cultural diversification. In this respect he characterized great religious art, for example, as providing an opportunity for the viewer to live simultaneously both on earth and in heaven through the luminous integration of all things in God, an integration that in his view constituted original human con-

---

35. Merton, "The Fall," in *Collected Poems,* 354.

sciousness.[36] For Merton, the artist, like the child, took nothing for granted, both being immune in their own ways from the familiar, preordained perceptions of conventional culture.

What counted for Merton was not the arrival at a given paradise, since this too could easily become a stale terminus of sorts. Rather, what was important were the qualities of paradisal vision, especially the transforming power of the imagination, which could construct other worlds. In the new light cast within these alternative worlds, one could return to and begin to transform the actual world based on a freshened perception of it. While there was no contradiction between Merton's paradisal vision and the dogmatic traditions of his church, he was, rather like Newman, whom he came to appreciate more and more toward the end of his life, inclined to challenge religious culture generally to commit itself to an evolution of theological understanding. Such theological organicism, which alienated some of Merton's Catholic readers, was crowned by his vision of what a heavenly paradise would encompass. An example is the following ecstatic entry from his journal in 1960 that was prompted by the dawning of a spring day: "With my hair almost on end and the eyes of the soul wide open I am present, without knowing it at all, in this unspeakable Paradise. . . . Oh paradise of simplicity, self-awareness—and self-forgetfulness—liberty, peace."[37]

Apart from seeing the artist and the mystic as centers of paradisal consciousness, Merton looked toward the child as a locus of such consciousness. There are few images as pervasive in Merton as that of the child, and childhood appears to have fascinated him both in an actual and in a mythic sense. Merton's idealized mythos of the child acted as a lodestar for the actual child that in some ways he remained throughout his life. He accepted Karl Barth's distinguishing between the two kinds of childhood in speaking of Mozart, who as a young prodigy was denied childhood in an actual sense but whose music revealed him to have been a child in the "'higher meaning'" of the word.[38] In some ways Merton's

36. Merton, "True Legendary Sound," in *Literary Essays*, 29; Merton, "Louis Zukofsky—the Paradise Ear," in ibid., 128; Merton, "The Monk and Sacred Art," 232.
37. Merton, June 5, 1960, in *Turning toward the World*, 7.
38. Merton, *Conjectures of a Guilty Bystander*, 3.

relationship with his church and with his order was childlike in an actual sense. As is apparent from his widely read autobiography, *The Seven Storey Mountain* (1948), following the deaths of all of the members of his immediate family he turned to the Church and in particular to the monastic community at Gethsemani in Kentucky with the gratitude of an orphan child. By his own account his first abbot, Dom Frederic Dunne, was a supportive, fatherly figure, and while his relationship to his next abbot, Dom James Fox, was problematic and strained, Merton was dedicated to the end to obedience to his superiors, even if doubtful in particular instances about the judgments rendered by them. In addition, one could argue that in his handling of the romantic relationship with M. in 1966 he was grateful to be rescued from that entanglement by the paternal intervention of his abbot.

The unconscious appears in Merton's writings as a link between actual and mythic childhood, since it converted incidents into symbols. An example is the dream that he recounted in his journal in 1965 in which he found himself in a place where he had been as a child and where he had encountered the black foster mother whom (inside the dream scenario) he had loved in childhood. There is a possible indebtedness to Faulkner here, whom Merton was reading at the time and with whom he felt a firm sense of unity as both artist and contemplative. Perhaps reflecting his lifelong sense of alienation from his own mother, in the dream Merton distinguished between his natural mother and the black woman, whom he paradoxically sees as having given him a "new *life*."[39] In some ways Merton's feelings in the dream resemble those of the child in Flannery O'Connor's story "The Artificial Nigger," a story with which he was familiar. Thematically, the dream also touches on Merton's intense reaction to the civil rights struggle of the 1960s. Both the biographical and the symbolic strands of the dream come together in Merton's realization in the 1960s, a realization that he developed in his journals, essays, and poems at the time: that his color was a badge of his incompleteness as a human being and as an American.

In *The Seven Storey Mountain* in the late 1940s, he considered the problematic nature of the relationship between actual and mythic child-

39. Merton, Feb. 4, 1965, in *Dancing in the Water of Life*, 202.

hood. Remembering his initial hearing of some of Blake's *Songs of Innocence* when he had been ten, he also recalled his literal understanding of the songs at that age, an age, he noted, already past that of the period of a child's most powerful imaginative vision.[40] By the age of sixteen, on the other hand, he had understood and been moved by Blake's symbolism. While Merton's assigning of imaginative receptivity to specific stages of childhood may be a matter of speculation, it is evident that he, like the romantics, thought about childhood in a mythic manner, stimulated by a consciousness of loss felt by the adult who had moved through childhood to what Blake called the world of experience. From this vantage point, that of the stranded and alienated adult, childhood loomed as a world of high imaginative vision supplanted by a flatter world of actuality. Childhood thus became for Merton a symbol of the starting point, a place where other choices might have been made than those that in fact had been made and thus a world that in this respect could be idealized. He attempted to recover the attributes of what he thought of as the child's vision: the openness, spontaneity, and imaginative readiness that so clearly mark his writings.

As with the other themes that Merton set forth in his writings, that associated with childhood had autobiographical roots. It is as if the facts of his life, as with everything else he focused on, came to possess a mysterious significance since they were part of a journey—of that he was in no doubt—that God had laid out for him. In the case of childhood this significance was intensified by his attachment, dating from his years in university, to Blake—and to a lesser extent to Wordsworth—who was himself absorbed by the spiritual and mythic import of childhood. Having been given permission to go beyond the monastic enclosure into the monastery woods in 1953, Merton encountered there the "child" of his English youth who had walked all over Sussex.[41] The autobiographical roots of the theme of childhood can also be seen, as has been suggested, in some of the dreams that he recorded in his journals, as in a dream he had in 1961 in which he was invited to a party. Swimming across a lake to attend the party, he encounters some women who are also going to

40. Merton, *The Seven Storey Mountain*, 85–86.
41. Merton, Feb. 16, 1953, in *Search for Solitude*, 32.

the party, but feels some estrangement from them, self-conscious about his "clerical garb." Approaching the shore and the house where the party is to take place, he becomes aware of the "beautiful water, magic water, from the depths of which comes a wonderful life to which I am not entitled, a life and strength that I fear." Recollecting the dream, Merton interpreted the water as a contact with the bliss of immortality, a destiny that lay ahead of him but from which he could draw strength in this life. However, having arrived at the house where the party is to take place, he meets with a divine Child who gives him pieces of bread, the "ritual and hieratic meal given to all who come to stay."[42] There are two children in the dream, one, Merton himself, who shyly separates himself from the women, the other the Child who is Christ. While the dream narrative, which in some respects recalls Blake's poem "The Land of Dreams," had personal roots, it also evolved into a psychological tale, which in turn crystallized into a contemplative vision. Although it is not clear how conscious he was of the sensual overtones of his pleasurable immersion in the water, he intended in his journals to be open to all aspects of experience. The self's journey involved a passage back and forth through all levels of his being so that the highest flights of the soul were characteristically rooted or made possible by previous, often more mundane, levels of experience. It was the whole picture that interested Merton, who resolved, as his journals testify, to leave nothing out.

In Merton's judgment childhood as a psychological state predisposed the mind to a primordial openness to experience that would later be modified by the selectivity and filtering of experience and knowledge encouraged in formal education. The primordial nature of the child's consciousness was linked to his belief that such consciousness had existed for all human beings in the past, even if within a mythic past buried deep within the psyche. The importance of the past in contrast to the future as a repository of paradisal consciousness was that it symbolized that such consciousness was possible in the present time since it had existed in the past. As with Rousseau, Wordsworth, and Rilke—whose *Duino Elegies* Merton particularly liked—he regarded the state of childhood as

---

42. Merton, *Conjectures of a Guilty Bystander*, 20. See also Merton, Sept. 12, 1961, in *Turning toward the World*, 161–62, for the earlier recording of this incident.

one in which a primal consciousness was in time corrupted by society. He expressed such a view in his posthumously published sequence on the contemplative life, "The Inner Experience": "The modern child may in the beginning of his conscious life begin to show natural and spontaneous signs of spirituality. He may have imagination, originality, a simple and individual freshness of response to reality, and even a tendency to moments of thoughtful silence and absorption. But all these qualities are quickly destroyed by the fears, anxieties and compulsions to conform which come at him from all directions." Similarly, Merton distinguished Sartre's writings from Ionesco's through what he thought of as the primordial, childlike qualities of Ionesco's imagination in contrast to Sartre's jaded "academic mumblings about freedom and 'engagement,'" the work of a "clever, mild little bourgeois."[43]

The idealization of the child in Merton's writings reached a high point of sorts in his angelic vision of Cuban children in his early poem "Song for Our Lady of Cobre:"

> The white girls open their arms like clouds,
> The black girls close their eyes like wings:
> Angels bow down like bells,
> Angels look up like toys,
>
> Because the heavenly stars
> Stand in a ring.[44]

While the poem contains echoes of Blake, it is substantially original and autobiographical in capturing the happiness of Merton's Cuban sojourn. The poem registers not only the paradisal suffusion of the child's perceptions but also the application of those perceptions in the racial harmony portrayed.

For Merton, the distinctive perceptual gifts of the child were suppressed by socialization, then later fortuitously rescued from oblivion on occasion through the imaginations of artists such as Ionesco who had

43. Merton, "The Inner Experience: Problems of the Contemplative Life," 271; Merton, Dec. 6, 1964, in *Dancing in the Water of Life*, 176.
44. Merton, "Song for Our Lady of Cobre," in *Collected Poems*, 30.

recognized the seriousness of the loss. In his own effort at reconstruction he put together a portrait of the mythic child, a survival of paradise in the imagination of a writer who had never lost sight of the shores of childhood. One of the distinguishing signs of the consciousness of Merton's mythic child was its *"primal* utterance," as he put it in an entry in his journal in 1960, a response not to words but to *"being."*[45] Merton's wariness about language here, later echoed in works such as *Cables to the Ace*, derived in part from the fact that he regarded language as one of the salient ways in which society obscured the child's fresh perceptions and unusual utterance by substituting the ponderous, abstract, and hackneyed speech of collective discourse. The effect of this substitution was the corruption of the child's imagination and the severing of its closeness to being.

For Merton, as for Wordsworth, the child's primal consciousness could be energized by the child's contact with nature. An example can be found in his suggestive early poem "Aubade: Lake Erie," in which the awakening children exclaim:

> "Here is the hay-colored sun, our marvelous cousin,
> Walking in the barley,
> Turning the harrowed earth to growing bread,
> And splicing the sweet, wounded vine."[46]

In the poem the children's pastoral consciousness is set off against a darker landscape of "gap-toothed" factories that foreshadow both the children's and the world's descent from innocence. Like the children in the poem Merton tended to depict nature as protective and responsive, as late, indeed, as 1968, the year of his death, when, looking out from his hermitage, he saw the sun rising in Aquarius spreading its protective wings over him.[47]

As is evident throughout Merton's writings, nature could have the effect, as Blake had intimated in his *Songs of Innocence* and as Emerson had

45. Merton, Aug. 30, 1960, in *Turning toward the World*, 36.
46. Merton, "Aubade: Lake Erie," in *Collected Poems*, 35.
47. Merton, Feb. 12, 1968, in *Other Side of the Mountain*, 55.

suggested in his influential essay "Nature," of restoring the child within the self, even into old age. Thus, in Merton's evocative poem "Evening," written in the 1940s, he described the cries of children at play as falling on "our deserted hearing / Clear as water." The poignant offsetting of the adults' vacant lives by the children's voices sprang not only from the liveliness of the children but also from the transforming imagination that was expressed in their play: "They say the sky is made of glass, / They say the smiling moon's a bride." In spite of his bleak picturing of adults in this poem, Merton was quite capable of acknowledging joyfully the presence of the child in the face of an adult. Having encountered an Italian American on the Upper West Side of New York in 1939, for example, he noticed that the man had a "good face and the eyes of a child." Even the intellectual could be a child, as he indicated many years later in *Conjectures of a Guilty Bystander*. Such a one, in Merton's view, was the poet Louis Zukofsky, who, he observed, spoke in the "paradise speech" of the child, not yet knowing the world as "alien" and anticipating nothing from it but joy.[48] In Merton's writings the child's vision is passionately inclusive, welcoming the unknown, rather like the children's open-armed response to the night sky above their heads in the above-mentioned poem as opposed to the unengaged response of the adults around them for whom the world had become an all too familiar affair.

In the poem "Evening," cited above, Merton developed the paradoxical idea of the child's weakness, portrayed as unwariness and ingenuousness, as a source of strength. He enlarged this conception in portraying the child's view of life as play as in fact a sign of the child's superior power. Similarly, in a letter to Jacques Maritain in 1963, he described ultimate reality as the "playing and dancing of the Child-God," and suggested that the most "serious" thing he could consider was the life of a Christian at "play." In addition, in an earlier letter to Boris Pasternak in 1958 in which he recounted a dream he had had, he said that he became aware in the dream of people who sadly failed to see their

---

48. Merton, "Evening," in *Collected Poems*, 41; Merton, Oct. 23, 1939, in *Run to the Mountain*, 69; Merton, *Conjectures of a Guilty Bystander*, 201; Merton, "Louis Zukofsky—the Paradise Ear," in *Literary Essays*, 130.

inner radiance and their "real identity," their relation to the "Child so dear to God who, from before the beginning, was playing in His sight all days, playing in the world."[49] The emblem of the child-God at play, which was drawn from the eighth chapter of the Book of Proverbs, is not hedonistic, but was meant to symbolize a deepening of the significance of all human activity when undertaken with the full use of one's faculties in a joyful relishing of a participation in being. A further instance of the child's weakness as strength occurred in the uncollected poem "Paper Cranes." There the unexpected strength of the child's vision is seen in the slight paper figures made by children as symbols of peace, figures that following the Second World War had achieved international recognition. In these folded pieces of paper, Merton maintained, the

> child's hand
> Folding these wings
> Wins no wars and ends them all.[50]

The child's vision wins, not in the sense that it literally halts all wars, but rather in the sense that the paper cranes prevailed on an imaginative level, mounting a visual argument, as it were, that has not and cannot be gainsaid.

Following William Blake, Merton generated in his writings antithetical worlds of innocence and experience centered on the child's vision, a vision with which, as has been suggested, he steadfastly identified. In his early journal *Entering the Silence,* for example, he wrote in 1952 that having passed through childhood he could no longer "believe the moon to be my own," and he came to feel the same, he added, about the stars and woods. He expressed this descent into the world of experience as a separation between the self and the nonself. The loss of the sense of unity with the surrounding world created a longing in human beings for what Merton called their "original name" and, in the social form of this long-

49. Merton to Maritain, June 11, 1963, in *Courage for Truth,* 38; Merton to Pasternak, Oct. 23, 1958, in ibid., 90.
50. Merton, "Paper Cranes," in *Collected Poems,* 740.

ing, for the consciousness of the "whole world at peace." Separated by the premature deaths of his parents from a trusting childhood awareness of living in a protective world, Merton as an adult recovered through his immersion in the Church his sense of belonging to a providential universe. This can be seen, for example, in a journal entry in 1967 in which, looking up at the night sky, he saw his "many friends," the constellations of the "Swan, Eagle, Perseus and Andromeda, Cassiopeia."[51] As was the case with his felt relationship with the saints, Greek mythological personifications united Merton with the procession of human beings whose childlike imaginations had in the ancient world peopled the night sky. This upward turning of the viewer's gaze expressed an inner truth that, intuitively grasped by the child, expressed a wisdom on which the adult might reflect. This was that creation implies a creator, who at the very least must be mirrored in creation.

For Merton, as for Blake, the adult's recovered innocence was tempered by the knowledge of evil and suffering. In *Zen and the Birds of Appetite* in the late 1960s, he postulated an innocence that was compatible with knowledge, arguing that the "two must go together" if one was to avoid the "emptiness" of the quietist, who lacked both wisdom and knowledge. In similar fashion Blake resisted turning the worlds of innocence and experience into separate antagonistic compartments that would have had the effect of impeding any effort at retaining a conception of the unity of being. In this connection, as scholars have now determined, Blake moved poems back and forth between his songs of innocence and experience, a sign of his awareness of the overlapping of innocence and experience within the fullness of being. In the journal kept on his visit to Asia in 1968, Merton illustrated the recovery of the child mind following the entry into the world of experience by relating a conversation with the Buddhist monk Sonam Kazi, in which they exchanged allegorical tales about abandoning habits of perception and of attachment to things. In one such story a Desert Father was described as having freed himself from such attachments and from the rutted life

51. Merton, July 5, 1952, in *Entering the Silence*, 488; Merton, "The Early Legend," in *Raids on the Unspeakable*, 126; Merton, Nov. 12, 1967, in *Other Side of the Mountain*, 10.

of the world of experience by weaving baskets and then at the end of each year destroying them.[52] Children could also exhibit the sort of innocence that follows experience, not necessarily the experience of guilt but of suffering. Thus, a little black girl who was killed in a racial incident in Alabama in 1963 was said in Merton's poem about her to provide a "lovely shade" in contrast to the "senseless platinum head" of the white doll in her hands. The doll symbolizes the destructive and racist culture that surrounded the little girl, whereas, as in Blake's well-known poem "The Little Black Boy," the shade provided by the black girl represents the innocence that follows experience, here the experience of suffering brought about by racial discrimination. The child's innocence, here portrayed as a precocious wisdom, makes her capable of cooling the fires of racism that Merton saw consuming American society in the 1960s. Once again, he portrayed the child archetypally as strong in its ostensible weakness. Echoing this sentiment, in 1958 he praised the "fragrance" of the Desert Fathers' simplicity and their resemblance to children; they could be so, Merton added, only by being "strong."[53]

In Merton's scheme of things the child's simplicity of vision protected it from the illusions of society's collective perceptions and mores. In his estimation this was Flannery O'Connor's childlike strength as a writer of fiction. He characterized O'Connor as like the child in the widely known story about the emperor's new clothes who innocently revealed the folly and vanity exhibited by the adults around him.[54] He returned to the story about the emperor's new clothes in the "Letter to an Innocent Bystander" in *Raids on the Unspeakable* (1966). In that essay he went on to characterize the child in the tale, the prototype of the innocent bystander, in a most original manner as the person who kept the "fault of the others from being criminal . . . nothing worse than foolishness." If the child had not been there, he continued, the complicit adult witnesses of the emperor's folly would have been not only foolish but insane and corrupt as well, adding that it was the child's cry that saved

52. Merton, *Zen and the Birds of Appetite*, 121; Merton, Nov. 2, 1968, in *Other Side of the Mountain*, 240.

53. Merton, "Picture of a Black Child with a White Doll," in *Collected Poems*, 627; Merton, Nov. 30, 1958, in *Search for Solitude*, 234.

54. See Merton, Notebook no. 14 (June 1964), Merton Collection, Bellarmine University.

them.[55] Merton appears to have meant that the child's visible harmlessness opened the minds of the adults in his surroundings who therefore had no reason to fear him. In this way, in an unthreatened and receptive state they were able to discover their folly without becoming angry or belligerent, and, in this way the child in Merton became, as in Wordsworth, father to the man.

The child's strength of vision, like the monk's, in Merton's view, proceeded from its condition as unaccommodated man, stripped, as he put it in a letter to a fellow monk in 1964, of even the attribute of "strong-mindedness" or forcefulness. While some might see this as inconsistent with the sometimes passionate tone of Merton's own voice, he was usually open to correction in his opinions, even when swept by irritation. Often in his journals, for example, he reasoned antithetically and dialogically with himself, searching for the open waters of the child's vision. Merton believed that the problem with strong-mindedness was that it shrank the field of vision to the dimensions of what was being strongly asserted rather than opened the mind to the possibilities of unity and inclusiveness that in his view constituted wisdom. Characteristically, he wrote in his poetic essay "Hagia Sophia" about the "impeccable pure simplicity of One consciousness in all and through all: one Wisdom, one Child, one Meaning, one Sister."[56] In "Hagia Sophia" he united the image of the child with the allegorical figure of holy wisdom, which he portrayed as female. The uniting of these figures was far from sentimental. For Merton, wisdom, the full conformity of intelligence to reality, was childlike in that it sprang from the pristine spark, the embodiment of reality that had been implanted in the soul by God.

A vision of unity involved not only objects within the mind's field of vision but also the perceptual process itself. Merton demonstrated such a unity formally in his poems through the use of synesthesia whereby the perceptions associated with one sense become transferred to another, thus uniting the senses not only with each other but with the broader governing perceptions that underlay them as well. An example occurred in the early poem "The Winter's Night," which concerned the nature of children's perceptions of the world. In that poem, awakening in the cold

55. Merton, "Letter to an Innocent Bystander," in *Raids on the Unspeakable*, 62.
56. Merton to Dom Ignace Gillet, Sept. 11, 1964, in *School of Charity*, 235; Merton, "Hagia Sophia," in *Collected Poems*, 366.

and dark, an apprehensive child declares that the moonlight "grated like a skate / Across the freezing river," while another sleepless child "hears" the starlight "breaking like a knifeblade / Upon the silent, steelbright pond." In the final stanza Merton as narrator and would-be child joins in the synesthesia exhibited by the children, listening as the moonlight "rings upon the ice as sudden as a footstep," while starlight "clinks upon the dooryard stone."[57]

The ontological significance of the child's vision was the subject of a number of Merton's poems, including the early poem "Birdcage Walk," which celebrated the power of the child's imagination. The poem grew out of a childhood experience when Merton had been in London walking with his uncle, Ben Pearce, in St. James Park. There they encountered an old man in gaiters whom his uncle identified as a bishop. In the seventeenth century Charles II, who had been fond of exotic animals and birds, had ordered caged birds to be placed in the park, thereby naming a well-known walk. In subsequent history the cages were removed, but the birds survived in the ponds and islands that enhance the park. Merton opened the poem with an imaginative re-creation of the original birdcage-lined pathway by writing "One royal afternoon," thereby connecting the gaitered bishop with the park's regal history. Through the figure of the Anglican bishop, whose appearance suggests the distant past, Merton as child entered that past through his imagination. With a surprising boldness, indicative of the felt *power* of childhood, he later recalled thinking that he had led the old bishop along the path. In any case, on the walk the bishop solemnly declares:

> "No bridge" (He smiled
> Between the budding branches),
> "No crossing to the cage
> Of the paradise bird!"[58]

This prohibitive declaration, in effect a call to the child to abandon the illusions of imagination, anticipates an important moment at the end of the poem when the child imagines himself as the royal fowler who re-

57. Merton, "The Winter's Night," in *Collected Poems*, 38.
58. Merton, "Birdcage Walk," in *Collected Poems*, 276. I am indebted to Patrick O'Connell for some helpful information and suggestions in connection with this poem.

leases the birds in spite of the aged bishop's observation that they were beyond reach on their islands. The child's imagination not only pushes through the barrier of the bishop's categorical denial, but also transcends his own initial vision of the bishop as someone who was locked in the world of experience through the allurements of pomp and authority. Thus, surprisingly, the child comes to see the old man as a "magic bishop," an even more striking triumph of innocence over experience than his seeing himself as the royal fowler.[59] If the bishop had been imprisoned within the world of experience by his own habits of mind, the young Merton could free him, as it were, through the transforming power of his imagination. Here Merton brought out not only the purity of the child's imagination but the daring and freedom of it as well, a freedom that, in general, socialization would in various ways suppress—just as the rare, exuberant exercise of the imagination by artists and mystics would help to bring it back.

The ontological significance of the child's imagination was also signaled in Merton's poem "Grace's House," the background of which he recounted in a letter to his old teacher Mark Van Doren in 1962. The letter grew out of Merton's astonishment in receiving a drawing from a little girl, a drawing that gave rise to one of his most admired poems. Reflecting on the child's vision, he wrote ecstatically that there were "circles within circles," and that if we chose we could safely "let loose in the circle of paradise the very wrath of God."[60] Merton recognized the child's paradisal vision in the way in which she drew her house:

> No blade of grass is not counted,
> No blade of grass forgotten on this hill.
> Twelve flowers make a token garden.
> There is no path to the summit—
> No path drawn
> To Grace's house.[61]

The reference to the "twelve flowers" in the drawing indicates the child's sensitivity not only to the expanse of grass but also to the individual

59. Ibid., 276.
60. Merton to Van Doren, Aug. 9, 1962, in *Road to Joy*, 45.
61. Merton, "Grace's House," in *Collected Poems*, 330.

blades, a perception of the one in the many for which Merton as a contemplative constantly strove. Furthermore, he depicted the child's vision as spreading concentrically outward from the center of her own being since we are told: "All the curtains are arranged / Not for hiding but for seeing out."[62] Given the introspective nature of Merton's and of the contemplative's life, this detail may strike some readers as disingenuous, but his view of the contemplative life was that it should look out from the ego toward the other, finally encountered as God. With the child's transforming imagination, Grace sees, without being aware that she sees, a paradise where all the animals are aware. The inclusiveness of Grace's vision is made even more complete through the amplifying, imaginative sympathy of the narrator. Thus, although Merton noticed in the drawing that there was no road to Grace's house, symbolizing the adult's exclusion from the child's vision, nonetheless for those like himself there was in fact a road, and his poem was that road.

A somewhat mystifying yet suggestive poem about the freedom of childhood is the poem "Landscape," which, like "Birdcage Walk," appeared in *The Strange Islands* in 1957. In a letter to some Anglican seminarians in the 1960s, Merton conceded that the poem was enigmatic, indicating that its theme was about the child's awakening to his or her own freedom while becoming aware of the hazards of freedom and of the safety felt in not exercising freedom. In this light one can make out some of the principal antithetical elements of the poem, especially the child's uncertainty about choosing a subject to draw. There is a further antithesis between the powerful male father figure in the poem, known as the Personage, and the protective maternal figure to whom the child remains securely attached. Attempting to decide what to draw, the child hesitates between boldness and fearful dismay. The stakes are portrayed as high as the child considers moving from his paradisal island home limned eternally—as in Wordsworth—with its "Interminable shore."[63] The poem incisively dramatizes the issue of childhood and freedom by showing the child's attraction to power, of which he or she has acutely

62. Ibid., 330.
63. Merton to Anglican seminarians, Nov. 11, 1963, in *Road to Joy*, 328; Merton, "Landscape," in *Collected Poems*, 277.

felt the lack, alongside an underlying apprehension that something precious may thereby be irrevocably lost. Nonetheless, the consciousness of choice is itself a development of sorts in the child's life, a consciousness whose full creative possibilities elude many. Some, Merton came to believe, will choose freedom without retaining childhood wisdom yet later recover the child's vision. Others will lose themselves entirely in socialized consciousness. In any case, it is necessary in Merton's presentation of childhood that the child exercise his or her freedom in order never to lose the sense of the importance of that freedom. Counterbalancing the descent into the world of experience, there was, Merton maintained, an innate child dormant within every adult.[64] This latent intuitive reserve, as real to Merton as a genetic code, he believed had an essentially ontological leaning toward unity. If the Personage in the poem "Landscape" invited the child in that poem to freedom and thereby to the possibility of danger by asking the child to choose what to draw, the paradisal child whom Merton believed to have been embedded in the human psyche would have answered: "Draw it all."

Never far from childhood in his own imagination and thinking, in Merton's view the child came to symbolize the freshness, intuitiveness, and unexpected strength that had been incorporated into being by the Creator. Drawn toward the future, the child, hungry for experience, unthinkingly came to treat the present moment dismissively, that present moment that Merton as an adult perceived as the center of reality. As has been suggested, as an adult Merton turned toward monasticism in part in order to preserve the child in himself. Moreover, his childlike character could be seen in his eclectic reading, though he moved easily and unself-consciously through diverse intellectual fields such as anthropology, psychology, philosophy, and natural science, spontaneously writing to authors whom he did not know but whose writings he admired. This often gave rise to significant exchanges, as in the correspondence with Czeslaw Milosz, Boris Pasternak, and Erich Fromm. Attempting to open his mind further to the unknown riches that lay before him, he swam about in a polyphony of different cultural voices, listening always, though, for the voice of the child. Archetypally consid-

64. See Merton, "Hagia Sophia," in *Collected Poems*, 365–66.

ered, the child became for Merton an exemplary symbol of the expansiveness of the primordial imagination. In turn the child's mind, ontologically speaking, became in his eyes a template for the self. The abandonment of this template meant losing the originality of the self and yielding to the subsequent absorption of the self into the collective mirror—paradise lost.

6

The Imagination and Art

Readers of Merton's widely known autobiographical narrative, *The Seven Storey Mountain,* will realize that the author had a ready and suggestive imagination. There was the scene, for example, in which sitting on the terrace of a hotel in Cuba he felt suddenly inspired by Mary, the mother of Jesus, to write a poem, which he immediately did, a poem that he appropriately called "Song for Our Lady of Cobre." Similarly, he later related a mysterious experience in which while in Olean in upper New York State where he was an instructor at St. Bonaventure College, he inexplicably heard the tolling of the bell of the monastery that he had visited in Kentucky and to which he would return for the rest of his life. There was also the unsettling episode in which also at Olean he found himself transfixed, while praying at night, by a vision of the "edge of the abyss" and by the apparition of a mysterious person whom he found himself unable to describe.[1]

While these are instances of what might simply be characterized as the psychological imagination, the sort of thing one might encounter in Poe or Rilke, Merton's interest in the imagination was primarily ontological. As with Blake and Coleridge, he was interested in the imagination as a means of attaining truth or reality either through imaginative discernment or through the creative joining of things together to restore their original unity, thus regaining a sense of the depth and authority of

1. Merton, Feb. 19, 1941, in *Run to the Mountain,* 309–10.

their being. In his early journal *Run to the Mountain*, he paid tribute to the power of Coleridge's imagination in depicting reality in contrast to Keats's imagination, which he described as dealing more with purely imaginary materials. Nevertheless, like Blake, Merton objected to a realism in art that involved the copying of the surfaces of things, which he saw as simply a form of materialism. Materialism was a salient, if not *the* salient, manifestation of evil, since it represented the failure of the imagination, which, more than anything else, as Michael Higgins has suggested, for both Merton and Blake marked the fall of humanity from grace. Indeed, in his M.A. thesis at Columbia, "Nature and Art in William Blake," Merton described Blake's view of materialism as "equivalent" to Hell: "It is almost, but not quite, complete nonexistence or death. So also believed," he added, "the Neo-Platonists." The triumvirate here of Blake, Merton, and the Neoplatonists expressed Merton's strongest intellectual leanings in many areas but especially those connected with imagination and art. His view of art, so derived, remained constant throughout his life, as can be seen in a letter in 1963 in which he declared his attraction to impressionist and expressionist painters and his profound dislike of "social realism."[2] Merton's fundamental objection to realistic or naturalistic art was that it stifled the imagination, which alone could offer alternative visions of reality to those presented by conventional thinking.

The unimaginative use of reason was another barrier to the ascent to truth in Merton's view. What Blake called the mind-forged manacles of reason, unaided by imagination, could, Merton argued, be seen in the behavior of a war criminal such as Adolf Eichmann, whose literalism of mind underlay a specious sanity that supported the massive destructiveness of the Second World War. Merton considered the sort of mind Eichmann and the other administrators of war seemed to him to possess in a prose poem titled "Chant to Be Used in Processions around a Site with Furnaces":

2. Merton, Oct. 10, 1941, in ibid., 435; see Higgins, *Heretic Blood: The Spiritual Geography of Thomas Merton*, 271; Merton, "Nature and Art in Blake," in *Literary Essays*, 426; Merton to a correspondent identified only as "My Dear Friend," [ca. 1963], in *Road to Joy*, 90.

For putting them into a test fragrance I suggested an
express elevator operated by the latest cylinder it was
guaranteed

Their love was fully stopped by our perfected ovens
But the love rings were salvaged. . . .

All the while I had obeyed perfectly. . . .

In my day we worked hard we saw what we did our
self-sacrifice was conscientious and complete our work
was faultless and detailed.[3]

The poem's dry, understated tone and phrasing mimic the step-by-step
process of reason unaided by imagination while showing the ironic contrast between an apparently rational surface order and the moral chaos
that can lurk just below that surface. The spiritual vacuousness of the
camp commandant is further revealed in his allusion to the "love rings,"
the wedding rings that were melted down by the Nazis, who in the midst
of their engrossing administrative duties are portrayed as nevertheless
conscious in a superficial and ironic sense of what the rings symbolized.

In his book *The Romantic Reformation*, Robert Ryan has observed
that for Blake the imagination was the "solvent of systems," that which
transcended the rigidity and narrowness of exclusively rational discourse. Ryan linked this view of the imagination to Coleridge's influential observation that the imagination dissolved things in order to re-
create them.[4] In some ways this description can help to illuminate Merton's
idea of the recombinant function of the imagination. Such a bridging by
the imagination could take extraordinary forms, as in Blake's startling
image of the marriage of heaven and hell, a yoking of disparate realities
to which Merton alluded in the opening section of *Cables to the Ace*. One
can observe such a combining of disparate elements in order to recon-
stitute reality in the poem "Two States of Prayer," from the early volume
Figures for an Apocalypse:

3. Merton, "Chant to Be Used in Processions around a Fire with Furnaces," in *Collected Poems*, 348.
4. Ryan, *The Romantic Reformation: Religious Politics in English Literature, 1789–
1824*, 231.

> In wild October when the low hills lie
> With open eye
> And own the land like lions.[5]

The baring of the landscape under the brisk October winds leads to the apt and original image of the hills lying with "open eye." The transposition of the open eye onto the autumnal scene does more than reflect the change in the seasons. It also conveys the sense of an alert, even aware, nature, similar in that respect to ourselves. This personified view of nature is further heightened by the image of the lions, which creates an impression not only of nonhuman awareness but of dangerous power as well. In this sense the scene registers the threatening onset of winter but in a way that, because of the tropes used, relates the seasons intimately to both animal and our own modes of being. This opening stanza of the poem thus prepares the reader for one of the states of prayer mentioned in the title, a fiery, unexpectedly aggressive assault on heaven. What is in the widest sense reconstituted here, then, is the reality of the surprising power of the soul extending itself toward transcendence.

In considering the poetry of Edwin Muir, Merton praised Muir's reconciling, through the use of the imagination, both the "inner and outer" human being and the present and past, seeking through the imagination the restoration of a "living unity."[6] Merton's eye was on the inclusiveness of the imagination, its ability to bring back together into a primordial unity that which through a weakness in vision or will had at some point become fragmented. A successful example of this use of the imagination occurs in the poem "Elegy for the Monastery Barn," which appeared in *The Strange Islands* in 1957. The poem, which is about the burning down of an old barn at Merton's monastery, begins with a whimsical tribute to the old barn as a somewhat dotty dowager:

> As though an aged person were to wear
> Too gay a dress
> And walk about the neighborhood
> Announcing the hour of her death.[7]

5. Merton, "Two States of Prayer," in *Collected Poems*, 150.
6. Merton, "True Legendary Sound," in *Literary Essays*, 33.
7. Merton, "Elegy for the Monastery Barn," in *Collected Poems*, 288.

At the beginning the tropes are humorous and of slight consequence, but the poem gathers significance when the barn's previous inhabitants and workers suddenly return:

> Look! They have all come back to speak their summary:
> Fifty invisible cattle, the past years
> Assume their solemn places one by one.
> This is the little minute of their destiny.
> Here is their meaning found. Here is their end.
>
> Laved in the flame as in a Sacrament
> The brilliant walls are holy. . . .
>
> Let no man stay inside to look upon the Lord![8]

Beginning with the innocuous image of the eccentric old lady, Merton slowly draws the reader into the flames, as it were, so that one sees the radical development of image and theme, here the images of death and transformation, including those of an apocalyptic intensity that an ambitious poetic imagination could accommodate. For Merton, it goes without saying, the poem was not just an exercise in imaginative creation but also a technique by which the mind could be brought to apprehend different levels of reality at once, not unlike Blake's fourfold vision. In this way the unity of being could be restored not only laterally, as it were, by bringing together diverse areas of experience, but vertically as well, by bringing together different *levels* of experience.

The transforming imagination in Merton's poetry was especially radiant in the poems of his youth, such as the "Song for Our Lady of Cobre" in which he recorded an inspired perception of racial harmony, an imaginative reconciling of diverse elements of a particularly sensitive and important kind. For this reason the poem is reproduced here in its entirety:

> The white girls lift their heads like trees
> The black girls go
> Reflected like flamingoes in the street.
> The white girls sing as shrill as water,
> The black girls talk as quiet as clay.

8. Ibid., 289.

> The white girls open their arms like clouds,
> The black girls close their eyes like wings:
> Angels bow down like bells,
> Angels look up like toys,
>
> Because the heavenly stars
> Stand in a ring:
> And all the pieces of the mosaic, earth,
> Get up and fly away like birds.[9]

The echoes from Blake, such as stars standing in a ring, reveal and enhance the visionary resonance of the poem. In an imagined universe in which the human spirit is depicted as second only to God, the stars, like the angels, are lesser beings, theologically and ontologically speaking, than the Cuban girls. In the poem's breadth of vision, human beings are shot through with a cosmic harmony marked in part by the black girls closing their eyes like wings. While the image is distinctly Merton's, it does recall Blake's image in "The Little Black Boy" of the black boy with his darker skin shielding the white boy from the burning rays of the sun.

Even though many of Merton's early poems were written in a time of ascetic monastic discipline, they frequently possess a joyful exuberance in which, because of the author's transforming imagination, it is difficult to separate the secular from the sacred. In the poem "A Psalm," for example, which was included in *The Tears of the Blind Lions* in the late 1940s, are the following lines:

> When psalms surprise me with their music
> And antiphons turn to rum
> The Spirit sings: the bottom drops out of my soul.[10]

While the image of rum here recalls a similar use in Emily Dickinson's poetry, Merton nevertheless took the image in a direction of his own. The comparison of the psalm with the rum is surprising yet apt, indicating the effect on his soul of the liturgical music, the opening up of the

---

9. Merton, "Song for Our Lady of Cobre," in ibid., 29–30.
10. Merton, "A Psalm," in ibid., 220.

responsive soul and the relaxing of its habitual restraints and boundaries as liquor would tend to do. The potentially negative connotations of the liquor are sublimated by being assimilated into the experiential and mystical context with no ill effects, thematically speaking. Thus, the imagination is portrayed as able to restructure the world in such a way that the unity achieved transforms all of the constituent parts.

In terms of Merton's interest in the imagination, it is worth recalling that throughout his life he was attracted to the poetry of Lorca, whose influence on Merton has been discussed by Patrick O'Connell.[11] Merton liked to use surrealist or quasi-surrealist elements in his poems, sometimes in the manner of Lorca and of Hart Crane, both of whose work he admired. He did this in such a way as not to give ascendancy to the subconscious as an end in itself but rather in order to enlarge the space inhabited by the imagination. An example occurs in his poem "The Bombarded City":

> Now let no man abide
> In the lunar wood
> The place of blood.
> Let no man abide here,
> Not even in a dream,
> Not in the lunar forest of this undersea.[12]

While lunar imagery is sometimes presented positively in Merton's poetry, here in this surrealistic setting it is sinister and frightening, particularly the "lunar forest of the undersea," an image that recalls Poe. Instead of illuminating the subconscious, however, as Poe would have done, Merton here uses the nightmarish scene to show the actual terror of war as greater by far than that of horrible fantasies about it that could grip the mind. Moreover, the imaginative image of the bony lunar light piercing the dark subconscious conveys an impression of death far more powerfully than would have been the case with an explanatory statement.

---

11. See O'Connell, "Under the Spell of Lorca: An Important Influence on Thomas Merton's Early Poetry," 256–86.
12. Merton, "The Bombarded City," in *Collected Poems*, 75–76.

There can be no doubt that Merton's respect for the cognitive value of the imagination derived in part from his heightened awareness of the mysteriousness of life and of the limits of reason. The words *mystery* and *mysterious* appear frequently in his writings, and he applied these words alternately both to religious truths and to the cosmos as perceived by the imagination. As a contemplative he accepted the resistance to human understanding posed by ultimate realities, as in his perception in 1941 that the "mystery" of the Holy Family lay not in the behavior and sayings of Jesus but rather in the hidden life that he shared with his mother and Joseph in the intimacy and "ecstasy" in which, as Merton construed it, the Holy Family lived. In the same journal he characterized the relation of Mary, the mother of Jesus, to the Church as a mystery "within mystery." Although Merton regarded artists as particularly predisposed to confront the ultimate mysteries of human existence because of their probing imaginations, he maintained in 1940 that the artist should be reticent about the mystery of what could not be explained. When in 1963 he was given an icon of Elias for his hermitage, his imagination stirred because of the light given off within the painting. At the same time, while he became aware of some of the specific sources of richness in the painting's figures and colors, he noted a final mysterious turning toward what he called the "blackness of the divine mystery." Later in the 1960s, reflecting upon the word *God*, Merton put forward the idea that that word was in fact a "non-word," a way of describing the deity in the Bible that nevertheless failed to explain the surpassing reality behind the word.[13]

At a less theological level Merton frequently depicted being as a mystery and the contemplation of being as partially illuminating although finally wrapped in mystery. In a letter to Mark Van Doren in 1954, he described the creational world as symbolic of a mystery that the contemplative could perhaps begin to understand. Nature was a deeply mysterious world to Merton, containing elements that teased the mind out of thought, leaving the core of the mystery undisturbed and inviolate. In

---

13. Merton, Jan. 11, 1941, in *Run to the Mountain*, 287; Merton, Sept. 2, 1941, in ibid., 393; Merton, Dec. 14, 1940, in ibid., 278; Merton, Apr. 24, 1963, in *Turning toward the World*, 315; Merton, *Opening the Bible*, 16.

addition, he perceived the self as an enigma in that the "real person" within it was shrouded in mystery, as he observed in *Conjectures of a Guilty Bystander* in 1966. In the same volume he described the mystery at the self's nucleus as "incommunicable," a reality that both lay within and transcended the boundaries of the self. It was not just that Merton perceived mystery within ultimate realities but also that he was attracted to it. In art, for example, he preferred the mysteriousness in the poetry of Dylan Thomas over what he regarded as the more transparent poetry of W. H. Auden or Louis MacNiece.[14]

Merton's attraction to the mysterious, which in terms of ultimate reality he associated with the vastness of the Creator's mind, was often associated in his writing with patterns of light and dark imagery. Drawing both on the romantic poets and on the Western mystics, his fascination with darkness is evident in a number of his early books, including *The Seven Storey Mountain*, the journals, and the early poetry. Who can forget the dramatic scene in *The Seven Storey Mountain* when, during his first night at the monastery, he was awakened suddenly by the clanging bells of the monastery tower drawing him through mysterious corridors until he found his way to the nave of the church and to light? For Merton, darkness was the visible form of the mystery of being in which at fortuitous moments a small light appeared. Such was his experience as a contemplative through which night became the most active and productive time for the soul:

> Most beautiful and peaceful darkness: is it the cave of my own inner being? . . . Here there is positive life swimming in the rich darkness which is no longer thick like water but pure, like air. . . . Everything is charged with intelligence, though all is night. There is no speculation here. . . . It is a strange awakening to find the sky inside you and beneath you and above you and all around you so that your spirit is one with the sky, and all is positive night.[15]

14. See Merton to Van Doren, June 3, 1954, Merton Collection, Columbia University; Merton, *Conjectures of a Guilty Bystander,* 134, 81; see Merton, Jan. 11 and Feb. 9, 1941, in *Run to the Mountain,* 288, 305.

15. Merton, Feb. 26, 1952, in *Entering the Silence,* 467–68.

The image of the sky within Merton's mind recalls Emerson's well-known image of himself as a transparent eyeball through which all of nature coursed. The image of the mind being carried upon a sea of darkness would appear to point to the unconscious and to the archetypes of the imagination stored within the psyche. Eclipsing the distractions brought about by daylight, the darkness described in the above extract made possible the awakening of the contemplative's imaginative perception. In this connection Merton explained to a correspondent at one point that darkness was the contemplative's light, while daylight, as in Wordsworth, engaged the "everyday" mind.[16]

In addition to darkness Merton responded to the half-light perceptible at dawn. Merton's journals and poems are filled with descriptions of dawns.[17] At such a time there was enough light to convey the outline of the tangible world, while there was also enough darkness to stimulate the imagination, which attempted to fill out what the eye could not quite make out. In a different kind of half-light, moonlit nights in his writings exude a balance of light and darkness sufficient to turn on the lamp of the imagination, drawing the mind out of its shell, as it were. In his poem "Nocturne" in *The Strange Islands*, Merton described night as "one-eyed" yet conveying a "wisdom" that "sails from God," the moon providing the observer with a simplified view in which the mind, undistracted by the plethora of daytime phenomena, was able to focus imaginatively on its own being and then on the singularity of being itself.[18]

Apart from this romantic use of the motifs of light and darkness, Merton absorbed from the Western mystics an analogous perceptual apparatus in the imagery of darkness that was associated with the apophatic approach of the mind to God. In 1959 in a letter to his artist friend Victor Hammer, Merton insisted that created light, though of great value, was a darkness in comparison with the light of holy wisdom, which for Merton was the light of the divine mind embedded in creation, particularly in the human mind. Similarly, in an essay on light and dark imagery in the writings of Saint John of the Cross, published in *Disputed*

16. Merton to Herbert Mason, Aug. 24, 1959, in *Witness to Freedom*, 263.
17. See O'Connell, "Merton's Wake-Up Calls," 129–63.
18. Merton, "Nocturne," in *Collected Poems*, 230.

Questions in 1960, he explained that it was not so much that the contemplative or mystic passed through darkness to light as that the darkness itself was the light. Merton here meant that darkness extinguished the lesser light of ordinary perception to make room for a greater enlightenment.[19] Nevertheless, he went out of his way throughout his life to explain that this perception of light and darkness involved not a rejection of the created world but rather a rediscovery of that world, now seen with restorative, spiritual intelligence. An example is his superb poem "Night-Flowering Cactus," which was published in *Emblems of a Season of Fury* in 1963:

> Though I show my true self only in the dark and to no man
> (For I appear by day as serpent)
> I belong neither to night nor day. . . .
>
> I neither show my truth nor conceal it
> My innocence is descried dimly
> Only by divine gift
> As a white cavern without explanation.
>
> He who sees my purity
> Dares not speak of it.
> When I open once for all my impeccable bell
> No one questions my silence:
> The all-knowing bird of night flies out of my mouth.[20]

The exquisite flower, which bloomed on only one night each year and was thus unseen, gave rise to a fertile silence in which the bird of night, an apt image, flew out of its mouth. While night was thus filled with riches for the mind's eye, the imagination—if not for the physical eye— Merton was careful not to diminish or dismiss the day, saying that the plant, though appearing differently in the daylight, belonged neither to day nor to night. Nonetheless, the focus here is not on being, whose

19. See Merton to Hammer, May 14, 1959, in *Witness to Freedom*, 5; see Merton, "Light in Darkness: The Ascetic Doctrine of St. John of the Cross," in *Disputed Questions*, 208–17.

20. Merton, "Night-Flowering Cactus," in *Collected Poems*, 351–52.

magnificence is unquestionable, but rather on perception, on the conditions that allow us to see that magnificence. In this perceptual context the distractions of the diurnal world, whether experienced by romantic or mystic, are seen to thwart deeper perception.

In Merton's scheme of things art arose out of the rich darkness of night and out of "beautiful cellars," as he put it in the fifty-third section of *Cables to the Ace.* Coming from parents who were both artists, he noted in *The Seven Storey Mountain* that he had always understood that art was "contemplation." Although his parents had not been religious contemplatives in any formal sense, their commitment to art was sufficient, Merton believed, to make them people who were in the world but not of it. Although he argued in his essay "Poetry and the Contemplative Life" (1947) and in *The Ascent to Truth* (1951) that the experiences of the artist and the mystic were distinct, thereby reflecting his own tension in the 1940s and early 1950s regarding his two vocations, he later acknowledged the cross-fertilization that occurred between art and mysticism. As early as *The Seven Storey Mountain,* he had indicated that he had from his earliest years regarded mystical and artistic experience as analogous, since both involved an intuitive perception of reality through an "affective identification" with the object contemplated.[21] Merton's language here recalls that of Jacques Maritain and Maritain's own imaginative application of Thomist philosophy to art in such works as *Art and Scholasticism* (1930) and *Creative Intuition in Art and Poetry* (1953).

Later in life, writing in *Zen and the Birds of Appetite* in the late 1960s, Merton acknowledged the contribution of Zen Buddhism, rather than Thomist philosophy, to art through its awakening in both the artist and the spectator of a primal spiritual consciousness. While Merton celebrated the artist's spiritual value, he lamented the unwarranted prophetic role that he believed had been thrust upon the modern artist's shoulders in the absence of credible ontological and spiritual insight in other parts of society, including institutional religion.[22] At the same time,

---

21. Merton, *Cables to the Ace,* in ibid., 431; Merton, *The Seven Storey Mountain,* 203, 202.

22. Merton, *Zen and the Birds of Appetite,* 90; see Merton, "Theology of Creativity," in *Literary Essays,* 360.

while he regretted the supplanting of religion and philosophy by art, he affirmed the function of art and of poetry in particular in making contact with the "inwardness" of things, as he put it in a lecture to novices in the early 1960s. In connection with his dual vocation as monk and artist, he suggested in an essay titled "The Monk and Sacred Art" (1957) that if the monk was a *"seer"* it was because he was also a *"maker,"* both in his work in the fields and in his more creative work. In this way he highlighted the interactivity of the cognitive and creative functions of the imagination, writing to Victor Hammer in 1963 that sometimes one could not "see a thing" unless one endeavored to "make something like it," adding that nothing came to be known except by being "changed in the process."[23]

Merton recognized the autonomy of the art object, its ability to act as a symbolic source of meaning to the spectator. Indeed, in a talk given to the novices at Gethsemani, he anticipated contemporary reader theory discussing the re-creation of a poem that occurred in the reader's imagination. Whether in the case of the reader-spectator or of the artist, Merton emphasized the connection of art to *seeing*. On one occasion he described primitive cave painting as essentially a celebration of the act of seeing and of the consciousness of seeing. Commenting on the painting of animals in the Paleolithic period, for example, he suggested that the animal so represented was made "luminous and transcendent" by the act of vision itself.[24] In *Conjectures of a Guilty Bystander,* he outlined what this sort of primitive artistic vision involved and what it did not involve:

> The cave painters were concerned not with composition, not with "beauty," but with the peculiar immediacy of the most direct vision. The bison they paint is not a mere representation of an animal, it is a sign, a *gestalt,* a presence of the unique and peculiar life force incarcerated in this animal. . . . This is anything but an "abstract essence." It is dynamic power, vitality, the self-realization of life in

23. See Merton, "Poetry and Imagination," Credence Cassette no. A 2076; Merton, "The Monk and Sacred Art," 232; Merton to Victor Hammer, Nov. 9, 1963, in *Witness to Freedom,* 8.

24. See Merton, "Poetry and Religious Experience," Credence Cassette no. AA 2804; Merton, *Mystics and Zen Masters,* 248.

act, something that flashes out in a split second, is seen, yet is not accessible to mere reflection, still less to analysis.[25]

Merton emphasizes here the inclusive vision of the Paleolithic artists, who captured the vital wholeness of their subjects rather than abstract ideas about them yet did not simply copy but rather *saw*, joining their minds to the animals they painted.

Thus, for Merton, the unifying inclusivity of art stemmed in part from its ability to unite the artist and the object of his or her contemplation. In a talk to the novices at Gethsemani he mentioned in connection with Blake's poem "The Sunflower" that, rather than being a statement about the sunflower, the poem depicted an intersubjective relationship between the poet and the sunflower that reflected a harmony of self and object whereby the poet and nature were, momentarily at least, in a state of communion. For Merton, this amounted to a restoration, in part at least, of paradise. In his own life as an artist he had experienced such harmony, as in the photographs he took on his trip to northern California in 1968 in which he saw not only the beauty of the sea rocks but also the "interior landscape" of himself in the implicitly collaborative photograph produced by both himself and nature. His comment on the photograph was that "what is written within me is there."[26] Regarding the intersubjectivity of artist and subject, or of artist and being, as it were, while he regarded the uniting action as initiated by the imagination, he did not see nature as epistemologically passive. Rather, like the romantics, he tended to perceive nature as cognitively helpful in expressing the surpassing vitality of the author of being.

In his reflections about Paleolithic painters, Merton demonstrated his valuing of those primordial states of consciousness that reflected a paradisal wholeness and joy. The primitive artist's act of seeing thus opened up a vision of what Merton thought of as the inherent perfection of being that, through the artist's imaginative discernment, informed his or her perception of actual beings. Inevitably, then, art introduced a per-

---

25. Merton, *Conjectures of a Guilty Bystander*, 280.
26. See Merton, "Poetry: The Angelic Realm," Credence Cassette no. AA 2908; Merton, May 22, 1968, in *Other Side of the Mountain*, 110.

ception of the ideal into the real or added it suggestively, like an underlying *pentimento*, a still visible reminder of the original, paradisal state of
being. Art was thus the "visible embodiment of the ideal," he suggested,
which the artist intuitively perceived in his or her "contemplation of nature." In this respect Merton's view recalls Shelley's pithy observation
that anyone who had encountered Sophocles' Antigone could never
again give to an actual woman a full measure of love. Similarly, regarding the effect of idealism in art, Charles Altieri has suggested that even
if modern readers had difficulty sharing Dante's faith, they could respond in a "speculative" way to the idealism in his work and thereby gain
a "fresh perspective" both on themselves and even on their own culture
and time.[27]

The thorny question of art as knowledge is one that Merton addressed from time to time, as in *The Seven Storey Mountain* in which he
declared that the actions and figures dramatized in literature were irre-
ducible and so not capable of being paraphrased since they belonged to
a different order of knowledge. In art, and particularly in literary art,
Merton maintained in an essay on William Faulkner that our deepest
human conflicts were enacted rather than analyzed or explained. This
was due to the fact that the essential idiom of art, the symbol, was a
unique instrument for joining the particular and the universal, a reflection of its inclusivity. In this matter Paul Ricoeur, with whose writings Merton was familiar, described symbolism as like a circuit in which
the symbol gives "rise to the thought, but thought always returns to and
is informed by the symbol," a structuring that helps to throws light on
Merton's view. Emphasizing the cultural inclusiveness of the artistic
symbol, Merton argued that in perusing Dante's symbols and myths, one
absorbed therein, without having to have it explained as such, a whole
system of medieval Scholastic philosophy and theology.[28]

In relation to knowledge, art that copied the original was, from Mer-

27. Merton, "Art and Worship," 115. Shelley's observation is alluded to in George
Steiner's *Real Presences*, 192. Altieri, *Act and Quality*, 329.

28. Merton, *The Seven Storey Mountain*, 180; Merton, "'Baptism in the Forest,'" in
Literary Essays, 96; Ricoeur, *The Symbolism of Evil*, 347; Merton, *The Seven Storey Mountain*, 123.

ton's point of view, of merely nominal value. The reason was that in order to deepen the knowledge conveyed, the artist's interpretive and creative imagination needed to be involved. As Merton put it in *Conjectures of a Guilty Bystander*, to convey the meaning of something substantial, "you have to use not a shadow but a sign, not the imitation but the image." Furthermore, as he wrote in his essay "Symbolism: Communication or Communion?" in 1968, the sign needed to incorporate a whole range of experience if it was to avoid the shallowness of allegory, which merely designated an abstraction. Jacques Maritain, whose writings Merton greatly admired, maintained that it was the artist's sensitivity to the concrete existential that saved his or her work from narrowness and so opened the artist's intelligence to the whole of reality, even if mirrored in the individual life and the singular incident. Merton saw the universal in art not only through the eyes of the contemplative but also through the Jungian archetypes drawn from the depths of the "common unconscious" of the human race. Speaking of Faulkner's well-known story "The Bear," for example, he noted that the symbols represented and evoked archetypal forms "anterior" to rational consciousness and spontaneously present in the mythic and religious literature of all times. In Merton's view symbolism operated on the basis of analogy to unite disparate parts of experience into a re-created whole. Indeed, in the case of certain writers, he argued in 1941, there hovered a metasymbol that encompassed a number of different works. He drew his ideas partly from Ananda Coomaraswamy, who, though writing on Eastern philosophy and religion, emphasized the role of analogy, as Thomas Aquinas had done, in bringing together "Heaven and Earth" within the purview of the mind and the self. In contrast to a decorative or merely expository use of figurative language, the symbol for Merton did much more than elucidate an idea or theme; rather, it pointed to the center or heart of existence. Because of the way in which symbols brought together different aspects of experience into a whole, he maintained that symbols could absorb apparently contradictory elements in a manner that would cause reason to recoil. In yoking such contradictory elements within artistic symbolism, even without reconciling them, Merton noted, the reader or spectator was led to a point beyond the contradictory fragments to a totality, being itself, that acted like a solvent for the separated and even os-tensibly conflicting fragments.[29]

He characterized the mimetic value of art as having a "transobjective subjectivity," as he termed it in a comment on the South American poet Alfonso Cortes.[30] In this manner Merton hoped to close the gap be-tween the subjective and other reality without, however, limiting art to realistic art. He explained this further in an important statement on modern art, and on abstract impressionism in particular, that he made in 1967:

> Beyond expressionism, which concerns itself with the frontiers of a subjective self where the individual rejoins the collective subcon-scious in archetypal symbols, there is another important direction in abstract art: the impersonal, objective, "constructionist" effort of men such as Mondrian, Arp, Calder, Le Corbusier. . . . Their work is objective not in the sense that it creates images or forms as pure objects but rather in the sense that it strives to integrate image and life in one reality, liberated from the human and accidental, a "pure reality" which is apprehended without "particularities of form and natural color." Here the encounter is not with the work of art in the mode of the traditional aesthetic experience but in a more univer-sal intuition like that of the mathematician or of the Zen master.[31]

No doubt reflecting his own admiration for his painter friend Ad Rein-hardt, Merton made a case for abstract expressionism based upon its de-piction of universal patterns of beauty and reality (in the widest possible sense) inherent in the psyche apart from the mind's store of narrative ar-chetypes.

29. Merton, *Conjectures of a Guilty Bystander,* 134 (an earlier version of this passage [Feb. 17, 1958] was included in *Search for Solitude,* 171); Merton, "Symbolism: Com-munication or Communion?" in *Love and Living,* 76; Maritain, *Creative Intuition,* 125–26; see Merton, "Notes on Sacred and Profane Art," 31; Merton, "'Baptism in the Forest,'" in *Literary Essays,* 98; Merton, Apr. 9, 1941, in *Run to the Mountain,* 340; Coo-maraswamy, *Transformation of Nature in Art,* 57; Merton, "Symbolism: Communication or Communion?" in *Love and Living,* 74.

30. Merton to Ernesto Cardenal, May 22, 1962, in *Courage for Truth,* 132.

31. Merton, "Art and Morality," 866.

Here one sees the broad freedom of Merton's approach to art, and one comes to understand his frustration at the conventionalism, narrowness, and staleness of much of the contemporary religious art that he encountered. One sees this freedom as well in his calligraphies and in his notes about them. He described his calligraphies, which were displayed in Louisville and at other galleries in the 1960s, as "ciphers of energy, acts or movements intended to be propitious," cautioning that their meaning was not to be found in "convention" or "concept." They should instead, he suggested, be regarded as "reconciliations," as "expressions of unique and unconscious harmonies appropriate to their own moment though not confined to it." By the same token, they should not, he warned, be associated with particular experiences or events. Nonetheless, he concluded, the calligraphies might still lead the way to "obscure reconciliations and agreements that are not arbitrary—or even to new, intimate histories."[32] Here, Merton pushed the mimetic range of art to the limit, suggesting its capacity to register the finest nuances embedded in the psyche in a way that he implicitly conceded might have struck some as "arbitrary" when such nuances were in fact real, if subtle, emanations of existence.

As well as rejecting any improper extraneous limiting of art, as in a moralistic censoring of art, Merton emphasized the freedom and spontaneity of art, as his calligraphies testify. In his "Message to Poets" he discounted the importance of calculation in preparing the work of art by observing that often the artist discovered the reason for having created the art object only well after its completion. It would seem that there was a personal as well as a theoretical basis for Merton's attraction to spontaneity and immediacy. The struggle that he had undergone in the 1940s and 1950s in which he felt divided by the vocations of contemplative monk and artist led him to use art, notably poetry, as a method of contemplation. In fact, writing to a correspondent in 1961, he described his writing as "meditating on paper."[33] In this light one is tempted to spec-

32. Merton, "Signatures: Notes on the Author's Drawings," in *Raids on the Unspeakable*, 180–81.
33. Merton to Dona Luisa Coomaraswamy, Jan. 13, 1961, in *Hidden Ground of Love*, 127.

ulate about Merton's rather minimal attention to revising, since revising would, one might suppose, tip the balance of his commitment toward the craftsmanship of art rather than toward contemplation. Merton may have seen his poems as opportunities for contemplation whose duration would last as long as the contemplative experience itself did. While any reader of the *Collected Poems* will soon become aware of the unevenness of Merton's poetry, the wonder is that so many of his poems are so accomplished.

Apart from these biographical considerations, however, his general view of poetry was that it captured the inspiration of the moment: "When the poet puts his foot in that ever-moving river," he wrote in "Message to Poets," using the well-known Heraclitean metaphor, "poetry itself is born out of the flashing water." Furthermore, the poet had best enter those rushing waters, he added, without a preordained frame of conventional or collective ideas so as not to risk the precious "immediacy" of poetry. At the same time, he considered symbols to be an entrance to a timeless reality, even if embedded in the linear, narrative structures that often surrounded them in art. The reconciling of the spontaneous and the timeless in the use of symbolism had to do with Merton's belief that perfect form was "momentary," as he put it in *Cables to the Ace* in the late 1960s: "Perfection and emptiness work together for they are the same: the coincidence of momentary form and external nothingness."[34] In choosing the momentary as the matrix of artistic creation, he attempted to maximize the presence of the imagination, the subconscious, and the unconscious and, through their patient uses of time, to minimize the intervention of reason and calculation. In addition, he was attracted to the immediate and spontaneous in art because of his long-standing fascination with surrealism. In this connection one can understand his attraction to Kafka's fiction with its "dream-like, free association dealing with subliminal events."[35] While the surreal might seem to mean that Merton was focused on the exercise of a highly individualized imagination, such was not the case. He regarded the surreal

34. Merton, "Message to Poets," in *Raids on the Unspeakable,* 161; Merton, *Cables to the Ace,* in *Collected Poems,* 421.
35. Merton, June 12, 1967, in *Learning to Love,* 249.

as issuing from a shared psychic substratum and thus as part of the communalizing effect of symbolism. Here again he turned to primitive art, which he maintained had unconsciously yet unerringly pointed the way. In Merton's view primitive art expressed a "deep communion" with all living beings, a sign of a recognition without the benefit of Western revelatory religion of the "ontological and natural principle" that all living things are "metaphysically one."[36]

He consistently stressed the inclusive and unifying effect of art, which he described as bringing together human beings, nature, and God in a "living and sacred synthesis."[37] In this matter he drew on the writings of Paul Tillich, through whom he was in turn introduced to the existentialism of Martin Heidegger. In *The Dynamics of Faith*, Tillich had underlined the role of the symbol in bridging the gap between subject and object, thereby foreshadowing Merton's view of symbolism as fostering a community of being. Here Merton also followed in the steps of the romantics, especially Blake, in highlighting the difference between the action of simile, with its implied separateness of things, and that of symbol, with its implied unity.[38] Thus, he suggested to Louis Zukofsky in 1967 that modern poetry should acknowledge both the physical and the symbolic resonance of experience, that one could do this, he had concluded, without sacrificing either the palpable singularity of the world or its broad ontological meanings.[39]

Symbolism was just one aspect of art's unifying effect in Merton's view. In a remarkable, posthumously published poem written in the late 1960s titled "The Originators," he outlined an aspect of the unity of artist and reader or spectator that would have surprised many:

> Because I chose to hear a special thunder in my head
> Or to see an occipital light my choice
> Suddenly became another's fate
> He lost all his wheels
> Or found himself flying.

36. Merton, "Symbolism: Communication or Communion?" in *Love and Living*, 71, 73.
37. Ibid., 60.
38. See Furst, *Romanticism in Perspective*, 186.
39. Merton to Zukofsky, May 5, 1967, in *Courage for Truth*, 293.

And when the other's nerve ends crowed and protested
In the tame furies of a business gospel
His feeling was my explosion
So I skidded off his stone head
Blind as a bullet
But found I was wearing his hat.[40]

Merton's dramatic picturing of the reciprocal relationship between poet and reader is here expressed in some momentous symbols, notably that of the bullet. He pictured himself writing out of his monastic seclusion yet influencing and being influenced by others. While the bullet is part of an innocuous circus motif, its startling and independent appearance as a symbol allows the reader to understand that Merton could not limit the emotional and social effect of his poetry on others, that that poetry might well have produced revolutionaries who spilled real blood, just as the revolutionaries beyond the monastic enclosure might well, through their fiery writings, have radicalized him. Merton thought that poets and artists, because of their awareness of the subconscious, were more likely than many to be responsive to signs of revolutionary ferment in their society.

More typical of his approach to the unifying effect of art was his perception of art as a fount of wisdom. In Merton's reckoning, poetic myth and "religious or archetypal symbol" were the natural venues of wisdom or what he generally called sapiential thought.[41] Placing his writing in this context, he believed that he had no "proprietorship" over his articulated thoughts, which were not originally or exclusively his, he insisted, and that even if they appeared to be his, they were not given just to him. It is important to interpret this as an example not of modesty on Merton's part but rather of his identification, not unlike Walt Whitman's, with the power that flowed through all human beings, some of whom were more articulate and intense than others. Thus, his writing expressed his connection to and communion with the world around him as readily and boldly as if he had fled his order and immersed himself in

40. Merton, "The Originators," in *Collected Poems*, 613.
41. Merton, "'Baptism in the Forest,'" in *Literary Essays*, 100.

the world beyond the monastic walls. In terms of Merton's relationship with the outside world, art made possible a kind of squaring of the circle, a series of "authentically personal images" that nevertheless grew out of a "common participation" in existence, as he put it in a prefatory note to *The Geography of Lograire*. Epitomizing this sort of thinking, he wrote to a Latin American correspondent in 1966 that no poet really matured until he or she had become "everybody."[42]

In addition to being someone who was conversant in a number of languages—English, French, and Spanish, to name a few—Merton was naturally conscious of the importance of language in art. He was at the same time interested in both clarity, a feature that characterized all of his prose writing, and inventiveness, which especially characterized his poetic writing. He conceived of language as a pliable, dynamic medium capable of enormous power in the hands of a good artist and a medium that linked the artist to all of being. Indeed, in Merton's eyes the whole world, including nature, was capable of speaking. This can be seen, for example, in his early poem "The Dark Morning," in which the narrator both watches and listens attentively to the "thin sentences" of the rain. The language of nature made Merton aware of the organic characteristics of language, and he bristled at the thought of a set of rules circumscribing language, preventing its leaping creatively into new forms. He thought of language as growing in the "same way as a tree, spreading out into the light." Following this sequence of thought, he described the language of art in an essay titled "Poetry, Symbolism, and Typology," published in 1953, as part of a "vital reactivity" wherein the words that had been placed next to each other by the artist released their associations to produce a new experience and a fresh perception of reality.[43]

Given such high expectations, Merton was disillusioned by the saturation of Western culture by institutional language, as is revealed in his long poem *Cables to the Ace*. He thought of this saturation as a smother-

---

42. Merton, "Author's Note," in *The Geography of Lograire*, in *Collected Poems*, 457; Merton to Ludovico Silva, Jan. 17, 1966, in *Courage for Truth*, 228.

43. Merton, "The Dark Morning," in *Collected Poems*, 29; Merton, Nov. 2, 1939, in *Run to the Mountain*, 83; Merton, "Poetry, Symbolism, and Typology," in *Literary Essays*, 327.

ing of the possibilities of language, and he noted in an essay published in 1969 titled "War and the Crisis of Language" that his own church appeared to have abandoned, at least in its liturgical language, the high eloquence of its own traditional discourse.[44] While Merton was open to inventiveness, he did not advocate replacing a sublime use of language with a banal one simply in order to modernize, as it seemed to him his church had done after the Second Vatican Council in the mid-1960s. Like George Orwell, Merton thought that public, particularly political, language in contemporary society had been corrupted by self-serving, ambiguous institutional jargon. In particular, in contrast to the opportunity that art perennially provided to deepen the capacity of language to represent experience, he regarded technological culture as having narrowed that capacity, as he indicated in a poem titled "Tower of Babel." In that poem the lofty potential of language is depicted as having been debased so as to permit language to adapt itself to

> first the machine,
> Then what the machine produces
> Then what the machine destroys.[45]

Continuing, Merton considered with alarm that in the West such technological discourse was all one had at hand to construct a picture of reality. This was language created by an uncritical, scientific enthusiasm to produce a version of "history" that, used as propaganda, would constrict and eventually destroy a more comprehensive and cogent version of history. Although "Tower of Babel" was an early poem, Merton continued to sound the alarm in a similarly titled verse play in *The Strange Islands* in the 1950s and in *Cables to the Ace* in the 1960s. In *Cables to the Ace*, in Orwellian fashion, he depicted the "Relaxed war-gods" as unlocking the newest "ministry of doors / With capital letters."[46] With associational imaging Merton juxtaposed the abstract and ponderous language of the military with the image of doors, rigidly fixed passages

---

44. Merton, "War and the Crisis of Language," in *The Nonviolent Alternative,* 236.
45. Merton, "Tower of Babel," in *Collected Poems,* 21–22.
46. Merton, *Cables to the Ace,* in ibid., 404.

that controlled the shape and mass of everything that passed through them.

Against such a social and cultural background Merton saw himself as an artist as having to devise a plan of escape, and he did so in the 1960s after reading Latin American writers such as Nicanor Parra and after having become familiar with Zen koans. In both cases he saw that language could be used reflexively and irreverently to construct a critique of itself and thus to liberate the mind from the numbing effect of collective and particularly of institutional discourse. He regarded writers such as Parra, Ionesco, and Brecht as having uncluttered the language landscape, as it were, sweeping away the rotten, hackneyed forms that many had haplessly begun to confuse with reality. Apart from the purging effect of irony, another approach to revitalizing language, he believed, was to use it creatively. In this connection one remembers that his first intention for his most famous work, *The Seven Storey Mountain,* was to have written the book in poetic prose, as he subsequently confided to his friend and publisher James Laughlin. Similar to a number of the romantic writers, he gravitated toward poetic prose or prose poetry in a reaction against the artificiality of the division between them and of the consequent loss of power to the writer who bowed to such an artificial division. In fact, Merton declared to a group of Anglican seminarians on one occasion that he liked best those of his poems that were "prosaic." In the late 1960s he became interested in "found" poetry, the use of existing phrasing, including prose, for poetic purposes, although he made it clear in a working notebook in 1967 that even such found poetry inevitably involved artistic selection. He employed such "found" poetry extensively throughout *The Geography of Lograire.*[47]

As a contemplative and artist Merton was fastidiously aware of the relationship between language and silence, having confided to Lisa Bieberman in 1967 that the relationship was one with which he had grappled for some time. He told her that, even in a nonartistic context,

47. Merton to Laughlin, Mar. 1, 1946, in *Thomas Merton and James Laughlin: Selected Letters,* 10; Merton to Anglican seminarians, Nov. 11, 1963, in *Road to Joy,* 329; see Merton, Working Notebook no. 26 (Feb.–Mar. 1967), n.p., Merton Collection, Bellarmine University.

as a first step it was important not to become too anxious to communicate and to be understood and justified.[48] Merton's valuing of silence as a contemplative in a sense put him in an antagonistic relationship to language and even to his own poetry, since even unspoken language could interfere with the ineffable atmosphere of contemplation. Immersed in silence the contemplative learned to make crucial distinctions that could be blurred in society at large where one easily lost sight of the sharp contours of experience in an environment saturated with noise and clutter. In the 1960s Merton read with enthusiasm George Steiner's book, *Language and Silence*, in which Steiner lamented the decay of language, especially in the public sphere, arguing that literacy had to be re-begun.

In *Cables to the Ace* (1968), Merton in a postmodernist fashion deconstructed institutional and collective discourse in order to reduce it to silence. The reason was that he perceived this language as having appropriated even the expression of emotional states and of the subjective life generally, thereby eclipsing the reality of the self. Following the linguistic maelstrom of *Cables to the Ace*, *The Geography of Lograire* (1969) reflects a regained use of language as intentional and meaningful, even if much of the language had been lifted from existing texts. *The Geography of Lograire* is a modernist poem, and as such combines verbal inventiveness with an assumption that language is fundamentally meaningful even if subject to abuse. The fact that Merton's long modernist poem followed his long postmodernist poem was not unusual in the case of someone whose relationship to literary history could be idiosyncratic. Of course, he had not been thoroughly a postmodernist in *Cables to the Ace* since he was ultimately hopeful about the possibility of noninstitutional and noncollective language being revitalized and renewed.

His most constructive approach to the problem of the hegemonic control of language by institutional and collective discourse was to rely on silence to withhold language until only the most significant utterance emerged.[49] Although this was Merton's position, one has to recognize

48. Merton to Bieberman, Apr. 15, 1967, in *Road to Joy*, 351–52.
49. See Merton, Working Notebook no. 34 (Dec. 30 [1967]), n.p., Merton Collection, Bellarmine University. See also Lynn Szabo, "The Sound of Sheer Silence: A Study in the Poetics of Thomas Merton."

that he wrote voluminously in various literary and nonliterary forms throughout most of his life. However, in his finest writings he was acutely sensitive to the balancing of silence and sound, and he praised such balance when he found it elsewhere. He marveled at the Gregorian chant with its restraint and pools of silence between the notes, its ability to lead the soul, as he put it, into the "infinitely more beautiful silence of God."[50] In connection with Dante's *Paradiso*, George Steiner made a similar suggestion about the power of language and silence to draw the soul upward. In the *Paradiso*, he wrote, words grew "less and less adequate to the task of translating immediate revelation. Light passes to a diminishing degree into speech; instead of making syntax translucent with meaning, it seems to spill over in unrecapturable splendor or burn the word to ash." In this sort of artistic context, instead of seeing language as the enemy as he had in connection with institutional discourse, Merton celebrated silence as the "mother of speech," noting that a "lifetime of silence" might in certain felicitous circumstances give rise to an "ultimate declaration" of "all we have lived for."[51]

Like Steiner, Merton turned toward the music of language in the case of poetic language not intended to be ironic. It was the music that drew Merton to Louis Zukofsky's poetry, music that he regarded as an axis between silence and sound. Sometimes sound could be used by the poet to punctuate and therefore to make the reader aware of the ocean of silence available to human beings, as in Ernesto Cardenal's poetry where, according to Merton, Cardenal injected the sounds of racing cars and trains into his poetry in order to point up the surrounding silence and loneliness. Similarly, within the modified life of contemplation that one could attempt even in mainstream society, Merton reflected in 1966 that one should listen not to the repeated phrases but to the language of the void, language that was neither spoken nor heard. On the other hand, as he acknowledged in a note that he wrote in connection with his verse play "The Tower of Babel," the restored unity that as a contemplative and artist he sought for all humanity depended not only on silence but also on the ability of human beings to "communicate the truth" to one

50. Merton, "In Silentio," in *Silence in Heaven*, 26.
51. Steiner, *Language and Silence*, 40; Merton, *No Man Is an Island*, 258.

another. In Merton's play a character who obviously has the support of the author says: "You must discover new words reborn out of an old time / Like new seeds from an old harvest." With such a hope in mind the people of the village, somewhat reminiscent of those in Keats's "Ode on a Grecian Urn," gather for a festival, flanked by houses that are dressed in "flags and vines." Furthermore, when they sing together, their song signifies that the "people are one."[52]

In large measure Merton's ideas about art and the imagination stemmed from romanticism, notably his central conception of the artist as seer. As a contemplative he regarded mysticism as analogous to art, commenting in an essay on art and morality that the work of art tended to "clarify" the "intelligence and heart" and that the experience of art was thus analogous to the "purity of religious contemplation." In addition, in "The Inner Experience" he noted that the language of the mystics was always "poetic."[53] Both art and mysticism in Merton's view drew on the imagination to carry the mind past the frontiers of the material world, though not past the actual world unless one chose to define the actual solely in empirical terms. As has been suggested, for Merton the imagination made possible the visualizing not only of alternate worlds of possibility but also of actual latencies and realities immanent and undisclosed in present reality and being. The cognitive value of the imagination lay in its ability to perceive a world in which unity replaced fragmentation both within the self and in the relationship of the self to others and to the cosmos. Such imaginative discernment Merton found in contemplatives such as the Rhineland mystics of the fourteenth century. Where art in Merton's view differed somewhat from mystical contemplation was in the creative role played by the imagination, the making of things by the artist as part of a shared participation in the original and sustained creativity of God. In this way both the artist and the imaginatively engaged reader or spectator discovered aspects of reality dis-

52. Merton, "Ernesto Cardenal," in *Literary Essays,* 324; Merton, Nov. 13, 1966, in *Learning to Love,* 160–61; Merton, "The Tower of Babel: An Explanation," in *Words and Silence: On the Poetry of Thomas Merton,* by Thérèse Lentfoehr, 154; Merton, "The Tower of Babel," in *Collected Poems,* 266–67.

53. Merton, "Art and Morality," 865; Merton, "The Inner Experience: Notes on Contemplation," 12.

cernible only through such creation. Furthermore, the created art object provided the reader or spectator with a concrete and enduring form, a symbol, that could provide each generation with a pathway to the spiritual and ontological realities that the artist had discerned.

Given his indebtedness to romanticism with its elevated, prophetic view of the artist, what is remarkable and distinct about Merton was his judgment that the artist should enjoy no special status, indeed that the artist was not only primarily a member of the human community but also through his or her art a builder of that community. Here one sees the inclusiveness of Merton's vision whereby the artist as an individual was seen to possess an innate ontological majesty and at the same time an indissoluble involvement in the whole human community. The two different views of art were accommodated by Merton's perception that if the artist had heard the music of the spheres, that music had its origin in a God who both created the music in the first place and recorded it for all time, so to speak, in the human psyche.

7

Myth and Culture

In a flourish of ideas contained in an unpublished notebook written in 1968 shortly before his death, Merton had concluded that the notion that human beings could live without myths was untenable and was simply another example of mythmaking.[1] He was conscious of the fact that in some periods of history, in particular in a scientific and empirical age, one could easily overlook the presence of the governing myths underlying a culture ostensibly committed to objectivity. He understood myths, or "mythdreams" as he frequently called them, to be clusters of ideas, including ontological and theological ideas, experiences, dreams, and desires about the total environment that found expression in each culture's narratives about itself. More formally, he defined myth as an "imaginative synthesis of facts and intuitions about them, forming an interpretive complex of ideas and images."[2] He not only understood myths to convey information or knowledge about a culture's picture of itself but also, more important perhaps, perceived a hierarchy of values within myths that became the basis of motivation for the members of a particular culture. Thus, those within an ostensibly scientific and rational culture such as that in the West would be motivated to act accordingly. In support of Merton's thesis one could cite the case of T. S. Eliot, who, although intellectually steeped in a humanist tradition, shaped his influ-

1. See Merton, Working Notebook no. 43 (1968), n.p., Merton Collection, Bellarmine University.
2. Merton, "Godless Christianity?" in *Faith and Violence*, 274.

ential essays about literature in a neoscientific manner so as to secure authority for them in a culture driven by a scientific ethos. Perhaps because he was opposed to the prevailing mythdreams of technology and progress, Merton was especially sensitive to the effects of sidestepping the prevailing mythdreams of a particular culture. He observed, for example, that when one entered the public arena with ideas and discourse that had not grown out of the culture's central mythdream, the language and themes simply sounded dead, and failed to attract attention. Fortunately, Merton believed, the prevailing mythdreams in the West had not quite obliterated the earlier mythdreams of Western culture—including those embedded in romanticism.

As a writer, and particularly as a poet, Merton fashioned myths of his own so as to construct a world in which new clusters of experiences, dreams, and values might compete with the dominant mythdream. One of the most ambitious of these mythdreams was that which Merton created in his large poem *The Geography of Lograire,* in the late 1960s. In that poem, as his friend Sister Thérèse Lentfoehr has indicated, Merton created a multicultural world parallel to that which existed in the world of realpolitik. On a smaller scale he frequently incorporated established myths in his writings in order to acclimatize his readers to myth and to the power of myth in the history of culture. An example is the poem "Fall, '66" in which he alluded to the myth of King Arthur, drawing meaning not only from the folk sources of the Arthurian legend but also from the Arthurian myth as filtered through literature, in this case Milton's poem "Mansus."[3] The effect of this was to trace the accumulated meaning of myth as it evolved through cultural history. He related the human need for beneficial cultural myths not merely to psychological and sociological but to the ontological and theological dimensions of human life as well. At the same time, although Merton recognized the value of scholars who had shown the myths in Genesis to be similar to other such myths in the religions of the Middle East, he was less interested in comparative religion than in the common myth, rooted in the psyche, that underlay these various religious myths.

3. Merton to Robert Barton, Aug. 11, 1967, in *Road to Joy,* 357.

In an effort to distinguish profound mythdreams from what he thought of as more superficial collective daydreams, Merton focused on the American space dream of the 1960s, a dream that he characterized as artificial and damaging primarily because it deflected attention away from more important mythdreams that were profoundly connected to human happiness. In the early 1960s he critiqued the dream of outer space in his poem "Why Some Look Up to Planets and Heroes" in *Emblems of a Season of Fury*. Analogously, in Merton's view, the shallow waters of the American consumer daydream, which marginalized deeper realities, had to be distinguished from the more fertile, complex, and archetypal depths of the common mythdream that underlay consumerism. The genuine mythdream was like an ocean on which the whole superstructure of culture floated, including, in the case of the West, for example, its logical and scientific discourse. This underlying mythdream with its wealth of imaginative energy implicitly called for a wider understanding of the role of the imagination and of the unconscious in culture, especially in cultures that tended to be dismissive about the imagination and the unconscious. Having severed its connection with its religious and sapiential traditions, traditions that had favored the interior life, Western culture had in Merton's view been left with a vacuum that had been uncritically filled by mythdreams that were the products of inferior imaginations.

Because he regarded himself as someone who, because of his wide interests, could move from one mythdream to another, Merton felt an unexpected closeness to the mythdreams of cultures ostensibly quite different from his own, such as that which underlay the cargo cults of the South Pacific. In the cargo cults Merton was primarily interested not in analysis but in synthesis, in the search for a "*common mythdream*" shared by all human beings.[4] Thus, he interpreted the cargo cult not simply as an attempt to gain material prosperity, a relatively shallow collective daydream as he would have termed it, but rather as driven by the common human longing for equity, the desire to be accorded the same value as other human beings. In connection with the cargo cults Merton regard-

4. See Edward Rice, *The Man in the Sycamore Tree*, 149.

ed his vocation as a solitary and a contemplative as a way of trying to circumvent the magnetism of the American mythdream and so open himself to the mythdreams of other cultures. In this respect he felt a kinship with those such as Gandhi, who, in reading the Westerner Henry David Thoreau, paradoxically rediscovered his own Eastern and Hindu traditions. So had Merton rediscovered his Western mysticism by acquainting himself with Buddhism, thereby becoming conscious of elements in Christianity that he believed he might not otherwise have noticed.[5] The effect was not only to add to his sense of the meaning of Christianity but also to make him aware of a larger religious reality in which both Christianity and Hinduism participated.

The most important work that exemplified Merton's commitment to intercultural understanding was his large poem *The Geography of Lograire* (1969), the poem that more than any other has attracted interest in academic circles in recent years. In this modernist, structuralist poem Merton drew on a variety of historical and anthropological sources in order to attempt to paint a picture of a common mythdream in which human beings wanted to be valued by one another. Dividing the poem into the four quadrants of the compass, Merton moved out imaginatively from his own mythdream with its personal figures and themes into the mythdreams of others, both individual and collective. The prologue to *The Geography of Lograire,* with its plethora of juxtaposed, often quasi-surreal images, reminds one of Hart Crane's proem to *The Bridge.* Crane was a favorite poet of Merton's, and he especially liked the ambiguous and suggestive open-endedness of Crane's metaphors and symbols. Merton wanted his own long poem to be an open project, rather like Pound's *Cantos* or Whitman's *Leaves of Grass,* a poem without end and beginning and without inhibiting spatial boundaries. In this way, in the North and South sections of *The Geography of Lograire,* Merton's personal mythdream flows into the collective mythdreams of other individuals and cultures and then out into a space into which others, including the reader, are invited. The poem is therefore, and this is where its structuralism is pertinent, a dialogic instrument for exploring cultural myths. In the words of the prologue to the North section of the poem:

5. See Merton, "Gandhi and the One-Eyed Giant," in *Gandhi on Non-Violence,* 3–4.

Geography.
I am all (here)
There![6]

In the South section of the poem, the quadrant in which Merton was living when he wrote the poem, he moves outward from Gethsemani and Kentucky to the American South and thence to what might have been seen as the very different cultures and mythdreams of Latin America and Africa. Each of the transitions in culture is signaled by a change in discourse as well as in subject matter so that the reader's initial impression is one of uncertainty, though increasingly not of confusion, as the poem's themes of unity and inclusiveness take root.

At a formal level Merton tied the sections of the sequence to one other by the use of a unifying motif: in the case of the South section, for example, that of eating. In the poem "Miami You Are about to Be Surprised," the population of south Florida, a place synonymous with pleasure, is advised: "You are going to be warned / By a gourmet with a mouthful of seaweed."[7] The gourmet in question is a tropical hurricane, a frequent visitor to Florida's shores. Here the hurricane appears as a mythical sea creature, an apocalyptic Poseidon bringing catastrophe to a hedonistic America.

The Miami poem, part 4 of the South section, is followed by "Thonga Lament," which is set in South Africa. The Bantu people are portrayed as trying to placate the gods of their ancestors, whom they regarded as divine and as capable of dooming them with a curse:

> You gave me life O Father
> But now you are gone
> Now you are secret
> Living in famous tunnels
> (But where?)
> Let us eat together in peace
> Let us not disagree
> That I and my children

6. Merton, *Geography of Lograire*, in *Collected Poems*, 498.
7. Ibid., 474.

> May live long here outside
> Out here in the air
> Without coughing or swaying
> Or losing balance and falling
> Into the tunnels.[8]

The motif of eating is here used to placate the cosmic forces at large so as not to incur their wrath. Merton juxtaposed the self-confident hubris of those in Florida with the insecurity of the Bantu to create the unexpected effect whereby the relatively primitive African culture is seen to exhibit a superior wisdom in not expecting the best of everything. Thus, the technological mastery of American culture is morally critiqued not only from within but also from without, from the viewpoint of a quite different culture, a culture with which an advanced culture might not ordinarily choose to identify itself. Through Merton's structuralist form the flow of meaning from one culture to the other occurs implicitly without the need for authorial comment.

Later, in part 5 of the South section of *The Geography of Lograire*, Merton focused on a Hottentot folktale, which again involved eating. In this tale a message sent by Moongod to human beings had been perversely altered by Hare so that instead of being told to hope for eternal life, human beings were left with a dismal message about the finality of mortality. Angered, Moongod cursed the hare and forbade the eating of it. Because of the mythic symbolism of eating as an assimilative, uniting activity, this exclusion of Hare symbolizes a kind of banishment or hell. The connection of the tale to Western culture occurs partly through the universality of the mythic form itself, the trickster tale, but more important through the mythic theme of the suppression of immortality and of paradise. In part 6 Merton reversed the point of view, showing the Bantu from the point of view of an actual white American missionary, W. C. Willoughby. Willoughby had been a professor of missions in Africa at the Kennedy School of Missions in Hartford, Connecticut. In his book he is revealed to have been a bigot not only with regard to aboriginal Africans but also toward Catholics and Buddhists, among oth-

8. Ibid., 475.

ers. The eating motif appears here in the form of medicinal salts that the missionary administered to those of the Bantu who, having converted to Christianity, went on to experience visions, an aberration that, in Willoughby's view, was efficiently curtailed by the administering of salts. Here, as with Hare, the food is not spiritually nourishing—nor is the condescending form of Christianity that it represents.[9]

In the subsequent "Notes for a New Liturgy," the food motif is more oblique, appearing in the form of strangled chickens in a ludicrous, hybrid liturgy that combined ancient tribal and Christian elements. The speaker for most of this section is a black African, Western-educated minister who moves easily and cynically from one religious mythology to the other but always with his social status and power as his major concern. Here again, Merton's source is important in throwing light on the dynamics of this section. In Bengt G. M. Sundkler's *Bantu Prophets in South Africa* (1961), the author observed that in South African society where the social status of the black was ordinarily inferior, ministerial positions in the church offered an opportunity for higher social status, even though only a handful of Bantu churches were recognized by the government. In Sundkler's view, in native African churches there existed a strong ambivalence toward the white people of Africa, with "opposition on the one hand, and on the other a desire to copy them and to demonstrate they can do as well as the Whites."[10] Merton's satirical treatment of the black religious leader focused on his absurdity, and might be mistaken by some readers for a racist treatment of black Africans. Merton exposed the absurdity of the black minister in part because he wanted to bring out the travesty that resulted when one culture borrowed superficially from another. In this case the superficiality amounted to a distortion brought about by the example of Western missionaries such as W. C. Willoughby. In *The Geography of Lograire*, Merton demonstrated that cultural borrowing was going on all the time, often with more lamentable consequences than if contact with another culture had not been made in the first place.

9. See Willoughby, *The Soul of the Bantu*, 112. Merton dealt freely with his source here, although Willoughby did write of using cathartics to deal with suspected cases of demonic possession.

10. Sundkler, *Bantu Prophets in South Africa*, 106–7.

Nevertheless, although fraught with pitfalls, intercultural contacts, Merton believed, offered the possibility of experiencing one's humanity in a new and valuable sense. This, at any rate, would seem to apply to part 8 of the South section of *The Geography of Lograire*, "Ce Xochitl: The Sign of Flowers," which centers on an important myth underlying Mexican culture. Here, the food imagery is connected with the fragrant god Xochipilli, the "Flower-Giver." Those participating in his feast, the reader is instructed, took their corn soup with a flower "Floating in the middle."[11] The beauty of the ritualistic dance celebrating the god Xochipilli is interrupted by a vulgar comment from a bishop who had regarded the precolonial religions as demonic. The bishop is portrayed by Merton as unable to see the richness of the culture before him and as therefore doomed to remain imprisoned not only within the narrow boundaries of his own culture but also within a superficial understanding of that culture.

The eating motif in the "Chilam Balam" part of the South division of *The Geography of Lograire* has to do with the burning of the maize of the Mayans, the staple of their diet, by the conquering Christians from Spain:

> With brimming tears
> We mourn our lost writings
> The burned books
> The burned men
> The flaming harvests
> Holy maize destroyed
> Teachings of heaven and earth
> Destroyed.[12]

In the caricaturist style of the great Mexican painter Diego Rivera, Merton portrayed the invasion of the Spanish missionaries as being as grotesque as that of their armies, obliterating forever the magisterial record of a culture that was, in Merton's view, in many ways superior to their own. Merton captures the dying Mayans movingly, elegiacally

---

11. Merton, *Geography of Lograire*, in *Collected Poems*, 480.
12. Ibid., 492.

recording their brutal exit from human history in a pageant of intercultural barbarism that becomes a bitter part of a larger theme of the ecology of culture in *The Geography of Lograire.* In the midst of this ecology was Merton's cultural accounting, his listing of many of those cultures that had all but disappeared from human memory, a loss that reaches poignantly into the emotional center of the poem.

The culture that most preoccupied Merton throughout his life was, not unexpectedly, that of the United States. In spite of the number of occasions on which, bristling under the strains of monastic institutionalism in the 1950s and 1960s, he thought of uprooting himself and living outside his adopted country, he regarded the United States as the most powerful and most influential country in the world and for this reason became increasingly determined to help in the shaping of its moral character and influence. He resolved to help to transform an America that mistakenly considered itself Christian into an America that actually was Christian. Merton's European background and his admiration for Latin American culture helped to create a critical distance between himself and his adopted country, thereby facilitating what has generally been acknowledged as his penetrating moral analyses of American culture. In his early writings he focused on America as a lustrous example of cultural promise and hope. In the early poem "Three Postcards from the Monastery" in *Figures for an Apocalypse,* for example, he asked rhetorically: "Who shall amaze us with the noise of your discovery, America? / Who shall make known to us your new, true name . . . ?"[13] Hidden away in the heart of the continent, Merton would make known America's *true* name, a name that he regarded as ideally synonymous with creational beauty.

Typical of Merton's early freshly optimistic observations about America were those recorded in his evocative Whitmanesque poem "A Letter to America," which appeared in *Figures for an Apocalypse:*

> America, when you were born, and when the plains
> Spelled out their miles of praises in the sun
> What glory and what history
> The rivers seemed to prepare.

13. Merton, "Three Postcards from the Monastery," in ibid., 154.

Buoyantly confident, the speaker proclaims the glory and history of America: "We hear them, now, in the Kentucky summer."[14]

When Merton was in the process of becoming a citizen of the United States in 1951, he approached the matter seriously, noting in his journal in February that citizens ought to recognize that they owed something to their country and that the United States was certainly "worth loving." On the evening before he became a citizen in June, he melted into his Kentucky surroundings with an awakened feeling of belonging to his adopted country that seemed heightened by the blazing sunset over the wooded hills, a "triumphant fire" that served as a sort of "anticipated celebration." In *The Seven Storey Mountain* he lyrically described his growing love for the landscape and for the continent to which he had pledged himself: "Oh, America, how I began to love your country! What miles of silences God has made in you for contemplation!" In another passage he described the American landscape as "big, vast, generous, fertile, and leading beyond itself into limitless expanses, open spaces." It was the American *land* that especially captured Merton's loyalty and passion, and he noted in his journal in September 1962 that "this is my place." When in October 1960 Merton visited the sisters of Loretto in an old Kentucky foundation that with its redolent suggestiveness of the "hundred Kentucky summers that had been lived in that building by nuns and the winters also," he felt utterly at home. It was the pristine character of much of the American landscape that attracted Merton, as in his initial response to the Abbey of Gethsemani as the only "real city" in America, a city in the "wilderness." Identifying himself with his fellow citizens, in 1964 he wrote to Jim Frost, a high school student, saying that "we Americans ought to love our land, our forests, our plains, and we ought to do everything we can to preserve it in its richness and beauty, by respect for our natural resources, for water, for land, for wild life."[15]

14. Merton, "A Letter to America," in ibid., 151–52.

15. Merton, Feb. 28, 1951, in *Entering the Silence*, 450; Merton, June 13, 1951, in ibid., 460; Merton, *The Seven Storey Mountain*, 310, 319; Merton, Sept. 6, 1962, in *Turning toward the World*, 244; Merton, Oct. 2, 1960, in ibid., 54; Merton, *The Secular Journal of Thomas Merton*, 183. In the original unedited journal Merton had written: "This is the only real city in America—in a desert" (Apr. 7, 1941, in *Run to the Mountain*, 333). Merton to Frost, Jan. 7, 1964, in *Road to Joy*, 330.

As Whitman had done, Merton identified in the United States moral qualities that he believed distinguished the best of the new world's emerging culture. Writing in his journal in May 1960 about a small book on racial segregation by Robert Penn Warren, he noted that Warren had taken a "typical American approach," which added up to "something decent" and reflected a "concern for reality," the reality of the South to which, as Merton put it, "I belong." On another occasion, writing to James Morrissey, the editor of the *Louisville Courier-Journal*, in November 1965, he described the American character as "tolerant and fair" and backed by a heritage of "open-mindedness." Similarly, in a letter to Susan Neer in December 1963, he criticized the attacks by white Catholics against black Catholics in Louisiana, calling for his fellow citizens to live up to "our American and Christian heritage of independent thought, devotion to justice and truth, fair mindedness, and fair play." Whereas Merton had balked at the stifling stratification of English society, he praised the ideals of egalitarianism embedded in American cultural history. Furthermore, while his disdain for American cities was almost generic, he was prepared to admit exceptions, as in the following entry in his journal in October 1960: "I renew my respect for the beauty and character of Cincinnati, its wide river, its hills, its misty views, its sudden corners. It is a good and real city."[16]

When Merton thought about the United States in a positive light, it was often about its earlier history. In late August and early September 1961 he wrote in his journal about his pleasure at hearing a biography of Lincoln read at refectory, remarking that America in those days was a "different country." Similarly, in 1961 he wrote to William Carlos Williams regretting the unfaithfulness of contemporary Americans to what he called the "original American grace." A particular focus of Merton's attraction to an earlier America was his respect for Thoreau, whose influence he acknowledged in a letter to Harry J. Cargas in 1966 when he observed that in his hermitage he was living a "Walden-like sort of life." He was particularly attracted to Thoreau, he added, as a "bridge builder" between East and West and by Thoreau's having expressed the

16. Merton, May 18, 1960, in *Search for Solitude*, 391; Merton to Morrissey, Nov. 21, 1965, in *Witness to Freedom*, 114; Merton to Neer, Dec. 22, 1963, in *Road to Joy*, 330; Merton, Oct. 28, 1960, in *Turning toward the World*, 61.

"real spirit of American personalism and freedom," its openness and readiness to "'listen to a different drummer.'" In 1962 Merton had written to Henry Miller saying that Thoreau was one of the reasons he had felt justified in becoming an American citizen. Thoreau symbolized for Merton that which he could not so easily find in European thought, a romantic consciousness that not only privileged the self but also, in an extension of this privileging of the self, embraced political dissent. In an essay in *Seeds of Destruction* he praised Thoreau as a nonconformist who seemed to "have believed that the American revolution had either misfired or had never really taken place."[17]

Merton's elegiac sense of the unfulfilled promise of America is evident in his poem "Christopher Columbus," which was part of the sterling collection *The Tears of the Blind Lions* (1949). Here, with long Whitmanesque lines Merton attempted to paint the idealized American mythdream in such a way that a contrasting awareness of its effacement in the twentieth century would be keenly felt:

> Suddenly the great Christ-bearing Columbus rises in the sea
> Spilling the green Atlantic from his shoulders
> And sees America through a veil of waters.
> Steam things low like cattle all around him in the rivers.
> Towers stand like churches on the rock, in a garden of
>   boats;
> Citizens look up like snap-dragons
> Crowding the streets and galleries and saluting heaven with
>   their songs.
> Music comes cascading down the stones until all walls
> Are singing the feasts of the saints in the light of
>   processions.[18]

With a deft use of superimposition, Merton portrays Columbus as Saint Christopher and as a mythic Poseidon striding into history with a vision

17. Merton, Aug. 27, 1961, in *Turning toward the World,* 156; Merton to Williams, Apr. 6, 1961, in *Courage for Truth,* 289; Merton to Cargas, Feb. 14, 1966, in *Witness to Freedom,* 171; Merton to Miller, Aug. 7, 1962, in *Courage for Truth,* 277; Merton, *Seeds of Destruction,* 75.
18. Merton, "Christopher Columbus," in *Collected Poems,* 207.

of the future in which the cultural riches of European Christianity were introduced into the garden of the New World. The actual future that materialized, however, turned out to be a lesser and paler place:

> And now the cities' eyes are tight as ice
> When the long cars stream home in nights of autumn. . . .
> But the children sing no hymn for the feast of Saint Columbus.
> They watch the long, long armies drifting home.[19]

In the turbulent 1960s Merton felt that he had a distinctive objectivity to bring to the problems of America because of his hybrid cultural background. He believed that he had been indelibly formed by Europe. He spoke about this aspect of his personal history in *The Seven Storey Mountain* when he described his return to Europe in 1925 as a return to the "fountains of the intellectual and spiritual life of the world to which I belonged," adding that it was France that grew the "finest flowers of delicacy and grace and intelligence and wit and understanding and proportion and taste." In August 1961 he reflected in his journal that the tone and value of his interior world had been created by "Christian and European culture," a culture quite different from that of the New World. Similarly, in *The Seven Storey Mountain* he recalled with pleasure that his attraction to the Abbey of Gethsemani had been related to its Europeanness, its architecture and culture being a statement that there was still something of the "bravery and simplicity and freshness of twelfth-century devotion, the vivid faith of St. Bernard of Clairvaux and Adam of Perseigne and Guerric of Igny and Ailred of Rievaulx and Robert of Molesme, here in the hills of Kentucky." Nevertheless, he concluded in his journal in 1967 that if in coming to a Trappist monastery in Kentucky he had come to a place with strong European roots, then this connection soon faded under Dom James Fox, whose cultural style was distinctly American. All the same, he was able to sustain his Europeanness by his friendship with those such as the Austrian American artist Victor Hammer, whose European culture Merton found "stabilizing" in contrast to what he regarded as the instability of American culture. More-

19. Ibid., 209.

192 Thomas Merton and the Inclusive Imagination

over, even though he had become an American citizen some years earlier, in 1956 he declared both himself and the expatriate novelist Julien Green, with whom he had been corresponding, to be essentially French.[20]

Merton's valuing of Europe reflected his cultural conservatism. Writing in his journal in August 1961 he praised the rhetoric of Saint Ambrose that had about it, he observed, a "solid dramatic quality," adding that the hymn melodies meant more and more to him because of their "European" quality. He also valued Europe because of its beneficial conservatism, its treasuring of a past associated with the development of Western culture, a past that appeared to be treated dismissively in the United States. In a comment in his journal in the summer of 1964 he indicated that Evelyn Waugh, whom he regarded as a quintessential European, wished to conserve "not what might be lost but what is not even threatened because it vanished long ago." Merton added that contemporary American conservatism as represented by Senator Goldwater in the 1960s, on the other hand, had ironically lent a hand to the "more rapid and efficacious destruction of what was sound and valid in the past." Safeguarding his own cultural independence, as late as 1966, two years before his death, he confided to Clayton Eshleman that his attraction to Spanish writing might conceivably have had something to do with the fact that he had been born only a few miles away from Spain and that he regarded himself, by birth at least, as a "French Catalan." Similarly, in a letter to Jonathan Williams in 1967 he declared that he lived "alone in the woods not claiming to be anything, except of course a Catalan. But a Catalan in exile who would not return to Barcelona under any circumstances, never having been there."[21] Typifying Merton's love of verbal play, this comment at a deeper level revealed his perennial consciousness of being rooted in a creational world that transcended borders. Nevertheless, his seemingly ingenuous claim of citizenship in

20. Merton, *The Seven Storey Mountain*, 30; Merton, Aug. 6, 1961, in *Turning toward the World*, 147–48; Merton, *The Seven Storey Mountain*, 321–22; Merton, July 27, 1967, in *Learning to Love*, 269; Merton, Aug. 14, 1956, in *Search for Solitude*, 64.

21. Merton, Aug. 29, 1961, in *Turning toward the World*, 157; Merton, Aug. [1964], in *Dancing in the Water of Life*, 131; Merton to Eshleman, Mar. 16, 1966, in *Courage for Truth*, 260; Merton to Williams, May 1967, in ibid., 286.

Catalonia did register the tension between his warm attachment to his hermitage home in Kentucky and his rather cooler relationship to the modern North American culture that surrounded it.

Ever seeking inclusiveness and balance, Merton sought a critical distancing in his assessment of Europe to match that which he had taken with respect to the United States. In *The Seven Storey Mountain* (1948) he criticized England as a place of "corruption," a "sweet and nasty disease of the soul that seemed to be rotting the whole of Europe, in high places above all."[22] In a similar vein, in the poem "Sports without Blood—A Letter to Dylan Thomas" in *The Strange Islands* (1957), he suggested that the preference of the English intellectual class for bloodless sports such as cricket and rowing had not prevented that class from endorsing and participating in the great wars:

> They have given the cricketer a grass heart
> And a dry purse like a leaf, Look!
> Look! The little butterflies come out!
> He was wounded, he was wounded in the wars
> Where the roots our umpires are.
> It is a funny death, when flowers undermine castles.[23]

Merton's clouded departure from Cambridge intensified his feeling of alienation about English academia, as can be seen in *The Seven Storey Mountain* where he recalled welcoming the freshness of an American university such as Columbia after his experience at Cambridge. At Columbia the professors were comparatively straightforward, he observed, with "none of the pompous beating about the bush, mixed up with subtle academic allusions and a few dull witticisms which was what you were liable to get out of almost anybody at Cambridge." If Merton had been attracted to the civilizing influence of British culture in some respects, he saw its limits, including its oppressive class system, a system that unfortunately reached, he believed, into the very heart of English religious life. In a pre–ecumenical age statement in *The Seven Storey Mountain,*

22. Merton, *The Seven Storey Mountain,* 126.
23. Merton, "Sports without Blood—A Letter to Dylan Thomas," in *Collected Poems,* 236.

he characterized Anglicanism as a religion that perforce bore the guilt of the upper class from which it was "inseparable." In a further jaundiced view of England in July 1962, he wrote to Charles Thompson about the "fumbling and bumbling," the "evasions and blind spots," that he saw as characteristic of "official" England.[24]

In the 1960s, looking at Europe as a whole, Merton also had some reservations, as he made clear in the "Author's Note" to *Seeds of Destruction* (1964), about the official and public support given by European monastic communities in the past to totalitarian movements. While in *Conjectures of a Guilty Bystander* (1966) he acknowledged that there remained in the United States some of the "best tendencies of European independence and liberal thought," he noted a gradual disappearance of certain features of European culture, and vowed that he would try to "preserve all the Europe that is in me as long as I live." Nevertheless, he was wary about identifying with Europe as a means of avoiding his responsibility toward America, especially in the 1960s when he believed that the Vietnam War gave every American citizen, including himself, a guilty status in the world's eye. Thus, writing in his journal in 1960, he undertook to avoid "passivity" in his behavior as an American.[25]

Apart from using his European upbringing to modify his relation to the United States, Merton created further objectivity in his view of America by conceptualizing it culturally in broader terms than was customary. For Merton, the United States was only a part of a hemispheric America, which he described as not merely a geographical entity but also a distinct and integral culture and space. In an essay on Ruben Dario in 1966 he spoke of the two Americas, the "Anglo-Saxon north and the Ibero-Indian south." Given his sensitivity to cultural diversity, evidently in this remark he meant not to overlook the cultural and racial complexity of the Americas but rather to indicate the kinds of culture that, broadly speaking, governed different parts of the hemisphere. In 1958 he declared in his journal that his lot was cast with the future of the

24. Merton, *The Seven Storey Mountain,* 138, 66; Merton to Thompson, July 19, 1962, in *Hidden Ground of Love,* 574.

25. Merton, *Seeds of Destruction,* xiii; Merton, *Conjectures of a Guilty Bystander,* 62, 257; Merton, Sept. 29, 1960, in *Turning toward the World,* 53.

whole of America, North and South. That future involved the emergence of the "voice of the new man who is rooted in the American earth," as he put it in a letter to Ernesto Cardenal in 1964, a voice that was paradoxically associated with the "silence" of the Indian.[26]

Merton thought of the American continent as having its own "vocation," a destiny, as yet unrealized, that would reflect that which was "free and spiritual," as he phrased it in a letter to Pablo Antonio Cuadra in 1958.[27] As he explained in his journal in February 1958, the vocation of the continent would flow from the vision of the leaders who were chosen from among the various peoples living on it. He cited Simon Bolivar as an example of someone who had played such a role in the development of a distinctively American culture. Enlarging on this idea, he wrote in his journal in 1958 that he wanted to have in himself something of the "*life and the roots and the belief and the destiny and the Orientation of the whole hemisphere*—as an expansion of something of God, of Christ, that the world has not yet found out." Seen in this sort of psycho-geographical light, Merton's thoughts about the destiny and vocation of South America were intimately connected with his thoughts about his own variegated identity. In some reflections about Simone Weil in his journal in 1965, for example, he observed that his attraction to Latin America might well have stemmed from its Europeanness. In this and in other reflections about the Americas, Merton thought in quasi-mythic terms in an attempt to construct a visionary model that incorporated both historical and imaginative meaning. That he was aware of the actual conditions of life in Latin America is evident in his observation in a letter to Cintio Vitier in 1963 that Latin American Christianity tended to identify itself with the policies of the State Department in Washington. On a mythic level, though, Merton seemed prepared to let his imagination take wing, which was almost inevitable considering that the only part of Latin America he had visited had been Cuba in

26. Merton, "Ruben Dario," in *Literary Essays*, 306; Merton, Apr. 20, 1958, in *Search for Solitude*, 194; Merton to Cardenal, July 12, 1964, in *Courage for Truth*, 146.

27. Merton to Cuadra, Oct. 13, 1958, in *Courage for Truth*, 181; Merton, Feb. 15, 1958, in *Search for Solitude*, 168; Merton, Mar. 4, 1965, in *Dancing in the Water of Life*, 213–14; Merton to Vitier, Aug. 1, 1963, in *Courage for Truth*, 237; Merton, Apr. 1940 (Havana, Cuba), in *Run to the Mountain*, 188.

1940. On that trip he had distinguished between the nakedness of Cuban culture, including Cuban poverty, and what he characterized as the squalid effect of attempting to hide poverty in some parts of the United States. As has been suggested, openness was one of the values Merton associated with the New World, and it was significant to him that he found it at times to be more present in Latin America than in the United States.[28]

In more particular terms, as a poet writing in the 1960s, Merton identified with the *writers* of Latin America in preference to the reflexive, academic poetry that seemed to be prevalent in the United States. Early in 1963, for instance, he wrote to Margaret Randall saying that he believed the best American poetry was being written in Latin America, because it opened itself to life in an ontological sense, an interest that in Merton's view most contemporary North American poets seemed less and less to address. He thought of his own poetry as reaching beyond what he called the "hermetic subjectivism" of many contemporary U.S. poets, so he told Cintio Vitier in 1965.[29] His consciousness of an affinity with Latin American writers was undoubtedly related in part to the fact that they came from a Catholic culture whose communal values, he believed, contrasted with the individualistic Protestant culture of the United States. He found himself especially alienated from the hegemonic nexus of individualism, Protestantism, and capitalism in U.S. culture. In this connection his reaction to the increasing ascendancy of technological capitalism in North American culture can be seen in his notes on a visit to an industrial park in Louisville with Dom James Fox in 1958:

> Surrounded by open fields with nothing whatever in them, not even thistles, marked "Property of General Electric. No Trespassing." The buildings are huge and go on forever and ever, out in the midst of their own wilderness. Stopped by guards, we signed in at the appropriate gate and promptly got lost in the maze of empty streets between the buildings, finally came out right. What struck me most

28. Merton to Randall, Jan. 15, 1963, in *Courage for Truth,* 215; Merton to Vitier, May 26, 1964, in ibid., 239.
29. Merton, Sept. 26, 1958, in *Search for Solitude,* 218.

was the immense seriousness of the place—as if at last I had found what America takes seriously.[30]

In the 1960s in *Conjectures of a Guilty Bystander*, Merton focused his thoughts about the dominance of technological culture in the United States on the automobile: "The attachment of the modern American to his automobile, and the *symbolic* role played by his car, with its aggressive and lubric design, its useless power, its otiose gadgetry, its consumption of fuel, which is advertised as having almost supernatural power . . . this is where the study of American mythology should begin." The problem with technocracy, as Merton saw it, and as philosophers such as George Grant and Charles Taylor have described it, was that it placed a priority on how things were done instead of on why they should or should not have been done. For this reason, in *Conjectures of a Guilty Bystander* in the mid-1960s, Merton acknowledged that technology could elevate and improve the life of human beings only if it remained subservient to their "*real* interests" and "true" nature; otherwise, it would inevitably degrade human life. In his journal in 1968 he wrote of technology as the American "Karma" in which what can be done "has to be done. The burden of possibility that has to be fulfilled, possibilities which demand so imperatively to be fulfilled that everything else is sacrificed for their fulfillment."[31] Although he was a modernist in some respects, particularly in matters of aesthetic form, Merton was deeply conservative in other ways, and he especially resented the tendency of technological culture to treat the past dismissively, as if it were inevitably and rightly slated for replacement.

What alarmed Merton was the joining of a heady technological culture in the United States with an energetic and rather narrow nationalism. He linked these two in his journal in 1964 when, in thinking about the Vietnam War, he recoiled at the "madness" of American "patriots" who seemed driven by "technological hubris." He balked at the prospect

---

30. Merton, *Conjectures of a Guilty Bystander*, 63, 230; Merton, May 16, 1968, in *Other Side of the Mountain*, 102.

31. Merton, Dec. 8, 1964, in *Dancing in the Water of Life*, 177; Merton, *Conjectures of a Guilty Bystander*, 74.

of the domination of the world by the technological culture of the United States, not simply because of the dehumanizing tendencies of that culture but also for the ecological reason that this would diminish the amount of cultural diversity in the world. As an example, he worried even at the prospect that the prayers of Western Catholics directed toward the Russians during the cold war period might, if successful, have led to a homogeneous Catholicism that would then have undermined the ability of different kinds of Catholics, Christians, and "others" to "challenge" and "complete us," as he put it.[32] Regarding this incompleteness, Merton was especially concerned, as can be seen in many areas of his writing, about what he perceived to be the lack of general knowledge about the rest of the world on the part of many in the United States.[33] Apparently speaking as a Europeanized American, Merton in 1959 also regretted what he considered the provinciality of public education in the United States, an especially unfortunate circumstance in a country that seemed to have the technological power to rule the world. Furthermore, he was not consoled by the role of institutional American Catholicism in this matter, arguing in a letter to Charles Thompson in 1962 that the Catholic press in the United States was fanatical in its attempt to destroy the "devil" of communism.[34]

The political polarization that characterized the cold war had in Merton's view obscured the faults of both East and West as cultures and, more important, overlooked the plight of those who demanded the most attention: the victims of the cold war and of the hot wars that the cold war had spawned. Thus, in an essay titled "Taking Sides in Vietnam," he declared himself to be aligned with the people who were being "burned, cut to pieces, tortured, held as hostages, gassed, ruined, destroyed," those who were the victims of both sides. At the same time, while he had reservations about the health of U.S. political culture, especially when inflamed by nationalism, he was not afraid, as he indicated in a letter in 1961 to Arthur Hays Sulzberger, chairman of the board of the *New York*

32. Merton to Arthur Hays Sulzberger, July 26, 1961, in *Witness to Freedom*, 160.
33. Merton, Apr. 10, 1959, in *Search for Solitude*, 272; Merton to Thompson, Sept. 7, 1962, in *Hidden Ground of Love*, 575.
34. *Merton*, "Taking Sides in Vietnam," in *Faith and Violence*, 110.

Times, to urge that readers in the United States better acquaint themselves with Karl Marx in order to challenge the present-day "pontiffs" of Marxism, a reference, it would seem, not only to leftists in the West but to those who had betrayed the principles of Marxism in Eastern Europe as well. Again, instead of being able to turn to his fellow Catholics for understanding, Merton noted in his journal in 1967 that the aggressiveness of U.S. culture had penetrated American Catholicism, giving it a "combative stance." The assimilation of American Catholicism by mainstream American culture galled Merton, since he saw the effect as having reached into his own monastery where, as he noted in his journal in 1959, the monks had taken to living more and more on the "'crucified' plane of the American Middle Class." Increasingly alienated from mainstream Catholicism in the United States, Merton considered giving up his American citizenship in 1966 as a gesture of his opposition to the involvement by the United States in the Vietnam War. In 1967 he considered living as a hermit monk in a monastic settlement in Chile, indicating that he wanted, among other things, to leave the United States and to live as the citizen of a country that did not possess nuclear weapons. He characterized the behavior of the United States during the Vietnam War as narcissistic and a confirmation of the worst tendencies of American nationalism, which he had always distrusted.[35]

As has been suggested, Merton's relation to his adopted country steadily darkened toward the end of his life. In contrast, writing in his journal in 1949, he had held up the hope of a transformation in the quality of American life "from within," a transformation to which he meant to contribute by persuading his fellow citizens to subordinate the dehumanizing currents of modern American culture to the "inner life and destiny" of human beings under the recognition of a "metaphysical absolute." In a letter to Abdul Aziz in 1962 he indicated that while there was "much good" in the American people, there was also much danger in a society that, in its radical privileging of individual freedom, left

35. Merton to Sulzberger, July 26, 1961, in *Witness to Freedom,* 160; Merton, May 27, 1967, in *Learning to Love,* 239; Merton, July 21, 1959, in *Search for Solitude,* 308; Merton, Mar. 15, 1966, in *Learning to Love,* 29; Merton, Sept. 11, 1967, in ibid., 290; on United States as narcissistic, Merton, Apr. 16, 1966, in ibid., 41; see Merton, Apr. 24, 1960, in *Search for Solitude,* 385.

everything to the "interplay of human appetites," assuming that everything would adjust itself automatically for the general good. Significantly, Merton identified himself in the letter as a "friend and brother of
people everywhere, especially those who are exiles and pilgrims like my-
self."[36] Although Merton, as has been seen, distanced himself from the
United States in this way on more than one occasion, it is worthwhile
noting that he did not leave the United States, although it is equally true
that Abbot James Fox did not and would not have countenanced such a
move. Nevertheless, Merton eventually accommodated himself to these
refusals by his abbot, and it is likely that, had he lived, he would have returned, more or less permanently, to his Kentucky hermitage, where in
any case a new abbot had replaced Dom James Fox in the late 1960s.

The urgency in Merton's essays about the United States in the 1960s
—as in *Seeds of Destruction* (1964), *Raids on the Unspeakable* (1966), as
well as the poems in *Emblems of a Season of Fury* (1963)—arose from his
apprehensive consciousness that the United States had fallen from its
Edenic, New World dream into "history like everyone else." In doing so,
Merton contended, the high democratic traditions of American political thought, even if far from untrammeled in the past, were particularly
vulnerable in the twentieth century when, through technological dis-
semination, many people expressed ideas and opinions that had been
fabricated for them.[37] In addition, he became alarmed at the vulgariza-
tion of the American ideology of individualism, as exemplified by the
publicized man in Chicago who had warded off potential intruders into
his fallout shelter with a machine gun. Amid such social alienation he
felt gifted by the enforced wanderings of his own existence to offer an
insight into the value of such varied cultural formation as he himself represented. By discriminating between the qualities of the various cultures
to which he had in some way become attached, he was able to use each
of these cultures as a sort of lever by which to perceive the others in what
he hoped was a more inclusive and objective fashion.

Over his lifetime Merton had become aware of the distinctive cul-

36. Merton, May 6, 1949, in *Entering the Silence*, 309; Merton to Aziz, Apr. 4, 1962,
in *Hidden Ground of Love*, 51–52.
37. Merton, *Conjectures of a Guilty Bystander*, 27, 86.

tural values of Europe, Latin America, and finally Asia. In the journal he kept on his trip to Asia shortly before his death in 1968, he used his growing knowledge of Asian culture as an unfamiliar lens by which he might more objectively perceive not only Asia but also the culture of the West and especially that of the United States. Against this background, Calcutta, for example, exhibited, it seemed to him, a madness of "confusion" and "despair" in comparison with America, which had become blighted by the "mad rationality of affluence." Similarly, in notes for a projected talk in Calcutta, which were later published in the *Asian Journal* as an appendix titled "Monastic Experience and East-West Dialogue," he contrasted what he termed the Asian habit of "nonhurrying and of patient waiting" with the Western passion for "immediate visible results." Through his encounter with Buddhism while traveling in the East, Merton was able to mount a challenge to the dominant rationalism, particularly in its disputatious aspects, of Western culture, as can be seen in his impressions of the great stone Buddhas in Polonnaruwa, Sri Lanka, in 1968, figures that struck him as quintessentially and ideally Asian.[38]

Though spurred by his recognition of the special value of Asian religious consciousness, Merton's reflections at Polonnaruwa reveal a maturing understanding of how one might think about all cultures. He had spent his life recording in his essays and correspondence the surges in consciousness experienced as he encountered writers and individuals from cultures other than his own. Through these contacts he sought knowledge not only of these other cultures but also of himself as part of a humanity whose vast and mysterious frontiers he intuitively perceived at a distance and to which he was determined to travel. In spite of Merton's growing misgivings about American society in the 1960s, he relied upon the distinctive openness and dynamism of that society to accommodate change both for itself and for the world. Taken as a whole, Merton's writings about America in relation to other parts of the world depict the fragmentariness of human culture and the consequent and

38. Merton, Oct. 19, 1968, in *Other Side of the Mountain,* 217; Merton, "Monastic Experience and East-West Dialogue," in *Asian Journal,* 313; Merton, Dec. 4, 1968, in *Other Side of the Mountain,* 323.

increasingly urgent need for completeness, a need that more than any other governed his mind in all things.

It may be objected in connection with Merton's mental journeying through different cultures with their various mythdreams that he in fact lived within few of the cultures that he thought and wrote about. As has been indicated, for example, apart from a visit to Cuba as a young man, he did not travel to Latin America. He did, however, have contact with Latin Americans, including some, such as Ernesto Cardenal, who became influential figures in Latin American politics and culture. All the same, following his entry into the monastery in 1941, his contact with other cultures was largely through reading about them. In Merton's view this might in some ways be regarded as fortuitous, since through the writers of the world he experienced these cultures at what he regarded as their deepest and richest levels. Thus, immersed in the travel journals of the fourteenth-century writer Ibn Battuta, for example, he was able to see a side of Islam that seemed invisible in the midst of the fundamentalist violence in Moslem culture in the 1960s. Such is the effect of the following passage from the East section of *The Geography of Lograire* in which Ibn Battuta's travels are commemorated:

> I sailed for the Maldives
> Where all the inhabitants
> Are Muslims
> Live on red fish lightly cooked
> Or smoked in palmleaf baskets
> It tastes like mutton
>
> These natives wear no pants
> Only aprons
> Bathe twice a day
> Use sandalwood and do not fight
> Their armor is prayer.[39]

In Ibn Battuta's narrative Merton found within Islam a principle of peace that had become obscured in some quarters. Furthermore, while

39. Merton, *Geography of Lograire*, in *Collected Poems*, 543–44.

the idyllic scene recorded by Ibn Battuta celebrated the harmony of a people in fortunate cultural surroundings, Merton did not single out older pastoral cultures as the only models worth emulating. There are a number of occasions in which he celebrated the civilizing aspects of culture, as in his comment in his journal in 1968 that an article he had read about Igor Stravinsky had lifted his spirits: "Just the encouragement of having a civilized man around—still!" Similarly, he praised the Oxford Anglican A. M. Allchin in 1963 for representing the best of the English universities, a "breadth, a simplicity, a sane traditionalism, a purity of vision and an originality that can only be combined in a really mature and developed culture."[40]

Thus, it was not civilization, particularly in its aesthetic aspects, about which Merton was wary, just as it was not primitivism itself that he idealized. This can be seen in his comment about the dark characters of Flannery O'Connor whom he mordantly described as two kinds of "very advanced primitives." For Merton, the primitive and the civilized both had the potentiality to restart culture and history in the direction of unity and inclusiveness. Because of his skepticism about the West, however, and its complicity in two world wars, a skepticism reflected in his early novel *My Argument with the Gestapo,* when Merton looked about for examples of a culture that was oriented toward wholeness, he found himself turning toward cultures that were not in the industrialized West. Primitivism in Merton's writings was thus a form of countercultural critique of a Western history that had given itself, nominally Christian or not, to dividing and conquering. He believed that the members of preindustrial cultures were far more likely than those in industrial societies to exhibit holistic cultures, cultures that those from technological cultures needed to explore in order to recover that part of themselves that had been left behind by the shift to technology. Furthermore, such a recovery, Merton believed, would incidentally alert those from advanced technological cultures about the humanity they shared with those in non-technological cultures. While Merton's approach might seem ingenuous to some, the Harvard biologist Edward O. Wilson has concluded that if

---

40. Merton, Mar. 12, 1968, in *Other Side of the Mountain,* 65; Merton, Aug. 10, 1963, in *Dancing in the Water of Life,* 6.

contemporary cultures in the West ignore their roots, surrendering their human nature to "machine-aided ratiocination" and their ethics and art to technological discourse, they will become "nothing."[41]

With his eye ever on cultural breadth, Merton regarded the Mayans as combining the values of both pastoral and urban living. Similarly, he saw the Zapotec people of Monte Alban in southern Mexico as having constructed a city-state devoted to creative activity and to ritual celebration.[42] He contrasted the centuries of peaceful life in Monte Alban with the restless belligerence of Western society that, he noted, had tended to focus aggressively on the future. Monte Alban, on the other hand, he characterized as having been centered on the present. In contrast to the precolonial culture of Monte Alban, he saw the West as having sacrificed wisdom to science in the post-Renaissance period when fully humanized cultures in his view needed to rely on both science and wisdom. In this light one can come to understand Merton's attachment to medievalism. Like the romantics of the late eighteenth and nineteenth centuries, the medieval period for Merton represented an alternative culture to the fast-developing technological regime that threatened to supersede every other aspect of culture in the West. Initially attracted to medieval culture through reading Etienne Gilson's *Spirit of Mediaeval Philosophy* in the 1930s, Merton liked the balance of spiritual culture and agrarianism that Gilson associated with the Middle Ages as well as what Gilson had maintained was the fundamental respect of philosophers such as Thomas Aquinas for individual worth and moral freedom. While Merton's attraction to medieval culture, like Gilson's, was selective, he did note the shortcomings of some aspects of late medieval culture when church and state became quite integrated, a mistake that in retrospect in Merton's view had cost the church more than the state in the long run by compromising the church's moral independence.[43]

Although in the late 1950s and early 1960s Merton became aware of

41. Merton, "Flannery O'Connor: A Prose Elegy," in *Raids on the Unspeakable*, 39; Wilson, *Consilience*, 326.
42. See Merton, *Ishi Means Man*, 67.
43. See Merton, Oct. 18, 1941, in *Run to the Mountain*, 440–41.

a need to participate in his own century with its preoccupations and problems, nevertheless he remarked in the spring of 1961 that he was still a "14th century man: the century of Eckhart, Ruysbroeck, Tauler, the English recluses, the author of the *Cloud*, Langland and Chaucer." He attributed his attraction to medieval culture to the effects of his solitude, which permitted him to be free, as he thought of it, from the "compulsion of fashion."[44] Indeed, as late as 1965 he insisted upon the relevancy of medieval culture, through which he claimed to have obtained an external vantage point on contemporary culture, enabling himself to discover not only what contemporary culture valued but also what it did not but might have possessed. For this reason Merton regretted the lack of Catholic, and therefore to this extent the lack of a medieval, consciousness in mainstream American society in contrast to Europe or Latin America. Furthermore, although his books of essays and poems in the late 1950s and 1960s, such as *Seeds of Destruction* (1964), frequently expressed a pronounced liberalism in social matters, he found himself stranded at times in the midst of a ferment for change in his own church in the 1960s, suddenly missing, for example, the austere, dignified music of the Gregorian chant. As was the case with primitivism, medievalism was a culture that Merton looked toward not as an end in itself but rather as a means of widening and enlarging his perspective on the modern age. Anyone who has read Merton's poetry from the late 1950s onward cannot help but see his interest in modernism. What makes his poetry distinct and interesting, though, is his ability to reproduce the images and discourse of his time while beneath the text, *pentimento*-like, there are vestiges of the past, often of the medieval past. The long poem *Cables to the Ace* (1968), which presented an ironic view of contemporary culture, offers an illustration of this in its third section: "Decoding the looks of opposites. Writing down their silences. Words replaced by moods. Actions punctuated by the hard fall of imperatives. More and more smoke. Since language has become a medium in which we are totally immersed, there is no longer any need to say anything. The saying says itself all around us. No one need attend. Listening is obsolete. So is

44. Merton, Mar. 11, 1961, in *Turning toward the World*, 99; Merton, Jan. 15, 1966, in *Learning to Love*, 7.

silence. Each one travels alone in a small blue capsule of indignation."[45] The word *decoding* contextualizes the use of language at the beginning of the passage as that belonging to the McLuhanesque twentieth century, symbolizing a technologically pragmatic flattening and narrowing of language. In an environment saturated with language of this sort, the speaker implies, one's use of language is mere smoke, and the only safety is to be found in silence and alienation. Beneath this resistant stand-off between language and silence lay the possible discovery of the benefit of a contemplative silence, a silence whose worth medieval mystics had well understood. In this backhanded manner, then, silence, in its beatific form, awaited discovery. Only when its spiritual and ontological value was discovered, the speaker in the above passage implies, would language be restored to its authentic purpose and value.

While Merton's identification with the culture of fourteenth-century mysticism might well appear anachronistic to many contemporary readers, his cumulative approach to culture allowed him to see his attachment to the Latin Fathers of the church, for example, as continuous with his interest in China, and in turn Confucianism, Zen, and Taoism, not to mention his interest in modern art. Such assimilation was part of Merton's attempt to form a culture that was his own yet also the world's inheritance. In speaking of this cumulative process of acculturation, Merton coined the phrase "transcultural maturity."[46] If sociology can be said to have put forward the view that society and culture were systematically distinct from the psychological lives of those who made up society and culture, then Merton's view might be said to be more psychological than sociological. Indeed, Merton saw myth, which he believed originated in the imagination, as forming a nexus between the self and the society, and, optimally, as with the Mayans, between the self and the highest communal values. While the sundry cultures that Merton attempted to assimilate all obviously had in common a basis in history, they sometimes, not unexpectedly, made history transparent about the nature of the human condition, thereby allowing one to move, fortuitously, through history into being.

45. Merton, *Cables to the Ace*, in *Collected Poems*, 397.
46. Merton, *Contemplation in a World of Action*, 211.

8

Individuation, Unity, and Inclusiveness

As a young man Merton's inclinations had been countercultural. Even later in life he looked back on the leftism of the 1930s, for example, as healthier than the conservatism of the 1950s in the United States, and later, in 1967, he described himself, along with activist intellectuals such as Daniel Berrigan, as on the "Christian non-violent left"—not "liberals" but Christian "anarchists." The term *anarchist* was one that Merton was pleased to attribute to other writers whom he admired, such as Boris Pasternak, and it is a term with which he himself identified from as far back as 1948.[1] While Merton sometimes characterized himself as a liberal, on the whole he preferred thinking of himself as an anarchist, because, like Berrigan, he believed that the liberal designation was too amorphous whereas anarchism, as with Thoreau, placed his allegiance squarely with the individual person and against the state. Thus, in 1961, he told Dorothy Day, herself a Christian anarchist and a profound influence on Merton, that he prized the personal liberty that was a part of anarchism. In this connection, he was wary of the trendiness of liberalism in the 1960s and its tendency to organize dissent within large groups, thus taking the risk of mounting a protest that was generalized and conventionalized. At the same time, he cautioned in *Seeds of De-*

1. See Merton, Apr. 8, 1961, in *Turning toward the World,* 106; Merton to Martin E. Marty, Sept. 6, 1967, in *Hidden Ground of Love,* 458; see Merton, Nov. 29, 1958, in *Search for Solitude,* 233. See also May 4, 1948, in *Entering the Silence,* 203.

struction in 1964 that freedom did not operate in a vacuum and needed to be guided by a "rational estimate" of reality in order to avoid becoming a blind affirmation of the will.[2] Here one catches a glimpse of Merton's fundamental affirmation of reason complemented by his balancing perception of the incompleteness of reason.

For Merton, genuine dissent always remained individual.[3] While in some respects he regarded the first monks as highly individualized, monasticism had, over the centuries, he contended, become so institutionalized that the time had arrived for monks to become antimonks. Merton's adoption of a hermitic life in the 1960s connected him psychologically and spiritually with the ancient Desert Fathers of Egypt and Syria who were, ecclesiastically speaking, the counterculture revolutionaries of their day. This was because they had opted for the desert as an alternative to the conventionalized settling of Christianity into the Roman Empire in a rapprochement of church and state that the Desert Fathers at the time and Merton in retrospect regarded with suspicion. Writing in his journal in 1965 Merton admitted that he thought individualistically about most things, all the while recognizing the limitations of individualism yet clinging to it in place of what he called a "superficial inadequate communal spirit." Indeed, it seemed to him that religion in general in the 1960s had become conspicuously and superficially harmonious and accommodating to all—an unfortunate sign: "Certainly, we preach the Cross, but not the cross of resistance; only the cross of submission," an unwise submission to power, he added, any power that adjusted itself to the Church.[4]

As far as the importance of individual dissent was concerned, Blake's influence on Merton was definitive, especially in contrast to the wavering political allegiances of Wordsworth and Coleridge. Merton did not hesitate to accept the mantle of social revolutionary, even if only in the nonviolent sense of the term, and he identified strongly with the protests of nonviolent revolutionaries such as Gandhi and Thoreau.[5] Gandhi, for

2. Merton, *Seeds of Destruction,* 99.
3. Merton, Sept. 10, 1960, in *Turning toward the World,* 44.
4. Merton, July 17, 1965, in *Dancing in the Water of Life,* 270; Merton, Apr. 30, 1963, in *Turning toward the World,* 316.
5. Merton to Jaime Andrade, July 1958, in *School of Charity,* 112.

example, generated political opposition, Merton noted in an essay in *Seeds of Destruction,* possessed of a "fully awakened and operative spiritual power." Similarly, in Merton's view, Thoreau's nonconformist dissent represented a hardy example of the American ideological tradition of individual freedom, as he wrote to Harry Cargas in 1965. He identified with Thoreau as both hermit and social dissenter, seeing the two ways of life as inextricably related. The social dissent of nonviolent protesters such as Gandhi, Thoreau, Dorothy Day, and Daniel Berrigan was in Merton's eyes informed by an enlightened moral objection to laws that were unworthy of the name. Nonetheless, because of his lifelong respect for law, his dissenting voice was a somewhat more conservative one than that of Thoreau, whose distrust of government qua government—particularly distant, centralized government—was unqualified. All the same, in 1966 Merton urged in *Conjectures of a Guilty Bystander* that the Christian had best throw in his or her lot with "revolution" and in this way transform society according to ideals that were not specifically Christian but generally beneficial to society. In a similar way he regarded the artist as a revolutionary who should, however, he stressed, "preach nothing," not even his or her own autonomy.[6] Rather, the artist should register dissent through the idiom of art itself in harmony with but not in imitation of other kinds of understanding and discourse.

Merton's dissenting spirit expressed itself in a series of books and essays in both prose and poetry through the late 1950s and 1960s. With titles such as "Letters to a White Liberal" and "Letters in a Time of Crisis," he confronted and attempted to diagnose a range of social issues and problems. Problems such as the tolerance of nuclear war weaponry and racial discrimination Merton related to a passive, materialistic population corralled in what he ironically termed in *Cables to the Ace* in 1968 as "the social cages of joy." Even within the Church with its pronounced spiritual ideals, there was an almost universal acceptance, he argued, of the justification of nuclear war in a given set of circumstances, an evil that Merton ascribed to a "nebulous" public discourse that lulled indi-

---

6. Merton, *Seeds of Destruction,* 228; Merton to Cargas, Feb. 14, 1966, in *Witness to Freedom,* 171; see Merton, *Conjectures of a Guilty Bystander,* 53–55; Merton, "Answers on Art and Freedom," in *Literary Essays,* 378.

vidual consciences to sleep. In this connection, in "Auschwitz: A Family Camp," written in 1966, he argued that the transformation of a civilized country such as Germany into a police state was made possible by the cunning manipulation of a large, well-meaning, but docile population.[7] With his eye on the social attitudes that made possible widespread evils such as racial discrimination, he observed that the black problem in the United States was in fact a white problem, and would never be resolved until it was recognized as such and until white Americans became ready to give up some of their property and wealth to atone for the wrongs inflicted by themselves collectively and individually both in the present and in the past.

As has been suggested, Merton's increasingly intolerant stance toward institutional consciousness and discourse in the 1960s reached into his view of religion and of his own church. Here he became increasingly restless about the heavy hand of institutionalized authority that seemed to him to block the church in its vital task of leavening society. Putting the matter bluntly, in 1968 he told Thomas McDonnell that while the Catholic Church presented itself as a "communion," it was operated in fact as a "collectivity," even a "totalitarian collectivity." In this connection he recalled the heavy weight of Irish Catholicism on James Joyce, an author whom he greatly admired, arguing that the Catholic Church had failed to recognize Joyce's "essentially *contemplative*" vocation.[8] In Merton's estimation the problem of Christendom's paralleling of and close relationship with the state had begun in the fourth century when the Christian Church became the official religion of the Roman Empire and in many respects adopted the organizational structure of that empire. The result, what has traditionally been known as Christendom, was from Merton's point of view a comfortable arrangement in which Christianity became secularized while civil officialdom had been only superficially affected by Christianity. Too easily, with such an arrangement, he reflected

---

7. Merton, *Cables to the Ace*, in *Collected Poems*, 395; Merton, "The Inner Experience: Some Dangers in Contemplation," 148; see Merton, "Auschwitz: A Family Camp," in *Nonviolent Alternative*, 150–59.

8. McDonnell, "Interview with Thomas Merton," 34; Merton, July 9, 1967, in *Other Side of the Mountain*, 140.

bitterly, there came about a society like the repressive regime of Franco's in Spain.[9] He portrayed the issue incisively in connection with the habitual and uncritical use historically by so-called Christian rulers of the Augustinian doctrine of the just war:

> The Christian may join the non-Christian in fighting to preserve peace in the earthly city. But suppose that the earthly city itself is almost totally made up of Christians. Then cooperation between the "two cities" takes on a new aspect, and we arrive at the conclusion that a "secular arm" of military force can be called into action against heretics, to preserve not only civil peace but the purity of faith. Thus Augustine becomes also the remote forefather of the Crusades and of the Inquisition. . . . The deficiency of Augustinian thought lies therefore not in the good intentions it prescribes but in an excessive naivete with regard to the good that can be obtained by violent means which cannot help but call forth all that is worst in man. And so, alas, for centuries we have heard kings, princes, bishops, priests, ministers, and the Lord alone knows what variety of unctuous beadles and sacrists, earnestly urging all men to take up arms out of love and mercifully slay their enemies (including other Christians) without omitting to purify their interior intention.[10]

One of the most unfortunate aspects of the history of Christendom, Merton believed, was the loss of the mystical dimension of Christianity in favor of its rational, judicial, and administrative aspects. This was especially harmful, he believed, because it was precisely this mystical or contemplative dimension that encouraged the full development of the self and an ineluctable consciousness of its inner freedom and therefore of its latent power of opposition to the state. Worse than this, he maintained, those in power in the Church had not infrequently used its institutional framework to permit injustice and inequity. Whether or not this was intended, he concluded, the complexities of the organizational structure had facilitated such policies and behavior. Certainly, Merton had felt this himself in the case of the censorship of his writings by his

9. See Merton, July 7, 1961, in *Turning toward the World,* 139.
10. Merton, *Seeds of Destruction,* 147–48.

order, particularly, but certainly not exclusively, the censorship of his writings on peace. In a gloomy comment to Rosemary Radford Ruether in 1967, he declared that monasticism had lost its soul through having been diverted from its independent purpose by a "perverse doctrine of authority-humility-obedience."[11] Doubtlessly, Merton here reflected his relationship with the man who was his abbot at the time, Dom James Fox, but it can be argued that that relationship simply made him aware of the pitfalls of corporate religious authority. Merton took his vows of obedience very seriously because he regarded such obedience as a means of freeing the deeper self from the ego, but he saw that in some ways such obedience could undercut the role of the monk as a potential social critic. As he indicated in an essay in *Seeds of Destruction* in 1964, he identified with primitive monasticism, which involved a loosely knit group of lay people living in solitude in informal communities under the direction of a spiritual leader, an arrangement that he was aware still obtained in the case of Hindu ashrams in the East. He saw the original monks, the Desert Fathers of the Middle East, as individuals in the very best sense, and his description of them in *The Wisdom of the Desert* (1960) made it evident that he wanted to emulate their independence of spirit:

> They seem to have doubted that Christianity and politics could ever be mixed to such an extent as to produce a fully Christian society. . . . The Desert Fathers declined to be ruled by men, but had no desire to rule over others themselves. . . . The society they sought was one where all men were truly equal, where the only authority under God was the charismatic authority of wisdom, experience and love. . . . What the Fathers sought most of all was their own true self, in Christ. And in order to do this, they had to reject completely the false, formal self, fabricated under social compulsion in "the world." They sought a way to God that was uncharted and freely chosen, not inherited from others who had mapped it out beforehand.[12]

In contrast to such an anarchic arrangement, modern religious superiors in Merton's view generally gave precedence to the "prosperity and

11. Merton to Ruether, Mar. 9, 1967, in *Hidden Ground of Love*, 504.
12. Merton, "The Wisdom of the Desert," in *Wisdom of the Desert*, 4–6.

reputation" of the order over the "values" of the individual monk, a situation that he believed could well and in certain cases undoubtedly did undermine the contemplative life of the individual monk.[13] Over the length of his life in the monastery, one can see that Merton changed in his attitude to his order and church, moving from an initial grateful sense of having found a home and family in the venerable traditions of his order and church to an increasingly tense awareness of the friction that attended his attempt to exercise his own powers as a contemplative in touch with the society around him. In an important entry in his journal in 1959 he vowed that he would think his own thoughts and write what he chose to write, leaving the "disposition" of his time and work to his superiors. In a similar vein, writing in his journal in 1963, he formulated a modus vivendi by which he undertook to maintain his obedience to his superiors while claiming the right to an interior freedom.[14] The sovereign value that Merton assigned to such freedom led him to challenge those within his church who believed that the moral pronouncements of the official church should override individual moral perceptions and decisions, a view that seemed to him to make a mockery of the liberty implicit in the Church's ostensible respect for the individual soul and for the freedom implicit in moral decision making.

Theorizing about these matters in 1962, he determined that in order to free the self from an identification with "collective archetypes," there was the need to further the process of *individuation*, a term that for Merton was devoid of the egocentric connotations of the word *individualism*. Thus, in 1966, struggling with the conflict between his loyalty to the Church and his individual perceptions, he justified his position on the basis of the fact that there were a number of diverse voices to be heard within the Church. There was the mainstream church, which on the whole he regarded as endeavoring, however inexactly, to be faithful to Christ's teaching; second, there was a "demonic" element that inevitably did not remain faithful to that teaching; finally, there was an alternate, dissenting, eschatological group, including himself, that attempted to

13. Merton, July 30, 1959, in *Search for Solitude*, 312.
14. Merton, Feb. 8, 1959, in ibid., 258; see Merton, May 10, 1963, in *Turning toward the World*, 318.

articulate authentic Christianity from a minority and ecclesiastically countercultural standpoint.[15] Nevertheless, having always attempted to reach a balance between personhood and the obligation toward unity, Merton wanted both to speak from the vantage point of his own conscience and to speak from the center of the Church.[16]

Although as a young man Merton had spoken disparagingly of Rousseau's *Confessions* in contrast to Saint Augustine's, there was much about his idea of individuation that resembled Rousseau's.[17] Rousseau had argued that individuals would develop well if permitted to grow without being diverted by society's attempt to mold them according to its collective consciousness. For Merton, the web of collective consciousness reached into the heart of his own monastic community, a manifestation of conventionalism and a smothering of the individual from which, he confided, one had to extricate oneself even while adhering to the community as one's community.[18] Because of his strong support for the idea of community, Merton straddled the line between communal living and individual thought, hesitant to lean too far in either direction. In *Disputed Questions* (1960), for example, he disparaged individualism as an instrument of "social atomism" that had led through its fragmenting effect to widespread "inertia, passivism and spiritual decay."[19] The reason was that individualism in his estimate had become a predominantly economic concept in Western society, relegating to a vague area of social responsibility moral decisions deemed to belong to a lesser order of priority.

In order to stay clear of the negative connotations of the term *individualism* while not rejecting the term *individual*, Merton began to rely on the term *personalism*. In this he followed the example of Etienne Gilson, who in *The Spirit of Mediaeval Philosophy* used the word *person* to designate a "free" being. By way of contrast Merton chose to use the word *individualism* to refer to individual "natures," human beings seen

15. Merton, Aug. 30, 1962, in *Turning toward the World,* 241; Merton, July 25, 1966, in *Learning to Love,* 101.
16. See Merton, Sept. 6, 1962, in *Turning toward the World,* 244–45.
17. See Merton, Sept. 13, 1939, in *Run to the Mountain,* 21.
18. Merton, Nov. 8, 1959, in *Search for Solitude,* 341.
19. Merton, *Disputed Questions,* x.

as biological and instinctive entities rather than beings capable of attaining wisdom and making free moral choices.[20] There was a danger of inconsistency in Merton's thinking, since in other contexts he valued the unconscious aspects of existence as experienced by human beings. He valued the unconscious, however, not in isolation but as part of a valuing of the totality of the human person. In this connection it can be said that in Merton's view wholeness was always not only preferable to but also greater than the sum of the parts.

Increasingly, especially in the late 1950s and throughout the 1960s, Merton, as had Jacques Maritain, made extensive use of the term *personalism* as in his allusion in 1968 to the "intense Christian personalism" of Blake's thought. As he explained in a talk given during his trip to Alaska in 1968, he shied away from the exclusivity of individualism because of its implicit setting up of barriers against the intrusion of or even the communal association with others. At the extreme, he believed, individualism could amount to a negation of others, leaving the individual free to follow his or her own self-interest while being impinged upon, not by communal consciousness, but only by the minimal need to obey existing criminal laws. Such a minimalist and potentially exploitative attitude to one's fellow human beings, he thought, would ultimately be destructive to society as a whole while incidentally debasing the humanity of the individuals within it. He viewed the issue not only as moral but as ontological as well. Thus, the individualist, driven by self-interest, not only whittled society down to the level of himself or herself, but in so doing also reduced the measure of humanity that he or she possessed. As Merton put it in *Conjectures of a Guilty Bystander*, the more one was able to "affirm others," to "say yes" to them in oneself, the more "real" one became.[21] Moreover, he regarded personalism as existentialist in that it included the full range of the person, who was thereby considered not merely as a sum of abstract qualities but rather as an individual

20. Gilson, *The Spirit of Mediaeval Philosophy*, 202; see Merton to Erich Fromm, Sept. 26, 1961, in *Hidden Ground of Love*, 315, and Merton to Philip Griggs, June 22, 1965, in ibid., 340.

21. Merton, "Blake and the New Theology," in *Literary Essays*, 11; Merton, "Prayer, Personalism, and the Spirit," in *Thomas Merton in Alaska*, 86; Merton, *Conjectures of a Guilty Bystander*, 129.

caught up in a full range of intellectual and moral choices and thus constituting a reality still in the making, as it were.

Merton's sense of balance regarding the boundaries of the person and the group was so fine that he doubted the sort of love in which two people attempted to submerge the personality of one in the other, a perception that grew out of his reading of Faulkner's novel *The Wild Palms*. On the other hand he approved of the way in which the individuated self could represent the group spiritually, as he believed Gandhi had done in India.[22] Reading Hannah Arendt's *Human Condition* in 1960, Merton believed that he had found a way to square the vexing question of the person and the group, first of all by dismissing a wrong approach. This he did by isolating as a false dilemma the conflict between the *individual* and *society*, arguing that these were, ontologically and morally speaking, two peas in a pod in that the same sorts of limited consciousness prevailed, largely materialistic preoccupations with anxiety and security.[23] The more useful and fascinating relationship, he argued, was that between the contemplative individual or person and the political sphere. Whether or not Merton underestimated the dynamism of the social sphere and overestimated that of the political sphere, his agenda was plain enough: the tension between the individual and the group could be a fruitful tension where the area of action in each case was unconventional and therefore open to change and growth. Resulting political change might, paradoxically, spring from an unexpected and ostensibly incongruous appeal to ancient traditions, as in Gandhi's tapping of the rich spiritual traditions of Hinduism in bringing about the social and political reform of India. Indeed, it was the application of these spiritual traditions to contemporary politics, Merton believed, that constituted Gandhi's originality. The extension of the self toward unity, which Merton regarded as the crown of the contemplative life, involved temporal as well as spatial movement. For example, he spoke of the value of revisiting the writings of the ancients, including those within his own Western tradition, in order to reconsider with a view to their possible

22. See Merton, "Faulkner Meditations," in *Literary Essays*, 536; see Merton, "Gandhi and the One-Eyed Giant," in *Gandhi on Non-Violence*, 5.
23. See Merton, May 14, 1960, in *Search for Solitude*, 389.

usefulness in the present truths that had been seen as remarkable in the past. Such truths were to be tested not merely theoretically through the scrutiny of reason but experientially as well.[24]

Merton's own relationship to society, both to his religious community and to society at large, is a complex question. Emerging from within the periods of solitary retreat that he experienced early in his monastic life and from his quasi-separate state as a hermit in the 1960s, he experienced powerful feelings of unity toward those immediately around him and toward those in the outer society. When in 1948, for example, he had to go to Louisville for the first time in seven years, he was surprised at his feelings of affinity for those around him on the city streets.[25] Although this was a modest affirmation in comparison with those that would come in the late 1950s and 1960s, it was essentially at one with those later scenes in that it expressed his emotional attachment to the people around him while rejecting the meretriciousness of the society that enveloped them. Similarly, in his early reclusive years in the monastery, freshened by his contact with nature and by the liturgical beauty of church ritual, he moved out from his cherished solitude toward a transformed sense of community with his fellow monks:

> At the end of the Night Office, when the whole choir sank into the darkness of death and chanted without the faintest light, I thought of the darkness as a luxury, simplifying and unifying everything, hiding all the accidents that make one monk different from another monk and submerging all distractions in plain obscurity. . . . The darkness is like a font from which we shall ascend washed and illumined, to see one another, now no longer separate, but one in the Risen Christ.[26]

Given Merton's later tensions at the monastery, especially with his abbot, Dom James Fox, this scene may strike some readers as ironic. Furthermore, given his pressing need from this time onward to leave the communal routines of the monastery and to retreat to a hermitage, tem-

24. See Merton, Sept. 8, 1960, in *Turning toward the World*, 42.
25. See Merton, Aug. 14, 1948, in *Entering the Silence*, 223.
26. Merton, Apr. 8, 1950, in ibid., 428.

porarily at first, then more or less permanently, one might wonder whether he was being disingenuous here in his professed feelings of unity with his fellow monks. In fact, his feelings for them in this scene were not primarily personal; nor were his radiant feelings in the scene at Fourth and Walnut, discussed earlier, for the people whom he encountered on the streets of Louisville. His feelings were ontological and aesthetic in that what he was attracted to in others was their shared participation as human beings in the color, movement, and spiritual emanations of being. This did not mean that his feelings were without sincerity but rather that they had a different kind of value.

In a similar light can one interpret Merton's warm feelings for the Trappist scholastics who were in his charge from 1951 to 1955:

> I am grateful to the scholastics simply because they exist and because they are what they are. And I am grateful to you, O God, for having placed me among them, and told me to be their Father. But finally I am grateful to you, O God, because I am more often alone. Not that I run away from them. Yet sometimes I do not know myself with them. At other times I find myself in them and with them. Indeed, direction is sometimes an experiment in recognition: they recognize something new in themselves and I in myself: for God recognizes Himself in us.[27]

The candor of this passage in Merton's journal, which he always knew would be read by others, is disarming. Here he laid out the alternating currents of his attraction both to solitude and to unity with others. While some might interpret the passage as indicating an evasiveness with respect to his ability to relate personally to others, the strong friendships that he made during his lifetime make it evident that he enjoyed such personal relationships. Furthermore, while there was a professional note in his relationship to the scholastics, that relationship was far richer than mere professionalism would suggest. Far from being patronizing, he looked to the students to provide him with a further glimpse of the existential range and therefore meaning of their shared humanity, not simply as a source of knowledge but also as a way of experiencing unity with

27. Merton, Feb. 12, 1953, in *Search for Solitude*, 30.

them. Because Merton, who was liked by the scholastics, nevertheless controlled his periods of solitude and involvement with his students, he was able to model for his students these alternating kinds of existence with their different values.

Since, except for medical visits to Louisville, including short visits to friends, and a few brief trips within the United States, Merton was prevented from traveling from 1941 until 1968, the year of his death, his contacts with people outside of the monastery were largely epistolary. Amid his prolific correspondence one notices that there were certain people with whom he felt a particular closeness: "There are people one meets in books or in life," he noted on one occasion, "whom one does not merely observe, meet, or know. A deep resonance of one's entire being is immediately set up with the entire being of the other." Here he was interested in a resonance that brought individuals together, even if they were physically separate, not on the basis of a common background but rather on the basis of a shared, heightened experience of being— whatever the separate and distinct manifestations of this experience might have been. In 1947 he wrote to James Laughlin, his lifelong friend and publisher, whose background, religiously, was very different from his own, that two minds that had turned toward God, their Creator, were thereby turned toward each other. Later, in 1959, he reflected about his feeling of affinity with the Buddhist scholar Daisetz Suzuki, hoping that they might come together on a common ground of spiritual truth rooted in a similar experience of the self.[28]

In "The Inner Experience," which was completed in the late 1950s, Merton declared that the life of the contemplative was primarily a life of unity and of the search for unity.[29] All the same, in earlier writings such as *Seeds of Contemplation* (1949) and *The Ascent to Truth* (1951), he had exhibited a triumphalist attitude that privileged Roman Catholic philosophy and theology. Gradually, his paradigm of religious unity shifted from that of a Catholic, institutional-centered matrix to a dif-

28. Merton, *Conjectures of a Guilty Bystander,* 170; Merton to Laughlin, July 17 [1947], in *Thomas Merton and James Laughlin,* 25; Merton, Apr. 11, 1959, in *Search for Solitude,* 273.

29. Merton, "The Inner Experience: Prospects and Conclusions," 340.

fuse cultural field in which the image of the author of being could be pieced together mosaically by contemplatives in various traditions. The unity experienced by the contemplative self, Merton believed, would be sufficiently profound and moving as to draw into itself the more superficial particulars that divided people of different cultures. Although the unity sought would be holistic, it would nonetheless preserve the self's identity, thereby avoiding the dissolution implicit in metaphysical systems such as pantheism. The same sort of balance applied to the uniting of different religious cultures.

In formulating his idea of unity, Merton managed to accommodate the points of unity perceived in the contemplative traditions of Christianity and Buddhism while acknowledging the fact that Christians tended to perceive spiritual unity as theologically grounded, whereas Buddhists characterized such unity as ontological and natural. Because of the strong creational consciousness developed in his later writings, Merton had no trouble in adopting a Buddhist perspective of being while retaining his Catholic theological underpinnings. The reason was that the unity he sought was not primarily doctrinal but experiential and so could be compared with the experience of other contemplatives in different traditions. Thus, avoiding the quagmires of philosophical and theological conceptualization, Merton could traverse the writings of different philosophical and religious traditions with an eye out for the similarities in reported experience. Before his sudden and unexpected death in 1968, he was planning to prepare a dictionary in which he compared the terminology used for mystical experience within the different religious traditions. He was not antagonistic to conceptual definitions in spiritual matters, of the sort that articulated dogma, for example, since he recognized the worth of a definition's clarification of an issue, but he cautioned against the use of such definitions to limit the reality addressed by the definition.[30]

He delighted in perceiving resemblances that became the basis of unifying perceptions, as in his observation that although a favorite poet, Louis Zukofsky, was a Jew, he was nevertheless also, quintessentially, a Franciscan in mind and attitude, even if he lacked the brown habit and

30. See Merton, Apr. 28, 1957, in *Search for Solitude*, 87.

sandals. Whatever their background Merton identified with those who had added to his understanding of humanity. He announced on one occasion, for example, that one had to either be a Jew or stop reading the Bible, which was so steeped in Jewish thought as to be unintelligible to anyone who was not "'spiritually a Semite.'"[31] On another occasion he described himself as a "Catholic Buddhist" of long standing as well as a Quaker. Explaining his Buddhist standing, he noted in a letter to Marco Pallis in 1963 that one could certainly follow the teachings of Christianity while at the same time being a "Chinese Buddhist in temperament" and having a "Buddhist outlook on life and nature." Although Merton knew that Buddhism was not theocentric, he admired and identified with the pronounced tendency toward cosmic unity in Buddhism, and believed that this approximated the experiential consciousness of certain medieval Western mystics. "Whatever Zen may be," he hypothesized, it was somehow "there in Eckhart."[32]

For Merton, the ontological unity perceived by Zen Buddhists had to do, as it had for the romantic poets and the great Western mystics, with the momentary dissolving of subject and object as the enabling step to an intuitive awareness of one's participation in being in its existential concreteness. Zen Buddhism took the business of contemplation off the page, as it were, relating Merton to a living tradition that his own church had largely placed on the periphery of its existence for the past hundreds of years. In this light one can understand the eagerness with which he looked forward to his Asian journey in 1968, especially the planned visits to Buddhist communities. It was not only their unifying consciousness and experience that attracted Merton to Buddhists but the way in which that unity was sought that was significant. Buddhism did not involve the suppression of opposites but a transcendence of them. In this way the endemic and intractable Cartesian dualism that had so complicated the Western sensibility could be overcome without confrontation or even a Hegelian synthesizing. In addition, although not theological

31. See Merton, "Louis Zukofsky—the Paradise Ear," in *Literary Essays*, 130; Merton, *Conjectures of a Guilty Bystander*, 5.
32. Merton to June Yungblut, Mar. 6, 1968, in *Hidden Ground of Love*, 641; Merton to Pallis, [July] 1963, in ibid., 465; Merton, *Zen and the Birds of Appetite*, 13.

or even metaphysical in the Western sense, Zen was open to the full range of being, the "noumenal and the phenomenal," as Merton put it.[33]

Although in the 1960s he claimed a unity of consciousness with Buddhist contemplatives, Merton was aware of some cardinal differences that might have daunted a more conventional Christian. For example, he believed that what Buddhist contemplatives called the self was what many Western contemplatives would have called God. What he risked in his acceptance of Buddhism on these terms was the charge that he had become a pantheist. Such labels did not disturb him because he knew where he stood ontologically and theologically even while conceding that his awareness and position were continually developing. Nonetheless, there is no indication that Merton ever considered abandoning his Christian beliefs because of his experiments with Buddhist meditation. Although he described Buddhist contemplation modestly as an enabling technique for any contemplative, he went further on occasion in categorizing Buddhism as a "cosmic religion" whose basic reality was the "metaphysical but impersonal ground of the cosmos." In terms of its broadness of scope, Buddhism in this manner could be compared in Merton's view with the Neoplatonism that underlay much of Western mysticism. Plotinus, the architect of Neoplatonism, had stressed the unity of being and the capacity of each "intelligence," as the scholar Richard T. Wallis has put it, to express the "whole Intelligible order from its own particular viewpoint." In *The Still Point: Reflections on Zen and Christian Mysticism,* William Johnston concluded that the reason contemplatives in various traditions could have similar experiences was that these were rooted in the "psychic life" of human beings that was fundamentally the same, Johnston argued, wherever and whenever it existed.[34]

Merton's search for unity led him to Confucianism, where, although he judged Confucianism an ethical philosophy rather than a religion, he nonetheless agreed with the first Jesuits in China about the "profound Catholicity of Confucian philosophy." He was not simply rushing headlong toward other religious cultures with a zealous desire for unity with

33. Merton, *Zen and the Birds of Appetite,* 37.
34. Merton, *Springs of Contemplation,* 222; Wallis, *Neo-Platonism,* 54; Johnston, *Still Point,* 184.

them; rather, as with Confucianism, whose moral principles seemed to him to resemble those that Thomist philosophers call natural ethics, he looked for the similitudes, as Whitman called them, that formed the psychological and philosophical basis for spiritual unity. As a young man Merton had been intrigued by the implicit unity between Christianity and Hinduism that he had discovered in reading the Hindu scholar Ananda Coomaraswamy, who had elucidated the links between medieval Scholasticism and Hindu mysticism. Indeed, in so doing, Merton later recalled in a letter to Coomaraswamy's widow, the Hindu scholar had led him toward Christianity. Coomaraswamy had made the point that since the seventeenth century, European philosophy and religion had moved toward "extroversion" and the autonomy of the individual, thereby losing the awareness of ontological unity that remained in Eastern philosophy and religion. Having been impressed by Coomaraswamy's work in the 1930s, Merton reminded a correspondent in 1961 that Christianity came to the West from the Orient. Merton himself had come to Christianity with the consciousness of its philosophical, if not always its historical, antipathy to what he called the "aggressive, materialistic and pragmatic" Western culture.[35] Coomaraswamy maintained that, like Hinduism, medieval Scholasticism, which formed the philosophical basis for Catholicism, identified being with intelligence and action. Having been introduced in this way to Hinduism and Christianity, with a consciousness of the latent unity between them, Merton went on to explore the similarities between the two religions, noting at one point that in the Bhagavad Gita there was a doctrine of "pure love" that resembled that taught by Saint Bernard of Clairvaux and a number of other Western mystics.[36] Ranging into yet other traditions in the 1960s, he announced that he had become "impregnated" with Sufism.[37] In the case of Moslem thought and culture, he might seem to have reached a difficult frontier, but he found in the contemplative outlook of Sufism a

35. Merton, *Mystics and Zen Masters*, 46; Merton to Dona Luisa Coomaraswamy, Jan. 13, 1961, in *Hidden Ground of Love*, 126; Coomaraswamy, *Transformation of Nature in Art*, 3; Merton to Joseph Tjo Tchel-oung, Apr. 28, 1961, in *Road to Joy*, 319.

36. Merton, "The Inner Experience: Society and the Inner Self," 131.

37. Merton, *Springs of Contemplation*, 266. On Merton's interest in Sufism, see Rob Baker and Gray Henry, eds., *Merton and Sufism: The Untold Story*.

basis for unity, and engaged in a correspondence in pursuit of this unity with the Sufist scholar Abdul Aziz. He sketched for Aziz the ramp that one might walk in crossing over between the two faiths, noting that, as Allah remained one being in performing diverse acts of compassion and mercy, in a similar way one might interpret the actions of the Trinity as an expression of the one God.[38]

Merton's peregrinations through other religions with their associated philosophies were not primarily intellectual but were rather a personal and in some ways urgent quest for a glimpse of ultimate reality experienced within the scope of his own life. As anyone who has read *The Seven Storey Mountain* will have recognized, he visualized ultimate reality not as the solution to an enigma but rather as the destination of a journey. For Merton, ideas were always associated with concrete, narrative events, one of the reasons his writing has been absorbing for so many readers. For this reason he looked forward to his trip to Asia in 1968 as a "going home," even though, as he readily conceded, he had never been to Asia "in this body."[39] The apex of his narrative entry into Asian religion came at Polonnaruwa, in what is now Sri Lanka, where he found himself overwhelmed by the sight of two enormous stone, reclining Buddhas:

> The vicar general, shying away from "paganism," hangs back and sits under a tree reading the guidebook. I am able to approach the Buddhas barefoot and undisturbed, my feet in wet grass, wet sand. Then the silence of the extraordinary faces. The great smiles. Huge and yet subtle. Filled with every possibility, questioning nothing, knowing everything, rejecting nothing, the peace not of emotional resignation, but of Madhyamika, of *sunyata*, that has seen through every question without trying to discredit anyone or anything— *without refutation*—without establishing some other argument. . . . I was knocked over with a rush of relief and thankfulness at the *obvious* clarity of the figures, the clarity and fluidity of shape and line, the design of the monumental bodies composed into the rock shape and landscape, figure, rock and tree. And the sweep of bare rock

38. Merton to Aziz, Oct. 18, 1963, in *Hidden Ground of Love*, 56.
39. Merton, Oct. 15, 1968, in *Other Side of the Mountain*, 205.

sloping away on the other side of the hollow, where you can go back and see different aspects of the figures. . . . The rock, all matter, all life, is charged with *dharmakaya*—everything is emptiness and everything is compassion. I don't know when in my life I have ever had such a sense of beauty and spiritual validity running together in one aesthetic illumination.[40]

The final mention of an "aesthetic illumination" should not be understood to mean that Merton was in the last analysis an aesthete. Aesthetic illumination for Merton, as he recognized it had been for Blake, was continuous with mystical illumination. In addition, the scene painted in the above passage captured dramatically the different order of spiritual consciousness exhibited by Merton from that of the disdainful cleric who accompanied him. This momentous opening of Merton's consciousness in the face of the closure of his companion's consciousness is followed by another, even more striking, opening of consciousness as Merton came to understand the iconic significance of the stone figures, whose expressions, through the mastery of the sculptors, were exquisitely expressive of Buddhist thought. That thought, he perceived, was openness itself, moving upward and outward from the visible expressions on the faces of the figures to the spaciousness of being and so to an area beyond philosophical disputation. The unity of the movement from stone to spirit was confirmed by Merton's observant registering of the fact that the figures appeared to grow out of the rock that surrounded them, not unlike the rustic cottages that Wordsworth described in his guide to the Lake District. Thus, the scene not only symbolized but, in the presence of an observer such as Merton, also epitomized the surging of being through the precision of form.

There were two main lines of unity that Merton followed: The first, which he attributed to Thoreau as well as to others, was a reaching out to other ontological and spiritual traditions. He felt indebted to Thoreau for Thoreau's having been a "bridge builder" between the philosophies of the East and the West.[41] The second approach to unity involved

40. Ibid., 323.
41. Merton to Harry J. Cargas, Oct. 13, 1965, in *Witness to Freedom*, 171.

a perception of an underlying intuition of *being* that permitted others to identify with a particular philosophy outside of their traditions. In this connection Merton characterized Gandhi as one whose political action had been based on a fundamental religious intuition of being that was common to Hinduism, Buddhism, Islam, Judaism, and Christianity.[42] Furthermore, in Merton's view there was no a priori reason to believe that contemplatives from these various traditions could not have been mystics in the Western sense. He was prepared, at least in principle, to validate a particular truth to which the adherents of a given philosophy or religion aspired, a truth that his own tradition might have historically come to overlook or understate.

Particularly distressing to Merton was the knowledge that since the late Middle Ages Christianity had lost the power and desire to welcome non-Christian cultural values, turning away from them instead as potential sources of heresy.[43] Resisting this cultural xenophobia, which he admitted had eased in the 1960s, he attempted to build within himself a cultural and spiritual edifice that included the voices of various religious and philosophical traditions. In this way, like Gandhi, he hoped to unite in himself the spiritual thought of the East and the West and so to prepare *in himself* the future reunion of divided traditions. He came to believe that he would be a better Catholic not by refuting "every shade of Protestantism" but by affirming the truths in Protestantism: "So too, with the Muslims, the Hindus, the Buddhists, etc."[44] It was at this point in his thinking he came to focus on what he came to regard as the most significant characteristic of unity—its inclusiveness. The extension of the self toward unity was generated by a perception of evil as disunity, a pulling into itself of the separated ego in the case both of individuals and of nations. In opposing such partisan perception, Merton focused on the history of culture as a history of amalgamation. From his earliest writings he had sought the high road of inclusiveness, demurring from the judgment of critics who had admired the description of nature in the poetry of Thomas Carew, for example, on the grounds that Carew's de-

42. Merton, *Seeds of Destruction,* 231–32.
43. See Merton, Aug. 20, 1963, in *Dancing in the Water of Life,* 11.
44. Merton, *Conjectures of a Guilty Bystander,* 129.

scriptiveness was not an end in itself but rather part of a larger picture in which the poet had attempted to incorporate the "effect of a natural object, with all its analogical properties, into the unity" of the poem's larger thematic design and subjects.[45] Similarly, in terms of Merton's gravitation toward the idea of inclusiveness, although he confessed that in his isolation in the monastery in the 1940s he had been subject to a "crude" theology that divided the natural and the supernatural, the sacred and the secular,[46] by the 1950s he had regained an awareness of the primacy of ontological wholeness, a quality that in 1960, for example, he said he admired in Lorca's poetry.[47]

Throughout his life he made it clear that the role of a contemplative like himself was to become a complete human being and to further this completeness in others. In part this completeness took the form of his becoming conversant with what Lawrence Cunningham has called the "modernist high culture of our time." In Cunningham's view Merton was distinctive as a major religious writer in entering the "larger world of cultural discourse" while remaining rooted in a particular religious tradition. Even within the confinement and ascetic strictures of his first decade in the monastery, Merton told James Laughlin that the monastic life, as shaped by Saint Bernard of Clairvaux and others, was admirable in its balancing of intellectual and physical labor.[48] At the same time, he believed emphatically that the contemplative life of the monk, which had been marginalized in Western if not in Eastern Christianity, had devolved in many instances into an unfortunate, doctrinaire narrowness.[49] For Merton such narrowness was the very essence of the absurd, a grotesqueness that overtook things when they became separated from their living ontological contexts.[50]

Such rigidity and narrowness required change, and change inevitably involved suffering. Looked at more constructively, suffering provided an

---

45. Merton, Nov. 3, 1940, in *Run to the Mountain*, 251.
46. McDonnell, "Interview with Thomas Merton," 28.
47. See Merton, Sept. 25, 1960, in *Turning toward the World*, 52.
48. Cunningham, introduction to *Thomas Merton: Spiritual Master*, 31; Merton to Laughlin, Oct. 3, 1950, in *Thomas Merton and James Laughlin*, 79.
49. Merton to Joseph Tjo Tchel-oung, Apr. 28, 1961, in *Road to Joy*, 319.
50. Merton, June 20, 1966, in *Learning to Love*, 324.

incentive to change based upon a sense of dislocation that in turn promoted ontological questioning.[51] If Merton's writings elucidated the philosophy and theology of suffering in a way that was not dissimilar from the view of suffering put forward in, say, Flannery O'Connor's fiction, nevertheless he did not depict pain and suffering with the sharpness and vividness that one finds in her fictional world. This difference arose from Merton's paradoxical conviction that suffering was in one sense a positive thing, an existential participation in a manifold richness of being even if it was no more than a negation of goodness and of being in a metaphysical sense. While such a view of pain might strike many readers as overly detached, Merton believed that suffering as a psychological experience frequently resulted from the friction caused by the gravitation of the ego away from the rest of the self, from others, and from God. Such suffering involved not simply pain but the consciousness of pain and the discovery of a revisualized and restructured existence that could and should follow the inception of such consciousness.

Merton's inclusive consciousness was therefore essentially celebratory. One of the most lyrical expressions of this consciousness occurred in "Hagia Sophia," a prose poem published in *Emblems of a Season of Fury* in which he focused on the innate treasure of wisdom in the psyche:

> There is in all visible things an invisible fecundity, a dimmed light, a meek namelessness, a hidden wholeness. This mysterious Unity and Integrity is Wisdom, the Mother of all, *Natura naturans*. There is in all things an inexhaustible sweetness and purity, a silence that is a fount of action and joy. It rises up in wordless gentleness and flows out to me from the unseen roots of all created being, welcoming me tenderly, saluting me with indescribable humility. This is at once my own being, my own nature, and the Gift of my Creator's Thought and Art within me, speaking as Hagia Sophia, speaking as my sister, Wisdom.[52]

Merton's acknowledging of the imprint of the divine intelligence within his own psyche as female reflected the bold inclusiveness of his reli-

51. See Merton, *Opening the Bible*, 67.
52. Merton, "Hagia Sophia," in *Collected Poems*, 363.

gious consciousness. While his selection of female traits such as mercy and tenderness might strike one in retrospect as somewhat stereotypical, his purpose was simply to balance the portrait of the divine as encompassing both genders in a period of religious culture in the West when such observations would have been regarded as avant-garde if not heterodox.

His goal was to restore wholeness to the image of God by replacing the patriarchal image that had been passed down through the ages in the West. In addition to this form of incompleteness, he more than once noted the "absurdity" of his incompleteness as a celibate monk, cut off from intimacy with women.[53] Without sentimentally idealizing the relationship between men and women, he acknowledged his incompleteness as a celibate monk, the price he had paid, so to speak, for his vocation to solitude. At the same time, it can be said that as a monk he had a number of platonic friendships with women, and recognized the value of these relationships in helping to complete him as a human being. This gratitude can be seen in his reaction in receiving a letter from his friend and literary agent Naomi Burton Stone in 1965, in which he paid tribute to her "mature" and "realistic" understanding and her "feminine" comfort. Also, he had had relationships with women, including sexual relationships, before entering Gethsemani. The long abstention from such relationships, though, might have caught him off guard in 1966 when he became romantically involved for a brief time with a young nurse. Although he did not, on the whole, deal generously and protectively with this young woman, he did understand that it was important for him, caught up in his own feelings as he was, to see himself as she, through her notes and letters, had come to see him and so thereby fill out the picture of his own reality.[54] Here one senses the existential concreteness of Merton's consciousness of the perils of incompleteness, an intuition that grew as indissolubly out of his own life as it had out of his interest in romanticism and in the contemplative traditions of East and West. With this awareness in mind, perhaps, he resolved in his journals

53. McDonnell, "Interview with Thomas Merton," 30.
54. Merton, Aug. 17, 1965, in *Dancing in the Water of Life*, 281; Merton, Sept. 6, 1966, in *Learning to Love*, 126.

to leave out nothing in an effort to make at least his *depiction* of himself less incomplete than it would otherwise have been.[55]

Regarding the self's movement toward inclusiveness, Merton rejected the separation of the self into separate streams of action and thought, arguing in *Conjectures of a Guilty Bystander,* for example, that the "true" philosopher and the "true" poet led lives in which philosophy and poetry were not separate activities or vocations but integral parts of their existence. What he reflected here was the sort of synthesis he believed had occurred in his own life in which the ordinary round of his existence had become integral with his teaching, his monastic duties, and his writing. In the midst of such a melting of distinctions, the self experienced its existence with a minimum of friction and abstraction and through intuitive insight became aware of its participation in humanity. This interfusion of the personal and of the universal underlay an unpublished manuscript titled "A Piece of the Continent" in which Merton indicated the social dimension of inclusiveness. There he argued in summary that the only way in which human beings could reach their innate ontological goals was to allow others to complete them as human beings while in turn reciprocally helping to complete others.[56]

In order to accomplish this, however, certain barriers had to be lifted. One of these barriers was that created by what he dryly called a "'perfectly safe'" consciousness. Such a consciousness, he added, which accommodated only "select" thoughts, in fact inadvertently poisoned itself. Better an "exposed" consciousness, he concluded, which, although a little "dirtied" by its openness, was freer and fresher than the protected consciousness.[57] A useful barometer with which to assess the "exposed" openness of Merton's own consciousness is that of his eclectic reading. In the index to his collected literary essays, under the first two letters of the alphabet, for example, one finds references to Henry Adams, Aeschylus, Conrad Aiken, Antiochus of Syria, W. H. Auden, Saint Augustine of Hippo, Francis Bacon, Charles Baudelaire, Henri Bergson,

55. See Merton, May 30, 1968, in *Other Side of the Mountain,* 110.
56. Merton, *Conjectures of a Guilty Bystander,* 267; see Merton, "A Piece of the Continent," n.d., n.p., Merton Collection, Bellarmine University.
57. Merton, Nov. 21, 1968, in *Other Side of the Mountain,* 289.

George Berkeley, John Berryman, William Blake, Dietrich Bonhoeffer, Hieronymous Bosch, Bertold Brecht, and Edmund Burke. Scattered through the *c*'s, *d*'s, and *e*'s one encounters references to Albert Camus, Marc Chagall, Noam Chomsky, Samuel Taylor Coleridge, Confucius, Constantine, Dante, Charles Darwin, Rene Descartes, John Dewey, Meister Eckhart, and Euripides. The range of Merton's reading was broad and unsystematic. He never knew in advance where his reading sorties would take him, and as often as not the authors he was reading led him to other writers. In addition, as he entered new terrain, he tended to arrange the writers in his head into constellations gathered around a particular interest. Under those who seemed to him to have been the principal shapers of modern thought and who should therefore be read, he urged monastic contemplatives in need of a basic understanding of the culture around them to read Marx, Darwin, Kierkegaard, Nietzsche, Freud, Jung, Adler, Lenin, Mao Tse-tung, Bergson, Dewey, Croce, Ortega y Gasset, Sartre, Heidegger, Buber, and those such as Teilhard de Chardin, Marcel, and Tillich who were Christian existentialists.[58] Merton's hospitableness to what some of his fellow monks might have termed secular knowledge issued from his fundamental conviction that the wider one's interests were on the human level, the more able one would be to understand the divine. Similarly, in the moral sphere, he contended that if one knew the good in whatever form it appeared, to that extent one knew God.[59]

One of Merton's techniques for achieving inclusiveness as a writer was his habit of pairing the objects of his thought—either antithetically or harmoniously. Essays such as "Rain and the Rhinoceros," "Atlas and the Fatman," "The Time of the End Is the Time of No Room," and "Art and Freedom," all well known to Merton readers, are examples. Whether the dualities chosen were antithetical or ostensibly compatible was of less importance to Merton than the charged field that was created as they were set next to each other, at which time the qualities and connotations of each part of the pair flowed irresistibly toward the other. A ready example is that of "Rain and the Rhinoceros" in *Raids on the Unspeakable*,

58. Merton, *Contemplation in a World of Action*, 31–32.
59. See Merton, Nov. 16, 1939, in *Run to the Mountain*, 88.

in which Merton appeared to have thematically polarized the person and society. Nature, he indicated in the essay, had providentially nourished the self, while society, represented grotesquely in Ionesco's absurdist play *Rhinoceros,* overran the self, compacting it with others into a homogeneous mass. The paradoxical effect of the self's sojourn with nature, however, as Merton's own solitude testified, was to create a sympathy toward other selves. Thus, the essay turned out to be not a polarization of the self and society but rather a study of the tension between the self and a highly collectivized society. In fact, it could be said that Merton's essay implicitly called for the beginning of a restructuring of society along freer, more decentralized lines. In the last analysis "Rain and the Rhinoceros" did not celebrate *absolute* solitude, just as it does not reject the idea of society as such. Instead of two mutually exclusive halves, then, the reader is left with an impression of fruitful possibilities generated by the initial dialectical juxtaposition of two very different things.

It is difficult not to think of Merton's method here and elsewhere in his writings as Hegelian, even if he did not always speak positively about Hegel. In his trenchant essay "Blake and the New Theology," for example, he contrasted Hegel unflatteringly with Blake, describing the opposites in Hegel's historical synthesis as colliding like "billiard balls," as opposed to Blake in whose writings and engravings opposites came together to "fuse in synthesis" as part of an ultimate and higher unity. Though one can appreciate Merton's privileging of a higher unity here, he may have been unfair to Hegel, since Hegel did in fact believe that opposites rose dialectically into a higher and richer synthesis toward a final, though nontheological, unifying of the material and the immaterial. With respect to dialectical thinking, Merton was fascinated as well by the way that some thinkers united heretofore disparate entities—as Pound had. If he had not read Pound, he once observed, he would never have realized that China and Rome had had "so much in common."[60]

External unification and inclusiveness depended in Merton's view on internal unification and inclusiveness. At some unspecified point, which was difficult to estimate because the process of unification and inclu-

---

60. Merton, "Blake and the New Theology," in *Literary Essays,* 6; Merton, Aug. 8, 1957, in *Search for Solitude,* 108.

siveness was so gradual and protracted, a person could trust himself or herself to act with spiritual maturity. A major impediment to such maturity was the isolation of one aspect of human experience as the focus of all of one's attention and energy. This could apply even to the privileging of the sacred at the expense of the secular, Merton believed, creating an artificial division where there ought to have been a reciprocal flow of meaning and significance. Thus, he balked in a letter to James Laughlin at the privileging of sexuality in the poetry of William Everson because Everson, a Catholic contemplative poet, had isolated sexual passion as something "sui juris all by itself in a sort of vacuum into which morality cannot enter." In this connection it is worth noting that in the essays in *Contemplation in a World of Action*, which were written in the late 1960s, Merton contended that Freud's emphasis on sexuality as the matrix of human behavior expressed, among other things, the psychoanalyst's cautionary and broadly moral view that one had to learn from one's new awareness of the power of the sexual drive in order to transcend it.[61]

Literature, Merton observed on a number of occasions in the final decade of his life, brought together existence and essence into the "whole" truth, as he had put it in *Thoughts in Solitude* in the late 1950s. In his pursuit of inclusiveness in the 1960s he became impressed by what literature and religion had in common, noting on one occasion in 1964 that *Moby Dick* spoke more eloquently about the spiritual life than many formal spiritual tomes. Following a meeting with Jacques Maritain in 1966, he came away with the conviction that against the background of the drought of strong theological and philosophical writing, a fresh and "living" way to approach theological and philosophical realities would be through "creative writing" and literary criticism.[62] In contrast to the abstractness of theological and philosophical speculation and argument, literature and art provided an existential form by means of narration and

61. Merton to James Laughlin, May 12, 1948, in *Thomas Merton and James Laughlin*, 34; Merton, *Contemplation in a World of Action*, 34.
62. Merton, *Thoughts in Solitude*, 63; Merton, Aug. 9, 1964, in *Dancing in the Water of Life*, 133; Merton to James Laughlin, Oct. 8, 1966, in *Thomas Merton and James Laughlin*, 301.

symbolism that enabled thematic ideas to grow out of flesh-and-blood contexts, as it were. In this way the universal and the particular, the idea and the thing, were united. Rilke's *Duino Elegies* and Eliot's *Four Quartets* helped Merton, he once said, not only in filling out his relation to his own time but also in providing him with ontological insight into his own life.[63] As opposed to the either/or structuring of philosophical discourse, in literature one found that truths, falsities, and moral rights and wrongs were not so easily distinguished and classified. The point, he noted, was to come to understand that "unless we know we are wrong we cannot be right, because the only thing we can successfully be right about is the fact that we are all wrong."[64] He did not believe that *any* wrong could become a right if seen in a particular light but rather that particular rights or wrongs could be reevaluated both in themselves and in terms of their moral weight within different perspectives. His was the viewpoint not of situation ethics but rather of the inclusivist who measured any one thing by the pervasiveness and strength of its participation in the whole.

One of Merton's most characteristic and illuminating comments on the subject of good and evil occurred in a rather Hegelian passage in his book *The Way of Chuang Tzu* (1965):

> The key to Chuang Tzu's thought is the complementarity of opposites. . . . Life is a continual development. All beings are in a state of flux. Chuang Tzu would have agreed with Herakleitos. . . . What is good and pleasant today may, tomorrow, become evil and odious. What seems right from one point of view may, when seen from a different aspect, manifest itself as completely wrong.
>
> What, then, should the wise man do? Should he simply remain indifferent and treat right and wrong, good and bad, as if they were all the same? Chuang Tzu would be the first to deny that they were the same. But in so doing, he would refuse to grasp one or the other and cling to it as to an absolute. When a limited and conditioned view of "good" is erected to the level of an absolute, it immediately becomes an evil, because it excludes certain complementary ele-

63. Merton, Nov. 29, 1965, in *Dancing in the Water of Life*, 319.
64. Merton to Mark Van Doren, Feb. 11, 1964, in *Road to Joy*, 47.

ments which are required if it is to be fully good. To cling to one partial view, one limited and conditioned opinion, and to treat this as the ultimate answer to all questions is simply to "obscure the Tao" and make oneself obdurate in error.[65]

Although Merton was here reproducing the thought of Chuang Tzu, his own view seems fairly evident. While good and evil retained their moral distinctiveness at any level, the weight they possessed in particular cases depended critically upon their *completeness* as concepts drawn from experience.

Paradoxically, Merton's attraction to inclusiveness arose from an existing and long-held tendency to discover the unusual in places where others had not. In the case of Coleridge's poem "The Rime of the Ancient Mariner," for instance, he saw or thought he saw that Coleridge's depiction of supernatural events was flecked with humor. Comparing Coleridge's poem with Horace Walpole's Gothic novel *The Castle of Otranto*, "The Rime of the Ancient Mariner," also Gothic in mood, nevertheless seemed to Merton with its water snakes and other slimy things to possess a subtle, underlying humor that prevented the work from acquiring the "cementlike solemnity" of conventional Gothic literature.[66] Whether or not one accepts his view about the presence of humor in Coleridge's poem, he was correct about there being a contrary, non-Gothic emotion generated by the water serpents, which convey an expansive sense of being that offsets the sober narrowness of the narrator's guilt-centered drama. Regarding the putative humor in the poem, he may also have been right about Coleridge's use of the grotesque, as in the image of slimy things that crawled with legs upon the slimy sea. This extravagant image presents the grotesque not as a Gothic horror but as an example of the ugly and absurd. In this way, with this extra window on his experience, the old mariner might be said to have reached the nadir of his spiritual journey in a contact with the plainness and ugliness of some aspects of being that he must accept in a gradual weaning of himself from hubris and a corresponding gradual embracing of all of being.

65. Merton, *The Way of Chuang Tzu*, 30.
66. Merton, Nov. 13, 1940, in *Run to the Mountain*, 258.

In his writings about history and culture, Merton also stressed the importance of inclusiveness. In the 1960s, for example, he told Thomas McDonnell that he thought the nation state, which Merton regarded as a collective projection of the ego, had overstayed its usefulness. In addition, in connection with science he came, after having read Teilhard de Chardin, to a belief in an evolutionary universe that included both matter and spirit. Even as early as 1957 he had rejected the old cosmology that had been a part of medieval monasticism, observing that modern contemplatives had no justification for living in a Newtonian universe or, "worse still, an Aristotelian one." For this reason, although he admired the architectural beauty of the great Gothic cathedrals of Europe, he argued against modern Christians identifying with such structures, which were no longer compatible with the social fluidity and openness of the cultures that surrounded them. Furthermore, such structures were not even faithful to Christianity itself, he added, which claimed, following Christ, to have no more need of physical temples than the human frame itself in which God had subsisted.[67]

Having delved into a book on quantum physics by George Gamow, Merton was enthusiastic about how modern physics had imaginatively transformed the way in which we look at the cosmos, comparing the scientific work of Niels Bohr with the thought of Heraclitus, who in Merton's view had arrived at a similar insight by intuitive means.[68] The comparison with Heraclitus recalls Merton's observation in his essay "Gandhi and the One-Eyed Giant" (1965) that neither the "ancient wisdoms" nor the "modern sciences" were complete in themselves.[69] By ancient wisdoms Merton meant not only those of Greece and Rome but those of Asia and of the aboriginal peoples of the Americas as well. The function of such wisdom in the modern age would be to offset what he regarded as a current ontological vacuum by providing interpretive schemes that, although conceived ages ago, might, like that of Heraclitus, philosophically illuminate the universe outlined by the new scien-

67. McDonnell, "Interview with Thomas Merton," 32; Merton, Nov. 2, 1957, in *Search for Solitude*, 132; see Merton, *Conjectures of a Guilty Bystander*, 273–74.

68. Merton, May 21, 1967, in *Learning to Love*, 237.

69. Merton, "Gandhi and the One-Eyed Giant," in *Gandhi on Non-Violence*, 1.

tific knowledge. In this connection it is apparent that if Merton was wary about the effects of technological culture, he nonetheless welcomed scientific inquiry, characterizing Einstein's imaginative and revolutionary repicturing of the cosmos, for example, as a great "'contemplative' achievement."[70] In contrast, what Merton found unsettling about the dominance of technological culture was its narrowness, a narrowness that was all the more troubling given the fact that many people had begun to live their lives entirely or nearly entirely within its conceptual boundaries and idioms.

Looking at culture from this wide angle, Merton concluded that for culture to grow there had to be a "communion" between the contemplative disciplines and science, "between the poet and the physicist, the priest and the depth psychologist, the monk and the politician."[71] His emphasis on "communion" illustrates the kind of inclusiveness that he sought and points up the difference between his approach and Hegel's. Even at the highest level, he believed, there could not be a fusion of all mind and all existence even if contained in the divine mind there was a complete understanding of reality. The reason lay in creation itself, which had been deliberately set free to be itself, so to speak, by the creative hand of God. In this matter Merton parted company with the intellectualism of Hegel's dialectical theory and was ill at ease with Hegel's exclusive reliance on logical as opposed to intuitive reasoning. In this latter respect Merton felt closer to Heidegger, who respected intuitive understanding and who rooted his philosophy existentially in being.

Merton's communal idea of inclusiveness not unexpectedly applied to the practical as well as to the ontological sphere. In *Faith and Violence* (1968), for example, he argued that the advantage of nonviolent protest as a way of resolving disputes lay in its invitation to an adversary, implicit in its "humility and self-restraint," to join in open and serious discussion. Such an approach was dialogic rather than dialectical. Moreover, from the crucible of such a confrontation could come new truths, psychological, political, and moral truths, for example, which then became available to all who were involved in the issue. Such spiritual

---

70. Merton, "The Inner Experience: Society and the Inner Self," 123.
71. Merton, "Symbolism: Communication or Communion?" in *Love and Living*, 79.

largesse could lead, if sufficiently noticed and adhered to over time, Merton believed, to a new kind of social relationship in which human beings not only were receptive to the truths set forth by their opponents but also incorporated these truths into their own lives for the sake of mutual harmony and for the good of those with whom they otherwise were at odds. Such behavior could, theoretically considered, become reciprocal and lead ultimately, Merton believed, to the manifestation of God within the human community.[72] While such an actual eventuality no doubt seemed unlikely to Merton, it was nevertheless conceivable and in any case indicated the path that the ultimate achievement of unity had to take. It was the path of love laid out by the Creator in the gift of life itself and historically embodied in Christ, whom Merton regarded as a perfect mirror of the divine. It is in this way that Merton's early christological consciousness and later existential, more impersonal ontological consciousness were reconciled. While the later Buddhist-like consciousness suspended Merton contemplatively in the waters of being, christological consciousness led him throughout his life to a more acutely active awareness of his involvement in the world. It was this consciousness in especial that led him to become a vigorous social critic in the 1960s. If creational ontological consciousness had conferred a trust in the cosmos and a grateful appreciation of its immeasurable beauty, christological consciousness stimulated the communal, socially engaged dimensions of his being.

The shift in Merton's writings from the ardent piety of *The Seven Storey Mountain, The Sign of Jonas,* and the early poetry to the more ontological emphasis of the later works can be seen as well in a comparison of *The Ascent to Truth*—an overtly philosophical and theological study from the 1950s—and later writings such as *Raids on the Unspeakable, Conjectures of a Guilty Bystander* and *Zen and the Birds of Appetite,* all of which dealt in their own ways with metaphysical themes. One cannot help but notice the relative dryness of Merton's ontological thinking in *The Ascent to Truth* in contrast to his passionate interest in the topic of being in the later work. Rather like Wordsworth's depiction of the universal passage from youth to middle age, Merton had evolved grad-

72. See Merton, *Faith and Violence,* 22; see Merton, *Opening the Bible,* 74.

ually from the peopled cosmology of his early works to the shimmering ontological stillness of the later writings. Even the figure of Mary in the beautiful prose poem "Hagia Sophia" is largely detached from the context of personal devotion and gathered up into a multidimensional depiction of the female element in being. Nevertheless, characteristically, in this entry from his journal in 1965, he attempted to reconcile the strands of Asian and Western consciousness in his overall outlook as a contemplative:

> I may be interested in Oriental religions, etc., but there can be no obscuring the essential difference—this personal communion with Christ at the center and heart of all reality, as a source of grace and life. "God is love" may perhaps be clarified if one says that "God is void" and if in the void one finds absolute indetermination and hence absolute freedom. . . . All that is "interesting" but none of it touches on the mystery of personality in God, and His personal love for me. Again, I am void too—and I have freedom, or *am* a kind of freedom, meaningless unless oriented to Him.[73]

Rather than substituting an impersonal ontological perception of ultimate reality for a historical and salvational one, as Huxley had argued in *Ends and Means* characterized the path taken by Western mystics, Merton embraced a synthesis of the two approaches. In his musing about the two contemplative traditions in the above passage, he might be thought to have wanted to have his cake and eat it too, but such a conclusion would miss the gist of his way of thinking. He regarded both the Christian and the Buddhist approaches to ultimate reality as incomplete, the Western approach relying on philosophical rationalism and on a belief in the impinging of the supernatural on history. What Western Christianity lacked in Merton's view, at least in its mainstream form, was a widely accepted and vigorous contemplative tradition that included intuitive ontological consciousness, whereas this was precisely the traditional strength, as he saw it, of Asian mysticism. Of especial interest in the above passage was his focus on "indetermination" and "freedom." Here, he shows how Asian, notably Buddhist, thought could be used to

---

73. Merton, June 26, 1965, in *Dancing in the Water of Life*, 259.

infuse the Christian concept of the self with a spaciousness that modified the Christian narrative of the soul's relationship to a personal God.
Buddhist consciousness expanded the narrative paradigm of child and
father to encompass the perception of the soul and self as spiritually continuous with the creativity and vastness of being and thereby in Merton's
hybrid consciousness with God as the epitome of being.

Merton's eclecticism and inclusiveness seem to have stemmed initially from a restlessness about who and what he was, spurred by the tragic
loss of his parents while he was still quite young. The subsequent and
perhaps associated motif of the journey that he adopted for *The Seven
Storey Mountain* presented a view of experience as unfulfilled but as
tending toward fulfillment. His fascination with Blake and with both
Christian and Eastern mysticism convinced him that his own sense of
incompleteness was not merely personal but universal and ontological as
well. His success and importance as a religious writer arose in part from
his having diverted attention away from a focus on dogma, which became the source of an embroiled American Catholicism in the 1960s,
and toward a focus on the self's unmediated encounter with ultimate reality. Increasingly in his journals and poems, often as fresh and vivid today as when they were written, Merton drew his readers away from ecclesiastical culture and toward solitude and the creational contingencies
of nature and time. The matter of time was especially important because
of his conviction that a consciousness of the primordial pointed the way
back to a unified consciousness and psyche. Merton was realistic enough
to know that the beginnings of life on earth were not as harmonious and
paradisal as he might have wished. What he tried to bring out, based
upon his experience as a contemplative, was the importance of the ingrained, archetypal, mythic memory in the human psyche that contained
the outline of an idealized state of wholeness. In this way and in contrast to a future-oriented eschatology similar to that which obtained in
conventional Christianity, human beings could have the consolation of
knowing that if wholeness had once existed, it could do so again. Furthermore, Merton's focus on the present as the time of psychic restoration and reunification made the transformations in consciousness that
he sought accessible.

His extension of himself into the past in a scrutiny of both highly sophisticated and primitive cultures allowed him to track the existence of an innate, psychic wisdom that he suggested persuasively had been marginalized both within traditional ecclesiastical rhetoric in the West and within the positivistic norms of technological culture. Merton insisted on the authenticity of this wisdom by drawing his readers to discover it in themselves through contemplation and through the ensuing emergence of the buried self. Once aware of its innate freedom, this self, ontologically attuned to its creator as a transcendent and also an immanent presence, would come to love being, and would thus be inclined to strive for its perfection, including its moral perfection. Thus would begin the transformation of society in ways exemplified, Merton thought, by contemplative revolutionaries such as Thoreau and Gandhi. In the final analysis he had more in common with Thoreau and Gandhi than with the mysticism of either Blake or Saint Teresa of Avila with their extraordinary visions. Though both Saint Teresa of Avila and Blake, for example, were phenomenological in conveying the experiential content of consciousness, the nature of that consciousness appears radically subjective in comparison with that which the reader encounters in Merton. In spite of his reservations about the limitations of reason, Merton on the whole wrote in a manner that was quite compatible with reason and was sensitive to the autonomous, physical reality of the external world.

Because of Merton's orientation toward inclusiveness, there is a need to comment on the frequently encountered image of him as an apophatic contemplative. When one considers the value of his writings as a whole, more than anything else they manifest an interest in and a celebration of the creational world. In some ways this appears out of step with apophatic consciousness, even if, as Merton frequently declared, apophatic consciousness did not imply a disapproval of or an alienation from the physical world. As an observer Merton brought out the detail, including the painterly detail, of the world before him. Even the central symbol of the dark night of Saint John of the Cross seems in Merton's hands not so much a fading out of the world as a brighter and more original image of it. In contrast to Saint John of the Cross, his attention characteristically seemed focused on this world in a gathering of the multiplicity of being into the ontological spaciousness of the present moment. Even what are thought of as the more austere writings of Merton, including the poetry that the critic George Woodcock called the poems of the "desert," though minimalist in form, are replete with life. In a poem such as "Love Winter When the Plant Says Nothing," for example, while one can observe the awakening of the inner eye amid the seasonal barrenness, the landscape that Merton depicted has just enough vivid features to stand as an evocative poem about winter. Intermediate between creational and apophatic consciousness and evident in poems such as "Song for Nobody" was Merton's distinctive projection of the silence of being, an immense presence dwarfing the sounds of more ephemeral realities that have been temporarily superseded, if not, within the interlaying of sound and silence, quite forgotten. The interplay of language and silence in Merton's writing reflected his attachment to both apophatic and creational contemplation. Creation drew him joyfully to speak about what he saw and heard, while apophatic consciousness made him aware that all speech would fall far short of expressing the existential reality of the creature or thing described. Apophatic consciousness was the stimulus, it might be said, for Merton's emphasis on inclusiveness. Beneath that emphasis lay his conviction that if language fell short in expressing being, then through inclusiveness he could offset the poverty of language in trying to capture the plenitude both of being and of consciousness, as can be seen in the polyphony of voices and cultural styles exhibited in a poem such as *The Geography of Lograire*.

Looking at Merton's expository writing about the spiritual life in the 1940s and 1950s, one can see why, polished though it was, he came, retrospectively, to prefer his creative writing. In contrast to the sometimes rather stylized books on meditation with their express, didactic purposes, in the journals and in the poems he resolved to include everything. He was motivated not by humility but rather by the desire to see and to show how thought arose within him, for the purpose not of reflexive analysis, but rather of freeing up the writing process, which in time became for him a primary method of contemplation. In the journals particularly one encounters the openness and candor that mark the relaxed style of the later period:

> Hot day, but dry and with breeze in the afternoon. Pleasant enough
> in the novitiate chapel.

I am wondering if I can perhaps begin to be more detached from my existence. Or to think of it, better to accept the unthinkable notion of it not-being. How insufficient are conventional meditations on death! I have the *responsum mortis* [answer of death] in me, and have spontaneously been aware of death as a kind of presence several times today.

Distinguish this from death-wish and frustration. It is at once an acceptance of not existing any longer (whenever I shall cease to exist in this state I am in) and a full acknowledgement of the good of existence and of life. In reality, it is the acceptance of a higher, inconceivable mode of life entirely beyond our own control and volition, in which all is gift. To resign oneself to not being what one knows in order to receive a totally unknown being from a totally unknown source and in that source.[74]

In order to avoid producing anxiety in the reader and so not to freeze out the possibility of a full response, Merton created an air of randomness at the surface of this passage. In unpacking the narrative, it is instructive to go to the end of the passage and then to work backward, attempting to restructure the reflection about his intimation of death along chronological lines. In real time, that is, in the original experiential sequence as opposed to the journal's reconstructed narrative time scheme, the intimation of death preceded the feeling of dissatisfaction with conventional spiritual writing about death. Thus, in terms of real time Merton felt quite unprotected in the thoughts that he was having about death, unprotected at least by any external source. Nonetheless, in real (as opposed to narrative) time he resolved to use the intimation of death to become, as he put it, more "detached" from his life, a resolution that in narrative time he places almost at the front of the narrative in order to demonstrate, in a gesture of reassurance to the reader, the value of that resolution. In effect he restructured the moment in order to provide the reader generously with a reassurance that he himself had initially lacked. At least as significantly, in terms of his own needs, Merton seemingly used the restructuring of the experience to adhere more easily to the asceticism of his monastic vocation while attempting to quiet his un-

74. Merton, Aug. 4, 1963, in ibid., 3.

easy apprehensiveness about the reality of death, whether imminent or not. But the passage goes deeper than this. What Merton discovered, as he absorbed the thought of death, was a countervailing consciousness present in the psyche that in accepting death he became liberated from the narrowness of the ego and led to an expectation of a transformed role in being, a level of consciousness that he had ostensibly sought but had in fact instinctively resisted due to the shadow of death. The ascending outcome of Merton's reflection is not merely a sentimental inference but rather, as the end of the passage indicates, a reasonable assumption that if death involved the fear of traveling to an undiscovered country, then that country would be pervaded by the same providential divinity that had brought about his personal existence. In a psychological, spiritual, and stylistic sense the interplay of real and narrative time formats enables the reader to follow both the chronological development of Merton's perceptions and the reflexive reshaping of those perceptions. In this way the reader witnesses the inclusiveness of Merton's imagination at a concrete, artistic level, and perhaps comes to realize why he has been recognized as one of the most fascinating writers of autobiography in the United States in the last hundred years.

The passage also illustrates Merton's contextualizing of his experience, a feature of his journal writing that extended throughout his life. Considering the passage as narrative, the opening words about the weather are typical of his journal entries. They set the scene unself-consciously and unceremoniously not in the expectation that such a notation would have any particular importance but rather just in case, in retrospect, it did. In fact, for the reader, the notation about the weather does have a useful purpose, as perhaps it did for Merton at some level, by providing his subsequent feelings of mortality with a setting of normalcy that had the effect of making those feelings appear natural and, more to the point, bearable. Merton's purpose was, as always, to place a particular experience within the whole canvas.

In time he crossed the relatively narrow threshold of his life as a Trappist monk in the 1940s into worlds of consciousness and culture that sometimes ranged quite far from his point of departure. On the whole, though, he evolved toward new states of consciousness and living not in order to deny the stated aims of his religion but in order to achieve them. If, under the influence of his early Thomist training, he distinguished hierarchically between biological and spiritual levels of human existence, then in his later writings he sought to redefine human nature according to criteria that were partly religious and, as has been shown in connection with works such as *The Geography of Lograire,* partly anthropological. Rather than exhibiting a dualism that pitted person against nature, in his later writings he proposed a more unified perception of human beings and indeed of all of being.

For this reason as well he welcomed the evolutionary theory of Teilhard de Chardin, who had traced the gestation of spirit from within matter. Merton's concept of personhood merged with this sort of unifying ontology in ways that were entirely suited to his sensibility because of his feeling of intimacy with the natural world. Just as he thought of the Creator as both above and within the world, so too did he regard human awareness as both within and beyond the instinctual level of nature. In many ways, as has been suggested throughout this study, he saw human beings, because of the benighted influence of modern technological culture, as having underestimated the distinctive character and strength of their own natures. Solitude and contemplation could awaken the self to the riches of the psyche, which contained a crystal of the divine. So awakened, Merton believed, the self would seek to restore the union of all life that had been broken apart by self-consciousness, as the romantic writers had testified, and by self-interest, as the mystics had stated.

Within the heart of one's being, however, Merton discovered, was an inscription in the psyche prompting one to reflect upon the richness of being, and having done so to find one's way back to the supernal source of both existence and consciousness. The way forward, he concluded, was through a canvassing of the plurality of being, a journey of sorts, not only toward the periphery but, even more important, toward the center. Merton's preoccupation with inclusiveness stemmed from his orientation toward what he called wisdom, a wisdom that he believed was innate. By wisdom he meant an awareness of the total contextualization of our existence, a consciousness of the full reality in which we are enclosed and are required to understand in order to discover how to live.

He regarded this essentially ontological understanding as overlooked and even dismissed within contemporary culture, which he judged to be myopically guided by an interest in technique. Adding to the difficulty, religious culture, he maintained, had traditionally been sectarian and therefore frequently at odds historically with its own lofty ontological purposes.

In the late 1930s Merton had been awakened to the spiritual dimension of reality by writers such as William Blake, Saint Augustine, and Jacques Maritain, who inclusively attempted to reconcile Thomist philosophy and romantic aestheticism. Following his indoctrination into Thomist philosophy and to a fixed ecclesiastical culture in the 1940s, Merton gradually returned to an assertion of intuitive consciousness under the tutelage of mystics such as Saint John of the Cross. In the same period he moved from the narrow pedestal of Catholic triumphalism to a perception of the ubiquitousness of reality and of truth. He came eventually to encounter the divine by staring at a bowl of carnations in a monastery chapel or in looking at the statues of two reclining Buddhas in a part of the world far away from his monastic home. What is interesting about Merton's ideology is its affirmation, without recourse to doctrinal framing, of the value of the individual psyche, of spiritual freedom, and of ontological inclusiveness, values that are asserted as goods in and of themselves. Indeed, what he ended up doing was revisualizing and enlarging the meaning of religious doctrine in the light of these values that came to him particularly through romanticism and mysticism. Although romanticism and mysticism had been marginalized within Catholic culture because of the dominance of Thomist philosophy, these intellectual currents became through him a significant part of that culture. In addition, because of his mingling of intuitive consciousness and naturalist notation, Merton joined an important naturalist-ontologist tradition in American literature, in turn influencing younger writers such as Annie Dillard who themselves became part of the same tradition. In addition, he has become an important figure in international religious culture as well. Rather like Wordsworth, Thoreau, and Whitman, Merton's significance as a writer stems especially from the expansive unity of his life and writing, especially the suggestive and evocative interfusion of incident and thought, observation and symbol, that heightens and intensifies the reader's perception and valuing of experience. While the diverse streams of form and meaning that flowed from Merton's burgeoning life make it difficult to see him as a systematic thinker, his thought was fundamentally coherent. In all of these respects his influence has been immense and, one hastens to add, salutary.

Bibliography

Abrams, M. H. *The Correspondent Breeze: Essays in English Romanticism.* New York: Norton, 1984.

Altieri, Charles. *Act and Quality.* Amherst: University of Massachusetts Press, 1981.

Aquinas, Saint Thomas. *Summa Theologiae: A Concise Translation.* Ed. Timothy McDermott. London: Eyne and Spottiswoode, 1989.

Augustine of Hippo, Saint. *The Confessions of St. Augustine.* Trans. E. B. Pusey. London: Dent, 1957.

Baker, Rob, and Gray Henry, eds. *Merton and Sufism: The Untold Story.* Louisville: Fons Vitae, 1999.

Bergson, Henri. *Duration and Simultaneity with Reference to Einstein's Theory.* Trans. Leon Jacobsen. Indianapolis: Bobbs-Merrill, 1965.

Blake, William. *Poetry and Prose of William Blake.* Ed. Geoffrey Keynes. 4th ed. London: Nonesuch, 1939.

Butler, Dom Edward Cuthbert. *Western Mysticism.* New York: Barnes and Noble, 1968.

Byatt, A. S. *Wordsworth and Coleridge in Their Time.* London: Nelson, 1970.

Carr, Anne E. *A Search for Wisdom and Spirit: Thomas Merton's Theology of the Self.* Notre Dame: University of Notre Dame Press, 1988.

Chandler, Alice. *A Dream of Order: The Medieval Ideal in Nineteenth-Century English Literature.* Lincoln: University of Nebraska Press, 1970.

Chesterton, Gilbert Keith. *A G. K. Chesterton Anthology*. Ed. P. J. Kavanagh. San Francisco: Ignatius Press, 1985.

Clubbe, John, and Ernest J. Lovell. *English Romanticism: The Grounds of Belief*. DeKalb: Northern Illinois University Press, 1983.

Coleridge, Samuel Taylor. *Select Poetry and Prose*. Ed. Stephen Potter. London: Nonesuch, 1933.

Coomaraswamy, Ananda. *Transformation of Nature in Art*. Cambridge: Harvard University Press, 1934.

Cooper, David. *Thomas Merton's Art of Denial*. Athens: University of Georgia Press, 1989.

Cox, Michael. *A Handbook of Christian Mysticism*. [England]: Crucible, 1986.

Cunningham, Lawrence. Introduction to *Thomas Merton: Spiritual Master*, 15–55. New York: Paulist Press, 1992.

Eckhart, Meister. *Meister Eckhart: An Introduction to the Study of His Works with an Anthology of His Sermons*. Trans. James M. Clark. London: Nelson, 1957.

Emerson, Ralph Waldo. *Essays and Lectures*. New York: Library of America, 1983.

Faricy, Robert. "Merton and Mysticism of the Mind." *Merton Annual* 11 (1998): 138–47.

———. *Wind and Sea Obey Him: Approaches to a Theology of Nature*. London: SCM Press, 1982.

Francis of Assisi, Saint. *Writings and Early Biographies*. Ed. Marion Habig. 3rd ed. Chicago: Franciscan Herald Press, 1973.

Frye, Northrop. "The Drunken Boat: The Revolutionary Element in Romanticism." In *Romanticism Reconsidered*, ed. Northrop Frye, 1–25. New York: Columbia University Press, 1963.

———. *Fearful Symmetry*. Princeton: Princeton University Press, 1947.

Furst, Lilian. *Romanticism in Perspective*. 2nd ed. London: Macmillan, 1979.

Gilson, Etienne. *The Spirit of Mediaeval Philosophy*. Trans. A. H. C. Downes. New York: Scribner's, 1936.

Grant, George. *Time as History*. Toronto: CBC, 1969.

Grene, Marjorie. *Martin Heidegger*. London: Bowes and Bowes, 1957.

Hart, Patrick. *Thomas Merton: First and Last Memories.* Bardstown, Ky.: Necessity Press, n.d.

Hartman, Geoffrey. "Romanticism and Anti-Self-Consciousness." In *Beyond Formalism,* ed. Geoffrey Hartman, 298–310. New Haven: Yale University Press, 1990.

———. *Wordsworth's Poetry, 1787–1814.* New Haven: Yale University Press, 1964.

Heidegger, Martin. *Being and Time.* Trans. Joseph Stambaugh. Albany: State University of New York Press, 1966.

Higgins, Michael. *Heretic Blood: The Spiritual Geography of Thomas Merton.* Toronto: Stoddart, 1998.

———. "A Study of the Influence of William Blake on Thomas Merton." *American Benedictine Review* 25:3 (1974): 377–88.

Holmes, John R. "The Surprising Orthodoxy of Merton's Blake." *Cithara* 20 (May 1981): 38–66.

Huxley, Aldous. *Ends and Means.* London: Chatto and Windus, 1938.

Inchausti, Robert. *Thomas Merton's American Prophecy.* Albany: State University of New York Press, 1998.

Johnston, William. *The Inner Eye of Love: Mysticism and Religion.* London: Collins, 1978.

———. *The Still Point: Reflections on Zen and Christian Mysticism.* New York: Fordham, 1970.

Jung, Carl. *The Undiscovered Self.* London: Routledge, 1958.

Kilcourse, George. *Ace of Freedoms: Thomas Merton's Christ.* Notre Dame: Notre Dame University Press, 1993.

Kramer, Victor. *Thomas Merton.* Boston: Twayne, 1984.

Küng, Hans. *The Incarnation of God: An Introduction to Hegel's Thought as Theological Prolegomena to a Future Christology.* Trans. J. R. Stephenson. New York: Crossroad, 1987.

Leigh, David. *Circuitous Journeys: Modern Spiritual Autobiography.* New York: Fordham University Press, 2000.

Lentfoehr, Thérèse. *Words and Silence: On the Poetry of Thomas Merton.* New York: New Directions, 1979.

MacGregor, Geddes. *Aesthetic Experience in Religion.* London: Macmillan, 1947.

Maritain, Jacques. *Art and Scholasticism*. London: Sheed and Ward, 1930.

———. *Creative Intuition in Art and Poetry*. New York: Pantheon, 1953.

McDonnell, Thomas. "An Interview with Thomas Merton." *U.S. Catholic* 33 (March 1968): 28–34.

McFarland, Thomas. *Romanticism and the Heritage of Rousseau*. Oxford: Oxford University Press, 1995.

McGann, Jerome. *The Romantic Ideology: A Critical Investigation*. Chicago: University of Chicago Press, 1983.

McInerny, Dennis. *Thomas Merton: The Man and His Work*. Washington, D.C.: Cistercian Publications, 1974.

———. "Thomas Merton and the Tradition of American Critical Romanticism." In *The Message of Thomas Merton*, ed. Patrick Hart, 166–91. Kalamazoo, Mich.: Cistercian Publications, 1981.

Merton, Thomas. "Art and Morality." In *New Catholic Encyclopedia*, 1:864–67. New York: McGraw-Hill, 1967.

———. "Art and Worship." *Sponsa Regis* 31:4 (December 1959): 114–17.

———. "Art of Poetry." Columbia University M.A. course notes [1938]. Merton Collection, St. Bonaventure University.

———. *The Ascent to Truth*. New York: Harcourt, Brace, 1951.

———. *The Asian Journal of Thomas Merton*. Ed. Naomi Burton Stone, Patrick Hart, and James Laughlin. New York: New Directions, 1973.

———. *The Behavior of Titans*. New York: New Directions, 1961.

———. *Bread in the Wilderness*. New York: New Directions, 1953.

———. *Cables to the Ace*. New York: New Directions, 1968.

———. *The Climate of Monastic Prayer*. Kalamazoo, Mich.: Cistercian Publications, 1969.

———. *The Collected Poems of Thomas Merton*. New York: New Directions, 1977.

———. *Conjectures of a Guilty Bystander*. Garden City, N.Y.: Doubleday, 1966.

———. *Contemplation in a World of Action*. Garden City, N.Y.: Doubleday, 1971.

———. *Contemplative Prayer*. New York: Herder and Herder, 1969.

———. *The Courage for Truth: The Letters of Thomas Merton to Writers*. Ed. Christine Bochen. New York: Farrar, Straus, Giroux, 1993.

———. *Dancing in the Water of Life: Seeking Peace in the Hermitage*. Ed. Robert Daggy. San Francisco: Harper, 1997.

———. "Day of a Stranger." *Hudson Review* 20:2 (summer 1967): 211–18.

———. *Disputed Questions*. New York: Farrar, Straus, and Cudahy, 1960.

———. *Eighteen Poems*. New York: New Directions, 1985.

———. *Emblems of a Season of Fury*. New York: New Directions, 1963.

———. *Entering the Silence: Becoming a Monk and Writer*. Ed. Jonathan Montaldo. San Francisco: Harper, 1996.

———. *Faith and Violence*. Notre Dame: University of Notre Dame Press, 1968.

———. *Gandhi on Non-Violence*. Ed. Thomas Merton. New York: New Directions, 1965.

———. *The Geography of Lograire: The Collected Poems of Thomas Merton*. New York: New Directions, 1969.

———. *The Hidden Ground of Love: The Letters of Thomas Merton on Religious Experience and Social Concerns*. Ed. William Shannon. New York: Farrar, Straus, Giroux, 1985.

———. *Honorable Reader: Reflections on My Work*. Ed. Robert Daggy. New York: Crossroad, 1989.

———. "The Inner Experience: Christian Contemplation." Part 3. *Cistercian Studies* 18 (1983): 201–16.

———. "The Inner Experience: Infused Contemplation." Part 5. *Cistercian Studies* 19 (1984): 62–78.

———. "The Inner Experience: Kinds of Contemplation." Part 4. *Cistercian Studies* 18 (1983): 289–300.

———. "The Inner Experience: Notes on Contemplation." Part 1. *Cistercian Studies* 18 (1983): 3–15.

———. "The Inner Experience: Problems of the Contemplative Life." Part 7. *Cistercian Studies* 19 (1984): 267–82.

———. "The Inner Experience: Prospects and Conclusions." Part 8. *Cistercian Studies* 19 (1984): 336–45.

———. "The Inner Experience: Society and the Inner Self." Part 2. *Cistercian Studies* 18 (1983): 121–34.

———. "The Inner Experience: Some Dangers in Contemplation." Part 6. *Cistercian Studies* 19 (1984): 139–50.

———. *Ishi Means Man*. Greensboro, N.C.: Unicorn Press, 1976.

———. *Learning to Love: Exploring Solitude and Freedom*. Ed. Christine Bochen. San Francisco: Harper, 1997.

———. *The Literary Essays of Thomas Merton*. Ed. Patrick Hart. New York: New Directions, 1981.

———. *Love and Living*. Ed. Naomi Burton Stone and Patrick Hart. New York: Farrar, Straus, Giroux, 1979.

———. *The Monastic Journey*. Ed. Patrick Hart. Mission, Kans.: Sheed, Andrews, and McMeel, 1977.

———. "The Monk and Sacred Art." *Sponsa Regis* 28 (May 1957): 231–34.

———. *My Argument with the Gestapo*. Garden City, N.Y.: Doubleday, 1969.

———. "Mystical Verse." *Catholic Poetry Society of America Bulletin* 4 (December 1941): 10.

———. *Mystics and Zen Masters*. New York: Farrar, Straus, Giroux, 1967.

———. *The New Man*. New York: Farrar, Straus, and Cudahy, 1961.

———. *New Seeds of Contemplation*. New York: New Directions, 1962.

———. *No Man Is an Island*. New York: Harcourt, Brace, 1955.

———. *The Nonviolent Alternative*. Ed. Gordon Zahn. New York: Farrar, Straus, Giroux, 1980.

———. "Notes on Sacred and Profane Art." *Jubilee* 4 (November 1956): 25–32.

———. *Opening the Bible*. Collegeville, Minn.: Liturgical Press, 1970.

———. *The Other Side of the Mountain: The End of the Journey*. Ed. Patrick Hart. San Francisco: Harper, 1998.

———. "Poetry and Contemplation: A Reappraisal." *Commonweal* 69 (Oct. 24, 1958): 87–92.

———. "Poetry and the Contemplative Life." In *Figures for an Apocalypse,* by Thomas Merton, 95–111. New York: New Directions, 1948.

———. *Raids on the Unspeakable*. New York: New Directions, 1966.

———. *The Road to Joy: The Letters of Thomas Merton to Old and New Friends*. Ed. Robert Daggy. New York: Farrar, Straus, Giroux, 1989.

———. "Romanticism." Columbia University M.A. course notes [1938]. Merton Collection, St. Bonaventure University.

———. "Romantic Poets." Columbia University M.A. course notes [1938]. Merton Collection, St. Bonaventure University.

———. *Run to the Mountain: The Story of a Vocation*. Ed. Patrick Hart. San Francisco: Harper, 1995.

———. *The School of Charity: The Letters of Thomas Merton on Religious Renewal and Spiritual Direction*. Ed. Patrick Hart. New York: Farrar, Straus, Giroux, 1990.

———. *A Search for Solitude: Pursuing the Monk's True Life*. Ed. Lawrence Cunningham. San Francisco: Harper, 1996.

———. *Seasons of Celebration*. New York: Farrar, Straus, Giroux, 1965.

———. *The Secular Journal of Thomas Merton*. New York: Farrar, Straus, and Cudahy, 1959.

———. *Seeds of Contemplation*. New York: New Directions, 1949.

———. *Seeds of Destruction*. New York: Farrar, Straus, and Cudahy, 1964.

———. *The Seven Storey Mountain*. New York: Harcourt, Brace, 1948.

———. *The Sign of Jonas*. New York: Harcourt, Brace, 1953.

———. *Silence in Heaven*. New York: Crowell, 1956.

———. *The Silent Life*. New York: Farrar, Straus, and Cudahy, 1957.

———. *The Springs of Contemplation*. New York: Farrar, Straus, Giroux, 1992.

———. *Thomas Merton and James Laughlin: Selected Letters*. Ed. David Cooper. New York: Norton, 1997.

———. *Thomas Merton in Alaska*. New York: New Directions, 1989.

———. *Thomas Merton on St. Bernard*. Kalamazoo, Mich.: Cistercian Publications, 1980.

———. *Turning toward the World: The Pivotal Years*. Ed. Victor Kramer. San Francisco: Harper, 1996.

———. *A Vow of Conversation: Journals, 1964–65*. Ed. Naomi Burton Stone. New York: Farrar, Straus, Giroux, 1988.

———. *The Waters of Siloe.* New York: Harcourt, Brace, 1949.

———. *The Way of Chuang Tzu.* New York: New Directions, 1965.

———. "The Wild Places." In *The Ecological Conscience: Values for Survival,* ed. Robert Disch, 37–43. New York: Prentice-Hall, 1970.

———. *The Wisdom of the Desert.* New York: New Directions, 1960.

———. *Witness to Freedom: The Letters of Thomas Merton in Times of Crisis.* Ed. William Shannon. New York: Farrar, Straus, Giroux, 1994.

———. *Zen and the Birds of Appetite.* New York: New Directions, 1968.

Mott, Michael. *The Seven Mountains of Thomas Merton.* Boston: Houghton Mifflin, 1984.

Nurmi, Martin. *William Blake.* London: Hutchinson, 1975.

O'Connell, Patrick. "The Geography of Solitude: Thomas Merton's 'Elias—Variations on a Theme.'" *Merton Annual* 1 (1988): 151–90.

———. "Keeping Pace with His Companion: Thomas Merton and Henry Thoreau." *Concord Saunterer,* n.s., 7 (1999): 114–49.

———. "Thomas Merton's Wake-Up Calls: Aubades and Monastic Dawn Poems from *A Man in the Divided Sea.*" *Merton Annual* 12 (1999): 129–63.

———. "Under the Spell of Lorca: An Important Influence on Thomas Merton's Early Poetry." *American Benedictine Review* 49:3 (September 1998): 256–86.

Plato. *The Portable Plato.* Harmondsworth, Middlesex: Penguin, 1977.

Raine, Kathleen. *Blake and Tradition.* 2 vols. London: Routledge and Kegan Paul, 1969.

Rice, Edward. *The Man in the Sycamore Tree.* Garden City, N.Y.: Doubleday, 1972.

Ricoeur, Paul. *The Symbolism of Evil.* Boston: Beacon, 1957.

Rousseau, Jean-Jacques. *The Emile of Jean-Jacques Rousseau.* Ed. William Boyd. New York: Columbia University Press, 1956.

Ryan, Robert M. *The Romantic Reformation: Religious Politics in English Literature, 1789–1824.* Cambridge: Cambridge University Press, 1997.

Shannon, William. *Thomas Merton's Dark Path.* New York: Harper, 1981.

Steiner, George. *Language and Silence.* New York: Atheneum, 1967.

———. *Real Presences.* Chicago: University of Chicago Press, 1989.

Sundkler, Bengt G. M. *Bantu Prophets in South Africa.* 2nd ed. London: Oxford University Press, 1961.

Suzuki, Daisetz T. *Mysticism: Christian and Buddhist.* New York: Collier, 1962.

Szabo, Lynn. "The Sound of Sheer Silence: A Study in the Poetics of Thomas Merton." *Merton Annual* 13 (2000): 208–21.

Thoreau, Henry David. *Reform Papers.* Ed. Wendell Glick. Princeton: Princeton University Press, 1973.

———. *Walden.* Ed. J. Lyndon Shanley. Princeton: Princeton University Press, 1971.

Thurston, Bonnie. "Thomas Merton on the Contemplative Life: An Analysis." *Contemplative Review* 17 (summer 1984): 1–8.

Tillich, Paul. *Dynamics of Faith.* New York: Harper and Row, 1957.

Underhill, Evelyn. *Mysticism.* Rev. ed. London: Methuen, 1960.

Waldron, Robert. *Thomas Merton in Search of His Soul: A Jungian Perspective.* Notre Dame, Ind.: Ave Maria Press, 1994.

Wallis, Richard T. *Neo-Platonism.* London: Duckworth, 1972.

Weis, Monica. "Beyond the Shadow and the Disguise: 'Spots of Time' in Thomas Merton's Spiritual Development." *Merton Seasonal* 23:1 (spring 1998): 21–27.

Williams, George H. *Wilderness and Paradise in Christian Thought.* New York: Harper, 1962.

Williams, Huntingdon. *Rousseau and Romantic Autobiography.* Oxford: Oxford University Press, 1983.

Willoughby, W. C. *The Soul of the Bantu.* New York: Doubleday, Doran, 1928.

Wilson, Edward O. *Consilience: The Unity of Knowledge.* New York: Random House, 1998.

Woodcock, George. *Thomas Merton: Monk and Poet.* Vancouver, B.C.: Douglas and McIntyre, 1978.

Wordsworth, William. *Poetical Works of Wordsworth.* Ed. Thomas Hutchinson, rev. Ernest de Selincourt. London: Oxford University Press, 1930.

———. *Wordsworth's Guide to the Lakes.* Ed. Ernest de Selincourt. London: Humphrey Milford, 1926.

Index